THE OFFICIAL BBCSPORT GUIDE

FORMULA ONE 2013

This edition published in 2013
by Carlton Books Limited
20 Mortimer Street
London W1T 3JW

10 9 8 7 6 5 4 3 2 1

A CIP catalogue record for this book is available from the British Library.

The publisher has taken reasonable steps to check the accuracy of the facts
contained herein at the time of going to press, but can take no responsibility
for any errors.

ISBN: 978-1-78097-244-2

Printed in Portugal

Opposite: Sebastian Vettel, Monaco 2012.

THE OFFICIAL BBC SPORT GUIDE

FORMULA ONE 2013

BRUCE JONES

CARLTON

CONTENTS

Right: Mark Webber celebrates winning the 2012 British GP, with Fernando Alonso and Sebastian Vettel also on the podium.

Jenson Button battles with Nico Hulkenberg at the 2012 season-closing Brazilian GP at Interlagos. Hulkenberg moves to Sauber for 2013, while Button gets a new team-mate, Sergio Perez.

ANALYSIS OF THE 2013 SEASON

This year's World Championship is the last before the switch to smaller engines in 2014. That change may tip the balance and give a currently less successful team the chance to shine, but, for 2013, expect Red Bull, Ferrari and McLaren to run at the front again. If we are treated to a season as jumbled as last year's was in the opening races, then we can look forward to another grand finale.

Formula One is going through a wonderful period, providing infinitely more exciting racing than it did in the past, thanks to there being more overtaking and also some nail-biting title races that are going all the way down to the wire. Sebastian Vettel dominated in 2011 but was made to fight for the title in last-round shoot-outs in both 2010 and 2012, as were Kimi Raikkonen in 2007 and Lewis Hamilton in 2008. In recent years, Jenson Button in 2009 was the only driver other than Vettel in 2011 to wrap up the title before the final round, and this is fantastic news for F1 fans.

For this year, there is just one change among the big three teams - Red Bull, Ferrari and McLaren - and this is Lewis Hamilton's departure to try his luck at Mercedes. Only a marked improvement in the Ross Brawn-run team's form and consistency will see him pitching for wins, let alone the title. In turn, that means that unless his replacement, ex-Sauber racer Sergio Perez, can get on to McLaren's wavelength immediately, then the McLaren attack will centre on Button, and that might mean a season not interrupted by so many failures.

Red Bull are sure to design a car that suits Vettel in particular, as he is the driver who earns their greatest rewards rather than team-mate Mark Webber. Likewise, Ferrari looks to Fernando Alonso, although Felipe Massa was at least getting up to speed again through last year to act as his wing man.

One of the most interesting considerations will be whether the team that became Lotus last year can stay as competitive as it was and so keep the big three on their toes. Certainly, Raikkonen still has the speed, and its title challenge will be boosted further if the fast Romain Grosjean can show more control and produce the finishes to match.

With Hamilton on board at Mercedes alongside karting team-mate Nico Rosberg, the atmosphere should be different from how it was when Michael Schumacher drew the limelight but failed to produce so many points. The big question is whether this team with its impressive designers can hit its targets.

Last year, Sauber came very close to toppling Mercedes and it has just replaced Perez with Nico Hulkenberg, a driver many tout as a future world champion. It's extremely unlikely that the Swiss team will manage to provide him and rookie Esteban Gutierrez with a car capable of winning, but he ought to score many points, especially if races are run in the wet.

The team that Hulkenberg has left, Force India, has finally been promised some investment in its facilities, which ought to help keep it in the hunt, this time with Paul di Resta as the undisputed number one driver.

Everyone associated with F1 was delighted in Spain last year when Pastor Maldonado gave Williams its first win since Juan Pablo Montoya won the 2004 Brazilian GP, but there's only guarded optimism that the team will continue its rediscovered form without a recognised, experienced driver who will steer clear of incidents as well as help develop the chassis.

Breaking with tradition, Toro Rosso let its drivers know long before last season was over that they had the team's approval and so were being kept for a second season. Daniel Ricciardo and Jean-Eric Vergne may even be able to dream that one day they might be promoted to Red Bull.

The three teams created to augment the grid in 2010 remain the slowest, even though Caterham, Marussia and HRT are all edging closer to the pace. However, money is tight and HRT seemed unlikely to last the winter after its owners realised that F1 costs money rather than makes it.

The best news is that the USA now seems to be accepting Formula One. Last year's United States GP in Austin has set the bar high for America's next new race in New Jersey, in 2014. If this can prove as big a hit, then F1 will finally put down roots here. Combine this with the arrival of Coca-Cola and Mastercard as sponsors, and Formula One is proving that if the show is good, then the rest will follow.

RED BULL RACING

There was much debate in the early part of last year about whether Red Bull had gained an advantage by using flexible wings, but you'd assume a car designed by Adrian Newey to be close to the edge and should expect no different in 2013.

Sebastian Vettel helped both himself and the team to a third title, but there are signs that the opposition, especially McLaren, are closing in.

Looking back over Red Bull Racing's incredible run of three consecutive Formula One constructors' titles won in 2010, 2011 and 2012, it's hard to remember that this was once the team that seldom ran ahead of the midfield when it started life in 1997 as Stewart Grand Prix. Indeed, even as recently as 2008, the team from Milton Keynes hadn't won a grand prix and ranked just seventh overall, embarrassingly one position behind its junior team, Scuderia Toro Rosso. Since then, however, with Adrian Newey leading the way on the technical front and Sebastian Vettel and Mark Webber providing consistent speed and guile from the cockpit, the wins have flowed in abundance and the titles have followed.

Last year's World Championship was certainly less of a dominant season for Red Bull Racing, after its 12 wins from 19 grands prix in 2011, but it was an unusual year for all the teams as not one of them managed to gain the upper hand and then keep it as they attempted to understand the tyres'

performance through the first half of the championship. What was interesting was the way that Webber bounced back from his 1:11 victory deficit to Vettel in 2011 and

ran with parity last year in a car that clearly suited him better than its predecessor. This, in turn, helped to strengthen the team's title bid.

KEY MOMENTS AND KEY PEOPLE

TEAM HISTORY
Jackie Stewart, three-time World Champion, formed a team to help elder son Paul go racing. This advanced to Formula 3000 and then, in 1997, to Formula One, with Paul retiring from racing to run the team. Johnny Herbert gave it a famous win in the wet at the Nurburgring in 1999 before it was bought by Ford and renamed Jaguar Racing for 2000. In 2005, Dietrich Mateschitz bought the team and turned it into Red Bull Racing, with its first win in 2009, followed by three titles in succession with Sebastian Vettel.

ADRIAN NEWEY
The designer considered to have the most fertile mind in Formula One made his F1 debut as chief aerodynamicist with Fittipaldi in 1980. After joining March, he worked on Indycar and sportscar designs before breaking new ground with the firm's 1988 F1 challenger. Lured to Williams in 1990, he helped the team to win five constructors' titles before joining McLaren in 1997 for more title success. In 2006, he moved on to Red Bull, adding three titles, starting in 2010.

2012 DRIVERS & RESULTS

Driver	Nationality	Races	Wins	Pts	Pos
Sebastian Vettel	German	20	5	281	1st
Mark Webber	Australian	20	2	179	6th

Another point of note in 2012 was that Red Bull Racing achieved fewer pole positions, and this explains why fewer wins came its way, as achieving one required a more varied range of race tactics than simply blasting away from the front. Those victories didn't start until the fourth round, at Sakhir, when Vettel won from pole with the fastest lap, with Webber winning two rounds later from pole at Monaco. Three rounds after that the Australian added another, overhauling Fernando Alonso's Ferrari at Silverstone. Vettel won again on the streets of Singapore, albeit only after Lewis Hamilton's McLaren retired from the lead, but drivers have to take whatever fortune throws their way. Then he added three more in the next three grands prix in Japan, Korea and India to pull him ahead of Alonso in the closing stages of the season, doing just enough to beat the Spaniard to the F1 crown in a dramatic last-round shoot-out in Brazil.

Unlike all of their immediate rivals, Red Bull Racing knew its 2013 driver line-up from early on once Webber had signed a contract extension. This removed an element of uncertainty that afflicted McLaren, Ferrari and Mercedes in particular and will thus have greatly assisted planning for this year's car. It also will have kept the best design tweaks within the team's four walls.

Encouragingly for all who support this dynamic team, the key ingredients have remained the same for the coming season, but it's clear that Newey, head of

aerodynamics Peter Prodromou and chief designer Rob Marshall are going to have to be on top of their game to stay ahead of the best offered by McLaren in the second half of last season.

Of course, no one can predict what is going to happen next year when a whole new series of engine regulations is adopted, but one would imagine that Newey and his gang are already thinking about how best to tackle this new set of parameters. For now, they will focus mainly on the immediate challenge of using their undoubted expertise in winning grands prix to stake their claim on this year's drivers' and constructors' championships, but all good teams plan ahead and there seems little reason to need to split up this group.

Demonstrating the attraction of success, the team has increased its financial backing from Japanese car manufacturer Infiniti and so will carry the team name Infiniti Red Bull Racing for the next four years.

FOR THE RECORD

Country of origin:	England
Team base:	Milton Keynes, England
Telephone:	(44) 01908 279700
Website:	www.redbullracing.com
Active in Formula One:	From 1997 (as Stewart until 2000, then as Jaguar Racing until 2004)
Grands Prix contested:	281
Wins:	35
Pole positions:	47
Fastest laps:	29

THE TEAM

Chairman:	Dietrich Mateschitz
Team principal:	Christian Horner
Chief technical officer:	Adrian Newey
Head of aerodynamics:	Peter Prodromou
Chief designer:	Rob Marshall
Head of car engineering:	Paul Monaghan
Engineering coordinator:	Andrew Damerum
Chief engineer:	Mark Ellis
Team manager:	Jonathan Wheatley
Test driver:	TBA
Chassis:	Red Bull RB9
Engine:	Renault V8
Tyres:	Pirelli

Team principal Christian Horner is never slow to celebrate when the team wins.
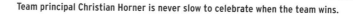

SEBASTIAN VETTEL

Sebastian has set himself quite a target for 2013, to make it four world titles in a row, but he is well equipped to do so. He had to work far harder for his 2012 crown than he did in 2011 and it will have made him an even better driver.

Everyone could see on his rapid ascent to Formula One that Sebastian was special, but not even his greatest fan will have predicted that he'd be World Champion by the age of 23, let alone a triple World Champion at 25. Yet this is how Sebastian's F1 career has shaken out since he scored that landmark victory in the wet at Monza with Scuderia Toro Rosso in 2008.

The subsequent move to Red Bull Racing for 2009 was the breakthrough, but it has still taken someone special to deliver. Certainly, last year was much less easy than 2011, as he won five times rather than 11, but he will have gained valuable extra experience as a result of this.

There is no doubt that Adrian Newey designs a supremely fast car with the very best handling. However, team-mate Mark Webber has won races in it but not titles, so Sebastian has proved himself as the man. There may come a time when Sebastian looks to see if he can deliver for another team, to prove that the title is down to him as well as the car. Indeed, there was talk last autumn that he might be thinking of moving to Ferrari in 2014, but the lure of winning for a team that

Sebastian will be all the stronger for having to really fight for his title last year.

clearly adores him is surely going to keep him at Red Bull Racing for years to come.

What Sebastian learned last year will stand him in good stead, having had to eke out maximum points even if that was for

fifth rather than victory, and the fact that Fernando Alonso got so close to depriving him of the title despite being in an inferior car will have rankled with Sebastian, as it implied that Fernando was the superior driver. Expect Sebastian to rise to another level to prove himself again.

TRACK NOTES

Nationality:	GERMAN
Born:	3 JULY 1987, HEPPENHEIM, GERMANY
Website:	www.sebastianvettel.de
Teams:	BMW SAUBER 2007, TORO ROSSO 2007-08, RED BULL RACING 2009-13

CAREER RECORD

First Grand Prix:	2007 UNITED STATES GP
Grand Prix starts:	101
Grand Prix wins:	26

2008 Italian GP, 2009 Chinese GP, British GP, Japanese GP, Abu Dhabi GP, 2010 Malaysian GP, European GP, Japanese GP, Brazilian GP, Abu Dhabi GP, 2011 Australian GP, Malaysian GP, Turkish GP, Spanish GP, Monaco GP, European GP, Belgian GP, Italian GP, Singapore GP, Korean GP, Indian GP, 2012 Bahrain GP, Singapore GP, Japanese GP, Korean GP, Indian GP

Poles:	36
Fastest laps:	15
Points:	1,054
Honours:	2010, 2011 & 2012 FORMULA ONE WORLD CHAMPION, 2006 EUROPEAN FORMULA 3 RUNNER-UP, 2004 GERMAN FORMULA BMW CHAMPION, 2003 GERMAN FORMULA BMW RUNNER-UP, 2001 EUROPEAN & GERMAN JUNIOR KART CHAMPION

BLASTING THROUGH THE JUNIOR CATEGORIES

Sebastian tore through the German karting series, but his talent was made even more obvious when he stepped up to cars in 2003. Having taken five wins in his first year in German Formula BMW, he took 18 in 2004 to be a runaway champion. Backed by Red Bull, he moved up to F3 in 2005 and finished fifth in the European series. Sebastian was then edged out by Paul di Resta in 2006, but winning two of his three races, both at Misano, in the more powerful Formula Renault 3.5 series proved his talent and Sebastian graduated to that for 2007. He won at the Nurburgring but quit after seven races – a few good F1 test runs for Sauber the previous year earning him his F1 racing call-up when Robert Kubica was injured in Canada. After this one outing, Sebastian moved to Toro Rosso. His first full campaign, in 2008, was marked by victory at Monza and so he was promoted to Red Bull Racing, landing the drivers' title for the first time in 2010.

MARK WEBBER

Last season was a good one for Mark as, although he still didn't land the world title he so covets, he at least re-established near parity with Red Bull team-mate Sebastian Vettel after being drubbed in 2011. Let's see what 2013 holds.

It's amazing to consider that last season could have turned into a decent one for this hard-working Australian, given that it took him until the sixth round even to step on to the podium, which was not a start to a campaign that would normally put a smile on anyone's face. Four fourth places, then 11th in Barcelona were his collection at that point, while Sebastian Vettel had bagged a win and a second place. Then, bang, Mark not only got his podium at Monaco but won the race. In an instant, his season was back on track and it wasn't long before the ink was dry on his contract extension to race on in 2013.

Clearly the Red Bull RB8 suited Mark better than the RB7 had in 2011 and, once the jumbled early-season form settled down, he was a match for his team-mate. Anyone who witnessed the way that Mark hunted down Fernando Alonso's Ferrari in the British GP, then passed it to win, could see that this was a driver getting back to the top of his game.

After that win at Silverstone, Mark failed to really claim the headlines, just as he failed to achieve another victory.

Mark had a better 2012 than 2011 and is sure to gather more victories in 2013.

He might have done so in Korea, where he was starting from pole, but Vettel jumped him at the start and, although the difference between them was really only the first few hundred metres of the race, it was enough for Vettel to put one over Mark again. So the gap between them came down last year, but the young German was still just that little bit better.

It will be interesting to see for which team Mark will race in 2014, as there have been rumours about him - much as there have about team-mate Vettel - joining Ferrari after Felipe Massa's one-year deal for 2013 comes to an end.

Mark is still chasing a world title, but this is his 12th season, so every race counts for him now.

TRACK NOTES

Nationality:	AUSTRALIAN
Born:	27 AUGUST 1976, QUEANBEYAN, AUSTRALIA
Website:	www.markwebber.com
Teams:	MINARDI 2002, JAGUAR 2003-04, WILLIAMS 2005-06, RED BULL RACING 2007-13

CAREER RECORD	
First Grand Prix:	2002 AUSTRALIAN GP
Grand Prix starts:	197
Grand Prix wins:	9
	2009 German GP, Brazilian GP, 2010 Spanish GP, Monaco GP, British GP, Hungarian GP, 2011 Brazilian GP, 2012 Monaco GP, British GP
Poles:	11
Fastest laps:	14
Points:	848.5
Honours:	2001 FORMULA 3000 RUNNER-UP, 1998 FIA GT RUNNER-UP, 1996 BRITISH FORMULA FORD RUNNER-UP & FORMULA FORD FESTIVAL WINNER

FORMULA ONE'S DEDICATED ATHLETE

Had his father's love of motorcycles not pointed him towards motorised sport, Mark might have followed his father on to the rugby field. However, karts beckoned, and after shining in Australian Formula Ford, Mark headed for Britain. He won the Formula Ford Festival and then called upon one of his father's rugby colleagues, superstar David Campese, to help him find the money to advance to Formula Three in 1997. After ranking fourth, though, Mark hadn't the budget to move up, so he accepted an offer from Mercedes to race in GTs. The lure of Formula One drew him back to single-seaters in 2000, when he raced in F3000. Second to Justin Wilson in 2001, Mark was given his F1 break when compatriot Paul Stoddart bought Minardi. A two-year stint with Jaguar proved his speed, and his first F1 podium followed with Williams in 2005, but his only victories were in the triathlons he loves to contest. Then his move to Red Bull Racing finally brought him his first win, at the Nurburgring in 2009.

FERRARI

Ferrari's management spent much of last year dissatisfied with the performance of their cars, but Fernando Alonso kept bringing in the results. If Pat Fry can orchestrate the building of a better chassis, then the fans will really have something to shout about.

Fernando Alonso will be praying Ferrari can build him a more competitive car so that he doesn't have to work as many miracles as last year.

It has been a few years since Ferrari was last the dominant team, and the *tifosi* are becoming impatient for a return to the glory days when they used to expect victory rather than pray for it.

Formula One has known few seasons as confusing as the first half of the 2012 World Championship, and there was no greater surprise than the Malaysian GP, when Fernando Alonso came out as winner in a race in which he really didn't fancy his chances. Indeed, the team was already holding crisis talks as to what to do to make the F2012 perform as it ought when the Spanish ace confused the issue by mastering the conditions in this wet/dry race. To the outside world, it was a great turnaround, but those within the team knew otherwise.

That Alonso continued at the head of the points table through the summer, picking up points in every race bar the Belgian GP, when he was removed from the running at the first corner as Romain

Grosjean clattered into and over his car, proved mainly his excellence rather than that of the F2012.

So, the team knows the size of the task ahead for 2013 if it's going to match the best on offer from McLaren and Red

KEY MOMENTS AND KEY PEOPLE

TEAM HISTORY
The world's most famous racing team has been in Formula One since the World Championship began in 1950. It started winning in 1951 and hasn't looked back, helping Alberto Ascari to the title in 1952 and 1953, Juan Manuel Fangio in 1956, Mike Hawthorn in 1958, Phil Hill in 1961, John Surtees in 1964, Niki Lauda in 1975 and 1977 and Jody Scheckter in 1979. After founder Enzo Ferrari's death in 1988, Michael Schumacher won five in a row from 2000 and Kimi Raikkonen was crowned in 2007.

STEFANO DOMENICALI
All Italians want to work for Ferrari, but few have felt this desire as strongly as Stefano, who grew up in Imola and watched the cars at the grands prix there. After joining the company, he started working at its Mugello circuit, then in its road car division. However, he moved across to the racing division in 1993, on the accounts side. His management skills earned him the post of team manager in 1998, and he duly succeeded Jean Todt as team principal in 2007.

2012 DRIVERS & RESULTS

Driver	Nationality	Races	Wins	Pts	Pos
Fernando Alonso	Spanish	20	3	278	2nd
Felipe Massa	Brazilian	20	0	122	7th

Bull Racing, perhaps with Lotus, Mercedes and even Williams pushing it hard. Pat Fry has now had two years since his arrival from McLaren, and so this is perhaps the season in which Ferrari will reap the fruits of his labours to give the team a more cohesive technical structure, one that will insulate it against panic if a car doesn't work as well as planned. After all, McLaren has known several horror seasons in the past decade when it has had to move mountains, with the season under way, to redesign and redevelop the car to make it more competitive. Team president Luca di Montezemolo is a man who wants results, so for team principal Stefano Domenicali this streamlining of the team structure will be reassuring, as it's said that his head will be the next one on the chopping block if things don't work well in the season ahead.

One other matter that needs to be addressed is that the team will require a stronger number two driver if it is to challenge for the constructors' titles it used to collect by the armful in Michael Schumacher's day. Felipe Massa was the number two driver in the German great's final year with Ferrari, showing well against him on occasion. However, since his head injury at the 2009 Hungarian GP, he's not been the driver he was and his reduced ability to collect points is hurting the team's push.

Of course, teams with strong number one drivers often don't want to do anything that might upset them, which means not bringing in a driver who has been winning with another top team, but it became increasingly clear through last year that Ferrari needed to act. It was too slow to secure the signature of Sergio Perez, a Ferrari academy driver after all, and so McLaren pounced moments after Lewis Hamilton announced that he was leaving the team for Mercedes. Then Ferrari dithered further and so it was left with the prospect of keeping a substandard but improving Massa on for a fourth year as its number two while other potential candidates sorted their plans to stay where they were or move elsewhere. That said, it's difficult when you might only be offering a one-year contract, as you have plans to sign a superstar for 2014 and beyond.

Quite who will be Alonso's team-mate in 2014 remains a mystery, but you can be sure that the queue for the job will be a long one.

"We must revamp our organisation and our working methods to try and be at the same level as the best, right from the first race, which for too many years we've failed to do."

Luca di Montezemolo

Stefano Domenicali spent the winter refining Ferrari's practices to produce a faster car for 2013.

FERNANDO ALONSO

Fernando produced a series of outstanding drives last year in a car that was seldom the best on track, keeping himself in the title hunt with Sebastian Vettel until late in the final round. Now it's up to Ferrari to produce a better car.

Fernando is a driver who seldom smiles, so engrossed is he in his work, so formidable his focus. Yet, in the days that followed his last-round failure to topple Sebastian Vettel and land the 2012 drivers' crown, he will surely have managed a little grin at the fact that he nearly pulled off one of the most impressive titles in memory. This was because the Ferrari F2012 he drove was seldom a match for Vettel's Red Bull RB8. Indeed, it was often not as fast as the McLaren MP4-27s and sometimes slower than the Lotus E20s. So the fact that he scored three wins and led the title race for much of the year was remarkable.

When you lose out by just three points, of course you look for the "what ifs", such as being removed from the Belgian GP at the first corner by Romain Grosjean and similarly by Kimi Raikkonen at Suzuka, but they both can find a few excuses. What will be remembered, though, is Fernando's relentless and successful hunting for points and the fact that his desire for another world title is every bit as strong as it was at the start of 2007, when he'd joined McLaren from Renault with the aim of achieving that very thing.

Fernando was pipped to 2012's title but will be all the stronger for his efforts.

Fernando has visibly turned Ferrari around and driven it forward, manhandling its cars to results that they didn't really deserve, so it's small wonder that the world's most famous team has him under contract until 2016.

The challenge will ramp up next year, as Vettel, perhaps by then a four-time champion, might be joining him at Ferrari and would surely give him a new challenge.

TRACK NOTES

Nationality:	SPANISH
Born:	29 JULY 1981, OVIEDO, SPAIN
Website:	www.fernandoalonso.com
Teams:	MINARDI 2001, RENAULT 2003-06, McLAREN 2007, RENAULT 2008-09, FERRARI 2010-13

CAREER RECORD

First Grand Prix:	2001 AUSTRALIAN GP
Grand Prix starts:	198
Grand Prix wins:	30
	2003 Hungarian GP, 2005 Malaysian GP, Bahrain GP, San Marino GP, European GP, French GP, German GP, Chinese GP, 2006 Bahrain GP, Australian GP, Spanish GP, Monaco GP, British GP, Canadian GP, Japanese GP, 2007 Malaysian GP, Monaco GP, European GP, Italian GP, 2008 Singapore GP, Japanese GP, 2010 Australian GP, German GP, Italian GP, Singapore GP, Korean GP, 2011 British GP, 2012 Malaysian GP, European GP, German GP
Poles:	22
Fastest laps:	19
Points:	1,364
Honours:	2010 & 2012 FORMULA ONE RUNNER-UP, 2005 & 2006 FORMULA ONE WORLD CHAMPION, 1999 FORMULA NISSAN CHAMPION, 1997 ITALIAN & SPANISH KART CHAMPION, 1996 WORLD & SPANISH KART CHAMPION, 1995 & 1994 SPANISH JUNIOR KART CHAMPION

WORLD CHAMPION IN KARTS AND F1

Fernando was clearly a star in the making even during his kart racing days. World kart champion at the age of 15 in 1996, he had to wait a further two years before being old enough to race cars and then elected to bypass a couple of levels to race in Formula Nissan in 1999, promptly winning the series. In 2000 he tried F3000 and starred in Formula One's immediate feeder formula, winning easily at Spa. Benetton boss Flavio Briatore gave Fernando his F1 break with Minardi in 2001. After spending 2002 as Renault's test driver, Fernando raced for the team in 2003, scored his first win in Hungary and then won ever more frequently to claim the 2005 and 2006 drivers' titles. In his year at McLaren in 2007 he fell just short of another title, and then he returned to Renault. In 2010 Fernando joined Ferrari and raced to five wins. His 2011 season wasn't as fruitful, but his position as team leader ensured that the team rotated around him, aiding his 2012 title push.

FELIPE MASSA

Improved results in the closing stages of last year saved Felipe's career with Ferrari, but his contract was extended only for one more year, so this will be a pivotal season for the Brazilian and will decide whether he stays on for 2014.

An upturn in form last autumn, once the Formula One show headed east from Europe, was what clinched an eighth year with Ferrari for Felipe. However, until he backed up his second place in Japan with fourth place in Korea, behind team-mate Fernando Alonso, his future was still in the balance as he simply hadn't been delivering in the way that a driver with so much experience should.

Felipe's contract for 2013 had been made marginally more secure when the man touted as his most likely replacement at Ferrari, Sergio Perez, was presented with the chance to drive for McLaren in place of the departing Lewis Hamilton. So the balance had already started to swing back Felipe's way, but his upturn was just in time to close the matter.

When looking to the year ahead, it must be a nagging thought for the *tifosi* that Felipe has not set the world on fire, and has been off the pace since returning to racing following the head injury he suffered at the Hungaroring in 2009. Having a driver who won't rattle Alonso's cage is one thing, but they need someone who will finish a place or two behind the Spaniard more often than

Felipe was back up to speed by late last season and must show that he can win again.

not if their beloved team is to claim the constructors' championship crown again.

Felipe's career, inevitably, is perceived as being in two parts, before and after his head injury, and if things don't improve dramatically, you can be certain that this

year he will simply be keeping the second Ferrari seat warm until a faster, hungrier driver of more proven race-winning calibre can be signed up for 2014. Sadly, Felipe is now a driver who will never become World Champion and he knows it. That he was so narrowly pipped to the crown by Lewis Hamilton in 2008 must make this reality all the more painful for him.

For all this, Felipe remains a really popular team player and is widely liked in the paddock, but most feel sure that he will be moving on.

TRACK NOTES

Nationality:	BRAZILIAN
Born:	25 APRIL 1981, SAO PAULO, BRAZIL
Website:	www.felipemassa.com
Teams:	SAUBER 2002 & 2004-05, FERRARI 2006-13

CAREER RECORD

First Grand Prix:	2002 AUSTRALIAN GP
Grand Prix starts:	173
Grand Prix wins:	11
	2006 Turkish GP, Brazilian GP,
	2007 Bahrain GP, Spanish GP, Turkish GP,
	2008 Bahrain GP, Turkish GP, French GP,
	European GP, Belgian GP, Brazilian GP
Poles:	15
Fastest laps:	14
Points:	704
Honours:	2008 FORMULA ONE RUNNER-UP,
	2001 EUROPEAN FORMULA 3000 CHAMPION,
	2000 EUROPEAN & ITALIAN FORMULA
	RENAULT CHAMPION, 1999 BRAZILIAN
	FORMULA CHEVROLET CHAMPION

AN UNCONVENTIONAL ROUTE TO F1

The early stages of Felipe's career followed the traditional pattern of national kart series, then junior single-seaters. In Felipe's case, he won the Brazilian Formula Chevrolet title in 1999. Moving to Europe in 2000, he was sensational, winning the European and Italian Formula Renault titles. He didn't have the money for Formula Three, so raced in the cheaper but more powerful F3000 Euro Series. This wasn't a top-rank category, but he won that and landed an F1 test with Sauber. He impressed and so found, suddenly, he was an F1 driver for 2002. With Ferrari showing interest, he became their test driver in 2003 before racing on for two more years with Sauber. Then, assisted by having his career managed by Nicolas Todt, he landed a Ferrari race ride in 2006. Teamed with Michael Schumacher, he wasn't disgraced and scored his first win in Turkey. He later came within a whisker of being champion in 2008, winning six times, but since the head injury he suffered in 2009 he has yet to rediscover his best form.

McLAREN

McLaren is a team which values continuity, but its hand was forced when Lewis Hamilton announced he was leaving, and so the team has signed Sergio Perez to race alongside Jenson Button as it seeks to land a championship title or two.

With Lewis Hamilton's departure to Mercedes, Jenson Button is now de facto McLaren leader and is sure to continue winning races.

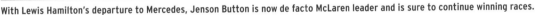

McLaren is a team that offers excellence from every angle, but team principal Martin Whitmarsh is only too aware that it hasn't always gone that final degree to turn wins into titles and is determined that this will be put right in 2013. Last year's campaign was a clear example, the team's form falling away before it came on strong to produce the best showing of all in the second half of the year following the introduction of updates at the German GP, by which time former McLaren racer Fernando Alonso had built up too much of a lead for them to catch him.

This year, after Lewis Hamilton's defection to Mercedes, and with Jenson Button being joined by third-year F1 racer Sergio Perez, the team is confident that it can deliver one or even both championship titles. Indeed, although he has yet to win a grand prix and question marks therefore remain as to his absolute potential, Perez signed a multi-year contract, so the plan is very much for him to become part of

the family, learn from Jenson's undoubted expertise, grow with the team and win with the team.

"It was a string of giant-killing performances, a trio of podiums and a killer fastest lap at Monaco that showed us

KEY MOMENTS AND KEY PEOPLE

TEAM HISTORY

Racer and engineer Bruce McLaren could have no idea what he was starting in 1964 when he followed former team-mate Jack Brabham into racing-car construction. The first forays into Formula One in 1966 were financed by success in building racing sportscars, most notably for Can-Am. However, Bruce won the 1968 Belgian GP to boost the team's reputation. Sadly, he died testing in 1970, but the F1 team blossomed, taking its first drivers' title in 1974, then enjoying all but total dominance in 1988 with Ayrton Senna and Alain Prost.

PADDY LOWE

After graduating in engineering from Cambridge University in 1984, Paddy moved into the world of motor racing three years later when he joined Williams to work in its electronics department. He made his name by running the active suspension project that did much to help Nigel Mansell win the 1992 title. McLaren signed him in 1993 and Paddy specialised in research and development, focusing on power steering, brake steer and the F1 simulator. In 2005, he became engineering director, and then at the start of 2011 he was promoted to technical director.

2012 DRIVERS & RESULTS

Driver	Nationality	Races	Wins	Pts	Pos
Jenson Button	British	20	3	188	5th
Lewis Hamilton	British	20	4	190	4th

FOR THE RECORD

Country of origin:	England
Team base:	Woking, England
Telephone:	(44) 01483 261000
Website:	www.mclaren.com
Active in Formula One:	From 1966
Grands Prix contested:	724
Wins:	182
Pole positions:	156
Fastest laps:	151

THE TEAM

Team principal:	Martin Whitmarsh
Managing director:	Jonathan Neale
Technical director:	Paddy Lowe
Director of engineering:	Tim Goss
Design & development director:	Neil Oatley
Sporting director:	Sam Michael
Aerodynamicists:	Doug McKiernan
	Andreas Ruhrmann
Head of race operations:	Simon Roberts
Head of vehicle engineering:	Mark Williams
Team manager:	David Redding
Chief race engineer:	Philip Prew
Test drivers:	Gary Paffett, Oliver Turvey
Chassis:	McLaren MP4-28
Engine:	Mercedes V8
Tyres:	Pirelli

that Sergio lacks nothing in terms of speed and commitment," explained Whitmarsh on signing the then 22-year-old Mexican from Sauber. "We've been monitoring his progress for some months and our task will now be to refine and develop his abilities as his career progresses."

Of course, the way that Perez fits in to the team is important to the success of this change in line-up, and Whitmarsh understands this. "Uniting Sergio alongside Jenson will give us a broad range of driver ability," says the team principal. "Jenson's unique blend of prodigious speed and canny race craft makes him formidably well armed to fight for victory on any grand prix circuit, while Sergio is still developing his palette of skills, and we're convinced that he's not only talented and quick but also that he's willing and eager to learn."

Furthermore, signing Perez has ended accusations that McLaren was too British and thus opened up the possibility of attracting sponsors from different regions, with Mexico's Carlos Slim – one of the world's richest men – having already been involved in developing Perez's career. Talk of Vodafone's deal reaching its conclusion at the end of this year could make any hook-up with Slim's Telmex consortium timely indeed.

Quite what technical director Paddy Lowe and his design team can deliver remains to be seen in this final year before F1's engines are downsized, but the lessons learned during the trying first half of the 2012 campaign will undoubtedly have been taken into consideration, and so while this year's MP4-28 is sure to be one of the most attractive cars on the grid, it might be even more attractive in the eyes of the team as it turns into the fastest car of them all.

The top teams are all expanding and diversifying, with Williams making notable progress in commercial uses of hybrid technology. However, McLaren is the most advanced, not only building its supercars that are starting to worry Ferrari and helping to shape the bikes ridden by Olympic gold medal winners, but also with its own Applied Technologies division helping top athletes, whether from cycling, rowing, sailing or canoeing, to improve their performance through the application of F1 measuring and performance analysis. So, McLaren expects success in all quarters, and a world championship title or two from its figurehead F1 wing would not go amiss.

"We won last year's final two grands prix on sheer pace and that achievement gave us an extremely solid platform from which to develop our 2013 car."
Martin Whitmarsh

Technical director Paddy Lowe (left) has team principal Martin Whitmarsh's full attention.

JENSON BUTTON

Lewis Hamilton's departure to Mercedes means that Jenson is de facto team leader, and the way that he not only sorted last year's car but flew in it shows his worth to the team as they bring in Sergio Perez to join him.

The 2013 season could be Jenson's greatest opportunity to add another drivers' title to the one he won with Brawn GP in 2009. Last year, he produced some moments of sublime skill, such as his wins in the season-opening race in Melbourne and the Belgian GP at the end of the summer, but if there was any luck going it seemed to be of the bad variety, whether it was a fumbled pitstop or a mechanical failure, rendering his bid for the title null and void with many races still to run after a good haul of points went begging. This year, with his silky skills, sympathetic use of tyres and the team's hoped-for design excellence, there's no reason why he shouldn't put things right.

What has always been so noticeable in recent years is the way that Jenson works with his team to find a solution to any performance shortcomings. As well as his obvious skills as a development driver, Jenson also arrives at the track with an empowering mental attitude, and that certainly helps get that extra bit of performance from his crew. Undoubtedly charming, there's an edge of steel to his nature when required, but he's not a man who makes enemies.

Jenson deserves a better run of luck in 2013 than last year.

After three years of having Lewis Hamilton as his team-mate, it's all change for 2013, with Sergio Perez joining, so there will be a new dynamic for the Woking-based team. However, this too will probably be a positive change for Jenson, as he has become clearly the team leader

and will be happy to assist the new boy while aware that the Mexican may well stretch him. Then again, he was confident enough in his own abilities to enter what many saw as a lion's den when he joined Lewis's team in 2010, where he went head to head with his fellow Briton and wasn't found wanting. This is clearly a big season for Jenson.

TRACK NOTES

Nationality:	BRITISH
Born:	19 JANUARY 1980, FROME, ENGLAND
Website:	www.jensonbutton.com
Teams:	WILLIAMS 2000, BENETTON/RENAULT 2001-02, BAR/HONDA 2003-08, BRAWN 2009, McLAREN 2010-12

CAREER RECORD

First Grand Prix:	2000 AUSTRALIAN GP
Grand Prix starts:	229
Grand Prix wins:	15
	2006 Hungarian GP, 2009 Australian GP, Malaysian GP, Bahrain GP, Spanish GP, Monaco GP, Turkish GP, 2010 Australian GP, Chinese GP, 2011 Canadian GP, Hungarian GP, Japanese GP, 2012 Australian GP, Belgian GP, Brazilian GP
Poles:	8
Fastest laps:	8
Points:	999
Honours:	2009 FORMULA ONE WORLD CHAMPION, 1999 MACAU FORMULA THREE RUNNER-UP, 1998 FORMULA FORD FESTIVAL WINNER, BRITISH FORMULA FORD CHAMPION & McLAREN AUTOSPORT BRDC YOUNG DRIVER, 1997 EUROPEAN SUPER A KART CHAMPION, 1991 BRITISH CADET KART CHAMPION

WAITING FOR F1 SUCCESS

For a driver who flew through karting, then the junior single-seater formulae, winning constantly, having to wait nine years from his grand prix debut with Williams until he finally became world champion must have been demoralising. Yet the journey that took him via Benetton and Renault to BAR/Honda finally yielded a first win in Hungary in 2006. Then, thanks largely to exploiting a loophole in the rules and running a double diffuser in 2009, he raced to six wins and the title with Brawn GP. Back in 1998, he won the McLaren Autosport BRDC Young Driver award and so it was fitting that he joined McLaren for 2010. This meant that he was pitting himself directly against Lewis Hamilton and this was seen as a brave move, as most paddock insiders reckoned that Lewis was the faster of the pair, but it was the making of Jenson as not only was he not disgraced but it was clear that some of the team started looking to him to drag them forward from any setbacks.

SERGIO PEREZ

Moving to McLaren is the break that this young Mexican's promising career deserves, and it's rare to be admitted to one of F1's top few teams, so he must grasp the opportunity provided by Lewis Hamilton's departure to show that he's a winner.

All the talk through the first half of 2012 was whether Ferrari would take a risk and pick Sergio to replace Felipe Massa after another campaign in which the Brazilian failed to match team leader Fernando Alonso for results. Yet, despite the clear evidence of Sergio's talents when he did everything but beat Alonso to the chequered flag in the wet at Sepang in his Sauber in the second race of the year, Ferrari put off making a decision. McLaren was therefore delighted that the Mexican was still available when it became clear that Lewis Hamilton was indeed quitting the team for Mercedes. In a flash, McLaren struck and tied up the deal.

So, what has McLaren landed? Sergio is a driver who displays something vital in Formula One's current guise: an ability to make his tyres last way longer than most of his rivals, thus affording the team the opportunity to employ a wider range of tactics to help him up the order. Take his drive to second place at Monza last September, when Sergio started 12th but stayed out 10 laps or more longer than his rivals on the hard rubber before pitting, and so rose to lead, before rejoining

Sergio must reproduce the form that led to second places at Sepang and Monza in 2012.

eighth and then advancing back to second with some excellent overtaking on the softer rubber. Perhaps the Sauber was lighter on its tyres than its rivals, but the splashes of speed he displayed leave people in little doubt that he will make

an impact at McLaren, where he has been described as the "perfect blend of youth and experience".

If there is to be any concern among McLaren fans about Sergio's signing it is that he appeared to go off the boil in the closing races of the season after agreeing to join the team. A glance at his results shows that after that second place at Monza he claimed just one further point in the final seven rounds, for 10th place in Singapore, during which time his Sauber team-mate Kamui Kobayashi collected 23.

Sergio is aware of what an opportunity this is, commenting when he signed for his new team, "I'm under no illusion that it is indeed a very big step, as it would be for any driver, but I'm ready for it."

TRACK NOTES

Nationality:	MEXICAN
Born:	26 JANUARY 1990, GUADALAJARA, MEXICO
Website:	www.sergioperez.mx
Teams:	SAUBER 2011-12, McLAREN 2013

CAREER RECORD	
First Grand Prix:	2011 BAHRAIN GP
Grand Prix starts:	37
Grand Prix wins:	0
(best result: second, 2012 Malaysian GP)	
Poles:	0
Fastest laps:	1
Points:	80
Honours: 2010 GP2 RUNNER-UP, 2007 BRITISH FORMULA THREE NATIONAL CLASS CHAMPION	

RACING IS IN THE BLOOD

It was always likely that Sergio would race, as not only was his father Antonio a racer – a Mexican Formula Vee champion – but his older brother Antonio was too, winning the Corona NASCAR series. His determination to make his mark was clear when he went from success in karting to Barber Dodge single-seaters in the USA and then moved to Germany, aged just 15, to live on his own and attempt to succeed in Formula BMW. He finished sixth in his second year, also having his first taste of power by racing in A1GP for his country, before moving on to Britain to try Formula Three. Sergio won the National class title and then raced in the main class in 2008, finishing fourth overall. GP2 followed, where he showed winning form in the Asian series before his first full campaign in 2009. It took until the second year of GP2 for Sergio to shine, finishing as runner-up in 2010 to Pastor Maldonado. In 2011 he became Mexico's fifth F1 driver when he stepped up with Sauber.

Precision pitstops are an essential component of race strategy and McLaren prided itself on achieving the fastest pitstops of all in 2012, but not all went smoothly.

LOTUS F1 TEAM

Changing the team livery to black and gold as it transformed itself from Renault to Lotus for 2012 seemed to change the team's fortunes and the Eric Boullier-led squad really did mix it with the big hitters, boding well for 2013.

Kimi Raikkonen settled back into F1 with aplomb. The question is whether he and Lotus will be able to expand on his one win.

Change can be confusing, and Formula One fans the world over probably spent the opening race of last season trying to work out which team was Lotus, which was Caterham and where the Renault team had gone. That wasn't good. Yet the team that had been Renault, running in the 1970s Lotus livery of black and gold in 2011 as Lotus Renault GP to rank fifth overall through the combined efforts of Nick Heidfeld, Vitaly Petrov and Bruno Senna, was still running black and gold cars, this time called Lotus, for Kimi Raikkonen and Romain Grosjean. Meanwhile, what had been Team Lotus in 2011 was still running its cars in dark green and yellow – Team Lotus colours from the 1960s – but this time as Caterham ... At least neither team tried to confuse the fans any further, as both raced on with Renault engines in their tails.

What impressed most in 2012, though, was that the new Lotus outfit was very competitive. Indeed, one of the features of last year's Lotus E20 was its balance, as the chassis produced by James Allison and his design team was clearly good to drive, whether in the hands of Raikkonen or Grosjean. Some reckoned that the car and its Renault V8 were good enough

KEY MOMENTS AND KEY PEOPLE

TEAM HISTORY

It needs to be explained that the team racing as Lotus in 2012 has nothing to do with the illustrious team that was founded by Colin Chapman in the 1950s. This team started life as Toleman, reached Formula One in 1981, starred with Senna in 1984, was bought by the Benetton family in 1985, raced on and won the title in 1994 and 1995 with Michael Schumacher, then was renamed Renault in 2002, before winning again with Fernando Alonso in 2005 and 2006. The team changed its name to Lotus in 2012.

ALAN PERMANE

Lotus's loyal track operations director has been with the team for 24 years, having joined in 1989 when it was Benetton. He started as an electronics technician and began travelling to the races in 1992. An assistant race engineer by 1996, working under Pat Symonds on Jean Alesi's car, he went on to engineer Giancarlo Fisichella, Jarno Trulli once the team became Renault, then Fisichella again. Promoted to chief race engineer in 2007, he took on the operations role in 2011.

2012 DRIVERS & RESULTS

Driver	Nationality	Races	Wins	Pts	Pos
Jerome d'Ambrosio	Belgian	1	0	0	23rd
Romain Grosjean	French	19	0	96	8th
Kimi Raikkonen	Finnish	20	1	207	3rd

to take a win, but it took the returning World Champion, back from his sojourn in rallying, until the 18th round to do it. Over the course of the season, Raikkonen suffered from being the less effective of the pair in qualifying, Grosjean from making too many mistakes that led to clashes and often to retirement, with none being more spectacular than his first-corner aerobatics in the Belgian GP. He will have learned from the subsequent one-race ban and perhaps will avoid similar over-exuberant confrontations in the future.

The step forward that this pair made for the team, all orchestrated by team principal Eric Boullier, who had had the confidence to employ them, helped the team advance from a distant fifth overall in the 2011 constructors' championship to rank a very solid fourth. This improvement was achieved with its first win since Fernando Alonso won the 2008 Japanese GP. However, its ranking came largely through collecting 10 podium finishes, up eight on its 2011 tally of two. Had Grosjean been less of a crash magnet, the team might even have beaten McLaren to third place overall.

While there have been changes of name and ownership in recent years, plus the destabilising loss of star driver Robert Kubica to injuries sustained in a rally accident, this team is capable of staying solid and even pressing forward, because it's still manned largely by a loyal workforce at its long-standing headquarters in Enstone, and it's their years of top-line experience that give the team its backbone. This bloodline goes all the way back to when Toleman entered F1 in 1981. The team personnel are settled not just in their jobs and how the team works, but also in their domestic lives, where they live, where their children go to school, and that's important.

Looking ahead to the 2013 season, the sensible thing for team chairman Gerard Lopez was always going to be to keep the same driver pairing, so that they could build on all the progress made last year. What will encourage them most is the fact that last year's car was a model of consistency, while some of their rivals were up at one grand prix and, sometimes inexplicably, down at another. This alone will give Raikkonen and Grosjean a platform from which to launch their attack.

"Last year we scored our first win with the Lotus name and with the continuity and stability that we have, I'm sure that we'll be fighting for podiums again."
Eric Boullier

FOR THE RECORD

Country of origin:	France
Team base:	Enstone, England
Telephone:	(44) 01608 678000
Website:	www.lotusf1team.com
Active in Formula One:	As Toleman 1981-85; as Bennetton 1986-2001; as Renault 2002-11; as Lotus since 2012
Grands Prix contested:	515*
Wins:	47
Pole positions:	34
Fastest laps:	54

* NB these stats do not include the 1977-85 period of the Renault manufacturer-entered team

THE TEAM

Chairman:	Gerard Lopez
Team principal & managing director:	Eric Boullier
Technical director:	James Allison
Deputy technical director:	Naoki Tokunaga
Chief designer:	Martin Tolliday
Head of aerodynamics:	Dirk de Beer
Operations director:	John Mardle
Track operations director:	Alan Permane
Team manager:	Paul Seaby
Race engineers:	Simon Rennie & Mark Slade
Test driver:	TBA
Chassis:	Lotus E21
Engine:	Renault V8
Tyres:	Pirelli

Principal Eric Boullier (left) and technical director James Allison (right) make a strong team.

KIMI RAIKKONEN

Kimi's Formula One comeback last year peaked with a dominant win in Abu Dhabi late in the season, and he backed this up with his quiet and effective manner. This year, he needs a faster car.

Kimi is the most unusual racer competing in the World Championship. He has been there, done that, won the drivers' title and now manages the near impossible by ensuring that he has as low a profile as can be. The 33-year-old Finn simply wants to race cars and doesn't want a minute of promotional duty outside the car if he can get away with it, as shown by his monosyllabic press conference performances. Attend a grand prix, though, and you have to have some sympathy for the drivers, as the calls on their time continue almost from dawn to dusk, especially if they're at their home grand prix. At least, as there's no Finnish GP, Kimi is spared that particular extra pressure.

However, in a sport that has just 20-something drivers on display at a grand prix, having one of the leading lights effectively opt out of everything except the time spent behind the wheel is not a desirable state of affairs, so one hopes that this leopard will change his spots for 2013 and at least smile for the cameras.

Some wondered how fast Kimi would be after two years away from Formula One, competing mainly in rallying, but

Kimi supplied driving excellence plus deadpan radio correspondence last year.

remarkably he slotted straight back into the level at which he had been performing for Ferrari in 2009, being very fast and making no mistakes. He wasn't driving a Ferrari, of course, but a Lotus for the team known formerly as Renault and before

that Benetton, and you knew that he was making it travel as fast as it would go. This meant one win and a trio of second-place finishes in Bahrain, Valencia and at the Hungaroring, plus thirds in Barcelona, at Hockenheim and Spa-Francorchamps.

TRACK NOTES

Nationality:	FINNISH
Born:	17 OCTOBER 1979, ESPOO, FINLAND
Website:	www.kimiraikkonen.com
Teams:	SAUBER 2001, McLAREN 2002-06, FERRARI 2007-09, LOTUS 2012-13

CAREER RECORD

First Grand Prix:	2001 AUSTRALIAN GP
Grand Prix starts:	177
Grand Prix wins:	19
	2003 Malaysian GP, 2004 Belgian GP, 2005 Spanish GP, Monaco GP, Canadian GP, Hungarian GP, Turkish GP, Belgian GP, Japanese GP, 2007 Australian GP, French GP, British GP, Belgian GP, Chinese GP, Brazilian GP, 2008 Malaysian GP, Spanish GP, 2009 Belgian GP, 2012 Abu Dhabi GP
Poles:	16
Fastest laps:	37
Points:	776
Honours:	2007 FORMULA ONE WORLD CHAMPION, 2003 & 2005 FORMULA ONE RUNNER-UP, 2000 BRITISH FORMULA RENAULT CHAMPION, 1999 BRITISH FORMULA RENAULT WINTER SERIES CHAMPION, 1998 EUROPEAN SUPER A KART RUNNER-UP, FINNISH KART CHAMPION & NORDIC KART CHAMPION

A MAN WHO WILL COMPETE IN ANYTHING

It's no coincidence that Kimi has competed wearing a helmet modelled on that of James Hunt, as he's a driver who, had he been born 25 years earlier, would have been just like the 1976 World Champion. Kimi isn't a driver who likes to be constrained by a modern PR role: he likes to race and then to party. In fact he might have been equally at home in the 1960s, when F1 drivers would also take part in the GT and touring car races supporting the grand prix. Instead, after he had rocketed from his car racing debut in Formula Renault to an F1 ride in a record-breaking 23 races, finished sixth on his debut for Sauber in 2001, won 15 races with McLaren and won the 2007 drivers' title in the first of three seasons with Ferrari, he simply broke free from the shackles. The World Rally Championship caught his imagination, so in 2010 he went and competed in that for Citroen. He even tried a couple of races on NASCAR's ovals, but Formula One drew him back.

ROMAIN GROSJEAN

Last year Romain showed emphatically that he has the pace to shine in Formula One, but it will be interesting to see whether he can keep his speed while managing to exercise some caution after a series of accidents in 2012.

This is a vital season for Romain, as he received considerable unwanted attention last year for his inability to avoid contact with other drivers' cars, particularly on the opening lap. Fortunately, Lotus team principal Eric Boullier remains a fan and has kept Romain on, giving him another chance when many in the sport – mainly those whose cars he had collected in collisions – called for him to be dropped, saying that he either took too many risks or lacked the spatial awareness for wheel-to-wheel combat. His one-race suspension was a humiliation but also a wake-up call, and it will be a measure of Romain's mind management and ability to heed advice – offered in particular after his spectacular mess-up at the start of the Belgian GP – if he can keep his speed while learning how to race at close quarters without taking his rivals out.

What was clear, though, was that the speed that helped Romain to Formula Three, Auto GP and GP2 titles translates well to Formula One, as he was every bit a match for his 2012 team-mate Kimi Raikkonen, World Champion in 2007 before his years away in other forms of motor sport.

Romain must demonstrate that he's learned from the clashes that spoiled last year.

Last year, third place in Bahrain and Hungary and second place in Canada proved Romain's credentials for mixing it with the Red Bulls, McLarens and Ferraris, but what is needed in 2013 is a run of solid results that are not interrupted by retirements.

Then and only then will Romain will be able to prove that he has what it takes to turn his speed into wins and perhaps even a world title. Certainly, some championship winners have reached Formula One with far inferior records, so there is no reason why Romain can't mature into the real thing if only he can sort out his demons and still dare to drive to his potential.

While compatriots Charles Pic and Jean-Eric Vergne are continuing their apprenticeships, Romain carries the proud tradition of French racers in F1 and the pressure is mounting, as the last Frenchman to win a grand prix was Olivier Panis in a surprise result at Monaco in 2006.

TRACK NOTES

Nationality:	FRENCH
Born:	17 APRIL 1986, GENEVA, SWITZERLAND
Website:	www.romaingrosjean.com
Teams:	RENAULT 2009, LOTUS 2012-13

CAREER RECORD

First Grand Prix:	2009 EUROPEAN GP
Grand Prix starts:	26
Grand Prix wins:	0
	(best result: 2nd, 2012 Canadian GP)
Poles:	0
Fastest laps:	1
Points:	96
Honours:	2011 GP2 CHAMPION & GP2 ASIA CHAMPION, 2010 AUTO GP CHAMPION, 2008 GP2 ASIA CHAMPION, 2007 FORMULA THREE EUROSERIES CHAMPION, 2005 FRENCH FORMULA RENAULT CHAMPION, 2003 SWISS FORMULA RENAULT 1600 CHAMPION

A WINNER AT EVERY LEVEL

Romain is one of those drivers who make their racing seasons count. Wins are good, but titles are better. He dominated the Swiss Formula Renault 1600 series in 2003; two years later he was the French champion, and two years after that the Formula Three Euroseries champion. In 2008, as well as racing in GP2 and winning the Asian series, he did some F1 tests with Renault, and it was with this team that he got his F1 break when he replaced Nelson Piquet Jr in mid-season after a strong start to his GP2 campaign. Things didn't gel and he wasn't retained, but a step down to race and win in GT1 sportscars in 2010 led to him returning to single-seaters in the Auto GP series later in the year, and this resulted in another title. He gambled on having another crack at GP2 in 2011 and won that title too, earning his right to a second bite at Formula One. This came with the same team, now racing as Lotus.

MERCEDES AMG PETRONAS

Ross Brawn has spent three years shaping the Mercedes team, delivering its first win last year. This year, though, the bar is set somewhat higher, and the signing of Lewis Hamilton to replace Michael Schumacher shows his ambition and intent.

Michael Schumacher has retired for good and so Nico Rosberg will have a very different team-mate for the season ahead: Lewis Hamilton.

Opinion was always divided as to whether Michael Schumacher's return to Formula One as a driver in 2010 after a three-year break was a good thing. The seven-time World Champion was 41 when he came back, and although the move helped fill his coffers it didn't add to his reputation, especially when it was team-mate Nico Rosberg and not he who scooped the team's only win in the past three years. Michael's best was third place in Valencia in a rare finish, and this wasn't enough. Perhaps it was unfair to expect him to win on his return, as the team that had cleaned up the year before when racing as Brawn GP didn't strike lucky two years in a row and thus didn't have the performance advantage that double diffusers had given Jenson Button and Rubens Barrichello in 2009.

The team was good, but team principal Ross Brawn has spent the years between then and now building up a technical and design line-up of impressive calibre. With Bob Bell leading from the front as technical

director, Aldo Costa as engineering director and Geoff Willis as technology director, combined with John Owen as chief designer and newcomer Mike Elliott in charge of aerodynamics, this year's drivers can expect the most competitive Mercedes

KEY MOMENTS AND KEY PEOPLE

TEAM HISTORY
Mercedes-Benz had a prodigious first spell in Formula One between 1954 and 1955, winning nine of the 12 grands prix it contested, with Juan Manuel Fangio and Stirling Moss leading from the front. Although the German automotive manufacturer became involved again when its engines were supplied to teams from 1994, Mercedes waited until 2010 before it had its own team in F1 for a second time, when it took over Brawn GP, with fourth place overall in 2010 and 2011 its best showing yet in the constructors' championship.

BOB BELL
One of the newer faces at Mercedes AMG Petronas, the team's technical director joined McLaren back in 1982 and ran its research and development department before working on its land speed record project in 1990. A move to Benetton as senior aerodynamicist followed in 1997, and the Ulsterman went on to have a brief spell at Jordan before returning when the team was renamed Renault and rising to become technical director. When Flavio Briatore had to step down, he became team principal. He joined Mercedes in April 2011.

2012 DRIVERS & RESULTS

Driver	Nationality	Races	Wins	Pts	Pos
Nico Rosberg	German	20	0	93	9th
Michael Schumacher	German	20	0	49	13th

yet. Indeed, Brawn is clear in this mission: "The potential is now there to match any team on the grid, which is the minimum standard for a Mercedes-Benz works team. Our task is now to translate that potential into on-track performance for this season and beyond."

Norbert Haug, vice-president of Mercedes-Benz Motorsport, agrees: "We know that it is time to take the next step, in order to deliver consistent front-running performances in the tradition of the Silver Arrows."

Last year, although the F1 W03 gave the team its first win when Rosberg was first home in China, the car would qualify well thanks to its clever double DRS but would then lose its way in races as the season wore on and so was not a challenger to the newly pacesetting McLarens, suffering in particular in terms of tyre degradation that left the drivers struggling for grip as the races went on.

Talking of drivers, Rosberg will be partnered by a new team-mate, as Lewis Hamilton is due to be installed on the other side of the garage after the most dramatic move on last year's driver market. Coaxing him away from the excellence of McLaren, Mercedes sold the move to Lewis on the basis that it is preparing a huge push in 2014, when new chassis and engine rules are introduced, convincing Lewis that he will have the ultimate package for the

season after this. Also, it made him realise that he wants a new challenge.

Non-executive chairman Niki Lauda is clear about what Lewis brings to the team: "When Lewis joins, it's a big change for everybody. It's high motivation as they all know that if they don't give him a decent car he won't win." The Austrian veteran even reckons that his arrival will motivate the team to produce a more competitive car for 2013 – "and I'm looking forward to what we can achieve together".

"If the car is competitive, and this is possible," Lauda continues, "then Lewis will win races. Also, the Hamilton effect will push Nico to go faster and Nico will push Lewis to go faster, and this is all you need in a team." Brawn concurs with this: "I believe that the combination of Lewis and Nico will be the most dynamic and exciting pairing on the grid in 2013 and I'm looking forward to what we can achieve together."

Perhaps the hardest thing for the team this year is to start forging an image of its own. Winning races will help, but too often last year its cars were mired in the midfield, largely ignored by the TV cameras and thus largely anonymous.

FOR THE RECORD

Country of origin:	England
Team base:	Brackley, England
Telephone:	(44) 01280 844000
Website:	www.mercedes-amg-f1.com
Active in Formula One:	As BAR 1999-2005; as Honda Racing 2006-08; as Brawn GP 2009; as Mercedes since 2010
Grands Prix contested:	246*
Wins:	10
Pole positions:	9
Fastest laps:	7

*NB This figure does not include the 12 races contested by Mercedes in 1954-55.

THE TEAM

Team principal:	Ross Brawn
Chief executive officer:	Nick Fry
Non-executive chairman:	Niki Lauda
Chief operating officer:	Rob Thomas
Technical director:	Bob Bell
Technology director:	Geoff Willis
Engineering director:	Aldo Costa
Chief designer:	John Owen
Head of aerodynamics:	Mike Elliott
Head of vehicle engineering:	Craig Wilson
Chief engineer:	Russell Cooley
Sporting director:	Ron Meadows
Test driver:	TBA
Chassis:	Mercedes F1 W04
Engine:	Mercedes V8
Tyres:	Pirelli

"I'm delighted to welcome Lewis to our team. The arrival of a driver of his calibre is a testament of Mercedes-Benz in Formula One and I'm proud he shares our vision and ambition for the success of the Silver Arrows."

Ross Brawn

Pride and relief were felt by Ross Brawn and Norbert Haug last year when Nico Rosberg won in China.

NICO ROSBERG

Nico and Lewis Hamilton were team-mates in karting, growing up in the sport together. Now they are together again at Mercedes, and people expect Lewis to get the upper hand once more, so it's up to Nico, a grand prix winner in 2012, to prove them wrong.

There had been flashes of speed from Nico ever since he made his Formula One debut in 2006, but it took until his seventh season for that promise to be realised when he raced to victory in the Chinese GP. In so doing, not only did he lay down a marker against illustrious Mercedes AMG Petronas team-mate Michael Schumacher but he became just the second son of a World Champion to win a grand prix, following Damon Hill's breakthrough at the Hungaroring in 1993. Whether Nico will go on, like Damon, to become a second-generation world champion remains to be seen.

For the year ahead, he will have a new team-mate to mark himself against: Lewis Hamilton, who has chosen to see whether Mercedes can guide him to his second world title after four years of trying without further success with McLaren. Of course, they know each other of old, and are good friends.

This might be tested, though, as the dynamic of the team is sure to change. That said, Nico seemed to come out on top when he was partnered with Schumacher, and his older compatriot was certainly a driver who expected to be the centre of

Nico welcomes Lewis as a friend, but we'll have to see how well they work together.

attention whether driving for Benetton, Ferrari or Mercedes.

What both Nico and Lewis will be praying for is that Ross Brawn can coax the Mercedes team to create a car that can not only show promise at the start of the year but then maintain that performance all season, something that it failed to do through 2012.

As it's his fourth year with the team, Nico will certainly have no trouble with the internal dynamics, and his smooth, considered driving style is one that ought to help them deliver results that match their potential, while the challenge of a new team-mate is sure to make him faster still.

What Nico has to remember is that he matched Schumacher in qualifying and came out ahead on points scored. The target will be set higher by Lewis, but he knows the team, is supported well by father, Keke, and is more than bright enough to adapt to changing circumstances. So, if he's mentally up for it, his biggest challenge yet in F1 might well be the making of him.

SON OF A CHAMPION

Although guided into a childhood of karting by his father, Keke – F1 World Champion with Williams in 1982 – Nico is unusual in racing circles in that he was encouraged to go to university too. However, racing won out. After driving for the same team as Lewis Hamilton in kart racing, Nico stepped up to single-seaters and won the German Formula BMW title at the first attempt in 2002, thus landing a car racing title a year before Lewis did. After showing good speed in two seasons of European Formula Three, Nico advanced to GP2 a year before Lewis and beat Heikki Kovalainen to the title. That was in 2005 and it earned him promotion to Formula One with Williams, impressing on his debut by taking fastest lap in Bahrain. After three more years with the team as it tried to rediscover its form, Nico moved to Mercedes for 2010 and compared well with team-mate Michael Schumacher, even beating him to be the one to give the team its first win.

TRACK NOTES

Nationality:	GERMAN
Born:	27 JUNE 1985, WIESBADEN, GERMANY
Website:	www.nicorosberg.com
Teams:	WILLIAMS 2006-09,
	MERCEDES 2010-13

CAREER RECORD

First Grand Prix:	2006 BAHRAIN GP
Grand Prix starts:	128
Grand Prix wins:	1
	2012 Chinese GP
Poles:	1
Fastest laps:	3
Points:	399.5
Honours:	2005 GP2 CHAMPION, 2002
	FORMULA BMW CHAMPION, 2000 EUROPEAN
	FORMULA A KART RUNNER-UP

LEWIS HAMILTON

Lewis Hamilton's switch to Mercedes was, without a doubt, the key move on the driver market for 2013, with Lewis surprising many with his decision to leave McLaren, the team that nurtured him from his karting days, in pursuit of new challenges.

To understand why Lewis elected to leave McLaren, a team of established excellence, to join Mercedes GP, a team that has won just once since it morphed from Brawn GP in 2010, is to understand an individual who wants to go his own way. The men who nurtured his career – father, Anthony, and McLaren supremo Ron Dennis – have been put behind him, and last autumn Lewis rejected team principal Martin Whitmarsh's attempts to match Mercedes's financial inducements to keep him at McLaren. Instead he chose to cut the tie, perhaps to gain more control over his own image rights and time, or perhaps simply to prove that he can win for a team other than McLaren.

There's no doubting that Ross Brawn has assembled a fine technical team at Mercedes, with Bob Bell, Aldo Costa and Geoff Willis, but it has to be seen as bold to leap from the team that ranked third last year to one that ranked fifth. Perhaps Lewis has his eye set more on 2014, when the new engine regulations are to be implemented and he feels that Mercedes will produce the best new engine.

For all the concerns about whether it's the right move, Lewis has a legion of supporters, people who believe that although he still makes occasional errors of judgement, he

Lewis proved his pace again last year and must be hoping his new car is fast in 2013.

remains the out-and-out fastest driver in Formula One. Niki Lauda, now non-executive director at Mercedes, is one. The three-time world champion said last year: "In a bad car, Lewis is the best driver as he's unbelievably quick and makes no compromise. You can ask, 'Why should I leave a competitive car?' but my argument is that if you're looking for a challenge then Mercedes is one. Think of it the other way around: if Schumacher couldn't get the team running up front in three years and you do it better, people will rate you much more highly."

TRACK NOTES

Nationality:	BRITISH
Born: 7 JANUARY 1985, STEVENAGE, ENGLAND	
Website:	www.lewishamilton.com
Teams: McLAREN 2007-12, MERCEDES GP 2013	

CAREER RECORD

First Grand Prix:	2007 AUSTRALIAN GP
Grand Prix starts:	110
Grand Prix wins:	21

2007 Canadian GP, United States GP, Hungarian GP, Japanese GP, 2008 Australian GP, Monaco GP, British GP, German GP, Chinese GP, 2009 Hungarian GP, Singapore GP, 2010 Turkish GP, Canadian GP, Belgian GP, 2011 Chinese GP, German GP, Abu Dhabi GP, 2012 Canadian GP, Hungarian GP, Italian GP, United States GP

Poles:	26
Fastest laps:	12
Points:	913
Honours:	2008 FORMULA

ONE WORLD CHAMPION, 2006 GP2 CHAMPION, 2005 EUROPEAN FORMULA THREE CHAMPION, 2003 BRITISH FORMULA RENAULT CHAMPION, 2000 WORLD KART CUP CHAMPION & EUROPEAN FORMULA A KART CHAMPION, 1999 ITALIAN INTERCONTINENTAL A KARTING CHAMPION, 1996 McLAREN MERCEDES CHAMPION OF THE FUTURE, 1995 BRITISH CADET KARTING CHAMPION

WIN AFTER WIN AFTER WIN

Some drivers reach Formula One after winning a few races here and there, landing not so much as a single championship title, but having enough momentum and sometimes finance to make the final jump from GP2. Lewis is from the opposite end of the spectrum, as he won title after title in karting, then continued this success through the junior formulae, being crowned at every level. Picked up by McLaren during his karting years, Lewis was then eased through Formula Renault and Formula Three. After taking two years to land the European crown, Lewis stepped up to GP2 and proved his pedigree by winning that as a rookie. What followed, when he made his F1 debut with McLaren in 2007 and was immediately a front-runner, confirmed his potential as a future world champion. Pipped at the final round in 2007, he landed the title at his second attempt in 2008. Race wins kept coming and, even with occasional mistakes while leading, he has produced some mesmerising drives, such as winning at Monza last year.

SAUBER

Watching a Sauber chase a Ferrari home at Sepang last year and then tear through the pack for another second place at Monza made one realise that this is a team that can hit the high notes. This year the excellent Nico Hulkenberg leads the attack.

It's a case of new season, new drivers as Nico Hulkenberg and Esteban Gutierrez come in to replace Sergio Perez and Kamui Kobayashi.

The loss of Sergio Perez to McLaren is a big one for this steadfast Swiss team, as he was the jewel in its crown, a driver truly capable of wringing the last fraction of performance from its cars in the races, and delivering the results that get teams noticed. Still, the Mexican driver's obvious skills in the cockpit and the fact that he was a member of the Ferrari academy meant that he was always going to move on, most likely to Ferrari. It was just a question of when. This is what happens when you're one of the teams without huge financial clout: it's like being a lower-division football team that has unearthed a player with rare talent.

When news broke late last September of Perez's departure to McLaren, to replace Mercedes-bound Lewis Hamilton, there was a sudden flurry of excitement when people thought that Michael Schumacher might continue his Formula One twilight years with the Sauber F1 Team, as he knew Peter Sauber from the days when he raced

sportscars for him in 1991 before he made it to F1, but his retirement is permanent this time.

This left the team with decisions to make on its driver line-up, and Kamui Kobayashi, who had been earmarked for

KEY MOMENTS AND KEY PEOPLE

TEAM HISTORY
Peter Sauber's team started in sportscar racing in the 1970s, honed from his own racing experience. After also building F3 cars, it joined forces with Mercedes for Le Mans in the 1980s and this looked to have paved the way for them to enter Formula One together, but Sauber went it alone in 1993, the team scoring its one victory in Canada in 2008, when it was in the third year of partnership with BMW. This ended in 2009, since when Ferrari engines have been used.

WILLEM TOET
Having been a race engineer in his native Australia in the late 1970s, Willem came to Europe in 1982 and worked on Ray Mallock's Group C sportscars. After joining Benetton as a wind tunnel engineer in 1985, he became Reynard's director of aerodynamics in 1991 and then returned to Benetton. He moved to Ferrari in 1995, filled the post of head of aerodynamics at BAR in 1999, arrived at BMW Sauber in 2006 and then had a spell at RML before coming back to Formula One and Sauber in 2011.

2012 DRIVERS & RESULTS

Driver	Nationality	Races	Wins	Pts	Pos
Sergio Perez	Mexican	20	0	66	10th
Kamui Kobayashi	Japanese	20	0	60	12th

FOR THE RECORD

Country of origin:	Switzerland
Team base:	Hinwil, Switzerland
Telephone:	(41) 44 937 9000
Website:	www.sauberf1team.com
Active in Formula One:	From 1993
	(as BMW Sauber 2006-10)
Grands Prix contested:	345
Wins:	1
Pole positions:	1
Fastest laps:	4

THE TEAM

Team principal:	Monisha Kaltenborn
Operations director:	Axel Kruse
Chief designer:	Matt Morris
Chief mechanic:	Urs Kuratle
Head of aerodynamics:	Willem Toet
Head of vehicle performance:	Pierre Wache
Team manager:	Beat Zehnder
Head of track engineering:	Giampaolo Dall'ara
Test driver:	Robin Frijns
Chassis:	Sauber C32
Engine:	Ferrari V8
Tyres:	Pirelli

possible replacement as he had fallen so far short of Perez in the first half of the season, suddenly looked more likely to stay on in the interest of continuity. Test driver Esteban Gutierrez was a possible, having won several GP2 rounds and finished third overall in F1's feeder formula. Furthermore, his signing would possibly have ensured the continued patronage of Carlos Slim, who backed Sauber with sponsorship from his Telmex concern. However, the matter was more than settled when Nico Hulkenberg, a driver rated even more highly than Perez, was coaxed to join from Force India, giving the team a team leader and thus allowing it to sign Gutierrez for the second seat.

It's not just on the driver front that Sauber has undergone change, as technical director James Key moved on last April, citing the reason that has been heard all too often before at Hinwil: he wanted to return with his family to England. If enticing technical brains away from that swathe of England known as Motorsport Valley is always difficult, keeping them has over the years proved just as hard. Key's loss will be keenly felt, as last year's Sauber, the C31, showed some real speed. Indeed, the C31 was arguably the most competitive car that the team has ever had. Yes, Robert Kubica won a race, the Canadian GP, in 2008, but the C31 was more competitive across the course of the season. Its particular

strength was race pace, as the car seemed very light on its tyres, which would yield dividends in the closing part of a grand prix. However, the flipside of this was that it wasn't very good at getting heat into its tyres and so was less than competitive in qualifying, which left Perez and Kobayashi with more cars ahead of them than they would have liked, limiting their progress up the order on race day.

In Key's place, Matt Morris was brought in from Williams, where he had been head of transmission design, to be Sauber's chief designer. For 2013, he and head of aerodynamics Willem Toet will be responsible for the C32.

The biggest change of all is to be found on the pit-wall, though, as founder Peter Sauber has stepped down and one-third team shareholder Monisha Kaltenborn has been promoted from managing director to team principal.

"Fighting against a big team like Mercedes GP is very, very difficult for us because we have simple limitations which they don't have."
Monisha Kaltenborn

Monisha Kaltenborn has a larger role now she's taken over from Peter Sauber as team principal.

NICO HULKENBERG

Nico is a driver on the move, not just from Force India to Sauber but up the scale. He's now seen as a Ferrari driver of the future, which is no surprise as he has long been tipped as a champion in the making.

Formula One can be a confusing arena, for both promising drivers and the sport's supporters, as drivers of great promise can be lost from view. After all, race for any team other than those whose cars fill the first three rows of the grid and the focus swings away from you. So it has been with Nico, this tall German who won at ease in Formula Three, A1GP and GP2 and then disappeared into the pack. His snatching of pole for Williams in the 2010 Brazilian GP was impressive, although some saw him as the lucky beneficiary of changing track conditions. Then a year on the sidelines as Force India's third driver in 2011 made him all but invisible again. Fortunately, things began to change in 2012, when his ability to pitch his Force India into battle with those driving for higher-ranked teams served a timely reminder that he is one of the stars for the future, definitely a world champion in the making.

Nico's results became ever stronger in the second half of the season, as shown by a fighting fourth in the Belgian GP but most especially with his race-leading drive in Brazil. That ended in his clash with Lewis Hamilton, but the point had been made that

Nico is now seen as a bright light, perhaps awaiting a move to Ferrari for 2014.

he's a driver who will deliver when he lands a ride with a top team. For the year ahead it's all change for Nico, as he has moved to Sauber. The deal to quit Force India was signed apparently after his excellent run to sixth place in last October's Korean GP,

when his passing of Romain Grosjean and Lewis Hamilton around the outside at Turn 4 was undoubtedly one of the best overtaking moves of the entire season. The switch to Sauber should be rewarding, since whatever Sergio Perez could wring from the Swiss car, Nico ought to be able to extract even more, given his superior racing pedigree.

They say that a wet track sorts the men from the boys, and Nico's expertise in the wet is already acknowledged, which is why a strong campaign this year for the Swiss team might just ease him closer to a race ride with Ferrari.

TRACK NOTES

Nationality:	GERMAN
Born:	19 AUGUST 1987, EMMERICH, GERMANY
Website:	www.nicohulkenberg.net/en
Teams:	WILLIAMS 2010, FORCE INDIA 2012, SAUBER 2013

CAREER RECORD	
First Grand Prix:	2010 BAHRAIN GP
Grand Prix starts:	39
Grand Prix wins:	0
	(best result: fourth, 2012 Belgian GP)
Poles:	1
Fastest laps:	1
Points:	85
Honours:	2009 GP2 CHAMPION,
	2008 EUROPEAN FORMULA THREE CHAMPION,
	2007 FORMULA THREE MASTERS WINNER,
	2006/07 A1GP CHAMPION,
	2005 GERMAN FORMULA BMW CHAMPION,
	2003 GERMAN KART CHAMPION,
	2002 GERMAN JUNIOR KART CHAMPION

A WINNER ON THE WAY UP

Few drivers reach Formula One with as many titles to their name as Nico did, as he won a title almost every year from his karting days on. Nico's first year in cars, 2005, was spent in Formula BMW and he pipped Sebastien Buemi to the title. His next stop was German F3, where he did well in an inferior chassis. What made his name, though, was his selection to race in A1GP as he beat higher-ranked drivers to land Germany the crown. Staying on in F3 in 2007, he trailed Romain Grosjean and Buemi but came back the following year and won it easily. He then dominated GP2 in 2009 and was selected to advance to Formula One with Williams. His best finish in 2010 was sixth in Hungary, but his proudest moment was qualifying on pole in changing conditions at Interlagos. Losing his drive to make way for Pastor Maldonado's arrival at the team left Nico as test driver for Force India in 2011, before the German landed a race seat again for 2012.

ESTEBAN GUTIERREZ

After two years spent on the sidelines at grands prix as Sauber's reserve and occasional Friday test driver, Esteban is stepping up to a full race seat this year thanks to continued financial backing from his home country, Mexico.

Esteban must be feeling that it was about time that Sauber promoted him to a leading role, as his association with the team goes back a long way. Their first connection was in 2009, when he had his first F1 test run. His form was good enough for him to become an affiliate in 2010, before being moved up to reserve driver from 2011. Naturally, Esteban continued racing, rising through GP3 by winning the title that first year, then spending 2011 and last year in GP2.

Having observed his development, Sauber team principal Monisha Kaltenborn decided that he had done enough to land a race seat in place of Kamui Kobayashi, saying, "Esteban has great talent and he's ready to take the leap. We mapped out his path to F1 and are in no doubt that we have a strong driver pairing for the 2013 season with Nico [Hulkenberg] and Esteban."

Obviously, the team has just lost a Mexican driver, with Sergio Perez having transferred to McLaren for 2013, and doubtless Sauber's Mexican sponsors, such as Telmex, Visit Mexico and Cuervo Tequila, have had a say in Esteban being brought in to give a Mexican focus to the team, especially in their closest race, the United

Esteban has a lot to prove in his rookie year as he follows in Perez's tracks.

States GP, which takes place across the border in Austin, Texas. Furthermore, there is talk of Mexico hosting its own grand prix again after a long gap since 1992.

The question as yet unanswered is whether Esteban is really the right man to

be performing at the sport's pinnacle, as he hasn't stood out in his two seasons of GP2. He won a race in his rookie season, whereas new team-mate Hulkenberg won five races and the title in his only year of GP2. Esteban ranked just third in his second attempt, so perhaps he's not the ultimate in young chargers.

However, there have been drivers before who have hit F1 and suddenly vaulted to a higher level of performance that has belied their relative inexperience and so Sauber must be hoping that Esteban can use his knowledge of the team, its personnel and its technology to do just that. Otherwise, the decision to take Mexican pesos rather than keep Kamui Kobayashi on for 2013 might look rather silly.

TRACK NOTES

Nationality:	MEXICAN
Born:	5 AUGUST 1991, MONTERREY, MEXICO
Website:	www.estebanracing.com
Teams:	SAUBER 2013

CAREER RECORD

First Grand Prix:	2013 AUSTRALIAN GP
Grand Prix starts:	0
Grand Prix wins:	0
Poles:	0
Fastest laps:	0
Points:	0
Honours:	2010 GP3 CHAMPION, 2008 EUROPEAN FORMULA BMW CHAMPION, 2007 UNITED STATES FORMULA BMW RUNNER-UP, 2005 MEXICAN ROTAX MAX KART CHAMPION

FROM MEXICO TO EUROPE

Esteban started racing karts in 2004, when he had turned 13. Success was almost instant as he won the Mexican Rotax Max Challenge title in his first full season, 2005, after which he was invited to race in the USA and then in the world finals in Malaysia. At the end of his 2006 karting campaign, Esteban tested a Formula Renault single-seater in preparation for his car racing career starting in 2007. Runner-up in the US Formula BMW series, Esteban advanced to the European series in 2008 and won seven of the 16 races to take the championship. He advanced to the European Formula Three series in 2009 and ranked ninth, but the highlight of his year was testing Sauber's F1 car when he was only 18 years old. His second international racing title was claimed in 2010, when Esteban won the GP3 series ahead of Robert Wickens by winning five of the 16 rounds. GP2 proved harder to crack across 2011 and 2012 with ART, although he won impressively at Valencia and Silverstone.

SAHARA FORCE INDIA

Form was good in 2012, with Paul di Resta and Nico Hulkenberg racing to fourth-place finishes against more fancied rivals. Money was tight, though, with both team owners facing funding problems, which cast a shadow over the team's long-term future.

Paul di Resta stays with Force India for a third year and must hope that investment arrives to move the team to the front of the midfield.

Like a shark, a Formula One team needs to keep swimming forward to thrive, and so Force India's top management knows that this is going to be a critical season for the team in which it must start scoring points on a more regular basis if it is to secure the backing required for long-term prosperity and growth.

Last year, even with the excellent Paul di Resta and Nico Hulkenberg leading its attack, the team dropped a place in the team rankings, falling from sixth in 2011 to seventh as Sauber moved up a place at its expense. As Formula One Management's travel money is distributed to the teams according to their ranking, with the championship-winning team being awarded the most, results are vital, not just for this year's budget but also for securing the team's future. With title sponsors becoming ever more difficult to find because of the world economy's unexpectedly slow recovery, this has taken on extra importance. In 2012 there

were reports that the companies of both team principal Vijay Mallya and chairman Subrata Roy Sahara had financial problems, with the former being hit hard by his loss-making Kingfisher Airlines and the latter being asked to refund 22 million investors in his micro-banking companies to the tune of $3.1 billion. Fortunately, last

KEY MOMENTS AND KEY PEOPLE

TEAM HISTORY
This is a team that has had many names. It began life in 1991 as Jordan, created as a step up from Eddie Jordan's successful F3000 team. Although fast from the outset, it took until 1998 to score its first win, through Damon Hill at Spa-Francorchamps. In 2005, when finances became tight, Jordan sold his team to Alex Shnaider and it was renamed Midland F1. Dutch sportscar-builder Spyker took over naming rights in 2007, until Vijay Mallya turned it into Force India for 2008.

SUBRATA ROY SAHARA
"Saharasri" gave the team a cash injection in 2012 and so added his computer company's name to the team's. He started his business career in 1978 and has expanded it to cover not only computers but financial services, life insurance, housing, print and TV media, healthcare and the IT sector. Now India's second largest employer after Indian Railways, he has long been involved with sponsoring sport, backing the national cricket and hockey teams for a decade and last year adding volleyball.

2012 DRIVERS & RESULTS

Driver	Nationality	Races	Wins	Pts	Pos
Nico Hulkenberg	German	20	0	63	11th
Paul di Resta	British	20	0	46	14th

November, Mallya sold United Spirits to Diageo and said that he'd invest $80m in the team's infrastructure.

In the light of this, despite improving form through 2012, no driver can feel entirely confident, should they stay with the team in the long term. Indeed, there was talk last autumn of Force India possibly having to look at replacing one of its hotshots with a driver who could bring with him a large budget. This would be great for an up-and-coming driver, as it would open a door at a midfield team, but the downside would be that it would reduce the internal competition that was so well balanced between di Resta and Hulkenberg last year, undoubtedly making each press just that little bit harder as they sought supremacy. Either, though, would provide a good role model for a younger driver, as both take such a professional approach to their racing, both in and out of the car.

One of the targets for technical director Andrew Green, Akio Haga, Ian Hall and Simon Phillips will be to design and engineer a car that races as well as it qualifies, as this was a problem last year, with lofty grid positions leading to promising performances that gradually weakened through the course of a race and often slipped away disappointingly in its later stages. Should they achieve this aim with the VJM06, then the workforce and their families will be filled more with hope than expectation when they trek

across the road for their annual works outing from their headquarters opposite the Silverstone circuit to the British GP.

As before, the Force India attack will be sharpened by the use of Mercedes V8s and transmissions sourced from McLaren, a combination of technical partners that certainly helped improve its pedigree last year when both Hulkenberg and di Resta claimed a fourth-place finish, at Spa-Francorchamps and on the streets of Singapore respectively. Yet the best was saved until last and, had he not slipped when trying to pass Lewis Hamilton's McLaren for the lead in the wet Brazilian GP, Hulkenberg could have secured the team's first win since its Jordan days.

Through the course of the team's life in F1, starting with its impressive debut season in 1991, it has raced under four names, although winning only in its Jordan days, but times are tough and future seasons could see it racing under yet another identity. The important part, though, is that this excellent bunch of racers from Silverstone continues to operate on motorsport's greatest stage.

FOR THE RECORD

Country of origin:	England
Team base:	Silverstone, England
Telephone:	(44) 01327 850800
Website:	www.forceindiaf1.com
Active in Formula One:	As Jordan 1991-2004; as Midland 2005-06; as Spyker 2007; as Force India since 2008
Grands Prix contested:	378
Wins:	4
Pole positions:	3
Fastest laps:	4

THE TEAM

Team principal & managing director:	Vijay Mallya
Chairman:	Subrata Roy Sahara
Deputy team principal:	Bob Fernley
Chief operating officer:	Otmar Szafnauer
Technical director:	Andrew Green
Sporting director:	Andy Stevenson
Chief designers:	Akio Haga & Ian Hall
Production director:	Bob Halliwell
Head of mechanical design:	Dan Carpenter
Head of aerodynamics:	Simon Phillips
Race engineers:	Gianpiero Lambiase & Bradley Joyce
Test driver:	TBA
Chassis:	Force India VJM06
Engine:	Mercedes V8
Tyres:	Pirelli

"We've every reason to be proud as last year we scored more points than in any previous season and given the tools that we have, which are mostly from the Jordan era, we've done exceptionally well."
Vijay Mallya

Team owner Vijay Mallya has promised a cash injection to update the team's technical facilities.

PAUL DI RESTA

Staying on for a third year with Force India, Paul has proved that he is more than ready to join one of Formula One's top teams, but the question is when the next such opening will become available.

It's so easy to say how well Paul has done in just two years of Formula One and treat him as a novice, but this is to overlook the years of experience he gained when a lack of money to graduate to GP2 led to him spend five years away from single-seaters, racing for Mercedes in Germany's DTM. The fine race performances that he has wrung out of his Force India since the start of 2011, displaying a remarkable ability to preserve the life of his tyres, are the result as much of applied intelligence as of his natural speed.

When his 2012 team-mate Nico Hulkenberg quit the team in favour of joining Sauber, and Sergio Perez filled the seat made vacant at McLaren by Lewis Hamilton's surprise departure, the Scot's options for 2013 dwindled last October to the point that he had to stay on for a third year with the financially troubled Force India outfit.

38

This may be no bad thing, as he will be an established team leader rather than an equal number one, but the big question is whether the Silverstone-based team can supply him with a car as competitive as last year's VJM05 became.

Paul is now the undisputed team leader and ought to benefit from the position.

The other question is how the Scot will react to the fact that he had been mentioned as a contender to move to McLaren when Hamilton was known to be looking to leave, or even to Mercedes when Schumacher retired, yet has moved nowhere. Timing is everything when landing a drive with a team that can offer a grand prix-winning car. In Paul, there is a driver fast and clever enough to grab any such opportunity. He's one of the most highly rated drivers now, and will be hoping that he still is when the next chance arises. If the VJM06 is competitive this year, then it really is make or break for Paul, as the driver merry-go-round looks set for a big spin for 2014 when the second seat at Ferrari becomes available. This will create a rare shuffling of the pack and he must ensure that his name is at the top of team chiefs' most-wanted lists.

TRACK NOTES

Nationality:	BRITISH
Born:	16 APRIL 1986, UPHALL, SCOTLAND
Website:	www.pauldiresta.com
Teams:	FORCE INDIA 2011-13

CAREER RECORD

First Grand Prix:	2011 AUSTRALIAN GP
Grand Prix starts:	39
Grand Prix wins:	0
(best result: fourth, 2012 Singapore GP)	
Poles:	0
Fastest laps:	0
Points:	73
Honours:	2010 GERMAN TOURING CAR CHAMPION, 2006 EUROPEAN FORMULA THREE CHAMPION & FORMULA THREE MASTERS WINNER, 2001 BRITISH JICA KART CHAMPION, 1998 SCOTTISH OPEN KART CHAMPION, 1997 BRITISH CADET KART CHAMPION, 1995 SCOTTISH CADET KART CHAMPION

ABLE TO RACE ANYTHING FAST

With a solid background of success in kart racing, including winning assorted Scottish and British titles from entry-level cadet karts to JICA level, Paul was an experienced racer when he tried cars for the first time in 2003. One of the people he beat in Formula Renault that year was eventual champion Lewis Hamilton. Paul advanced to Formula Three in 2005, winning the European title in 2006. Then, with money hard to come by, he accepted Mercedes's offer to turn to touring cars, competing in the DTM. He finished as runner-up in 2008, and went one better to be champion in 2010. By this time he had already done some F1 tests for Force India, a team he would be guided into for 2011 by its engine supplier Mercedes, the German manufacturer perhaps keeping an eye on him in case it needed him for its F1 team in the future. Paul showed immediately that he hadn't lost his feel for single-seaters as he raced well, finishing sixth in the Singapore street race.

BRUNO SENNA*

Many thought that Bruno had done enough last year to keep his Williams drive, but he was displaced by the team's reserve driver, Valtteri Bottas, and 2013 sees him starting with his fourth team in four years as he joins Force India.

The fit of Bruno and Williams seemed a good one, but there was a feeling that the team hadn't secured the points that its vastly improved FW34 deserved, which led to the management looking to make a change to its driver line-up. With the other driver, Pastor Maldonado, bringing in the bulk of the team's budget, it was always likely that the less flamboyant but more controlled Bruno would be the one shown the door to make way for a driver that they thought might drive the car that vital fraction harder and faster.

You had to feel for Ayrton's nephew last year as his best attempts to establish himself with Williams after half a season with Renault in 2011 were hampered by the fact that he had to sit out the first practice session on Friday at almost all of the grands prix. This was a contractual matter and gave the team's reserve driver Valtteri Bottas useful track time in his car. Useful for Bottas and for the team, that is, but certainly not for Bruno, as this lost session left him at an immediate disadvantage to team-mate Maldonado. In these days of such limited testing, track time is vitally important, so its loss was keenly felt. Fortunately, Bruno

Bruno will look forward to participating in the first Friday session, unlike in 2012.

has a cool head on his shoulders and so despite track time issues he continued to look, listen and learn. However, there really is no substitute for being out there, getting the feel of the car and the track through the seat of your pants.

Last year's results show that Bruno was seldom able to match Maldonado for outright speed. He was out-qualified 18 times to two by the Venezuelan, and was certainly never near winning, but his consistency was a help as he gathered 31 points, his best result being sixth place in the wet at Sepang. Yet, clearly, the team reckoned that Bottas might be that little bit faster, so Bruno was dropped for 2013.

There was talk of a transfer to Caterham, but it looked as if Vitaly Petrov was set to stay there. Then, when Nico Hulkenberg announced that he was moving to Sauber, this more interesting and certainly more competitive ride became Bruno's obvious choice. That Hulkenberg was able to use his Force India to challenge for victory in the final round, far ahead of the Williams duo, will surely have pleased Bruno.

A VERY LATE STARTER

Ayrton Senna's death at the 1994 San Marino GP nearly extinguished nephew Bruno's racing ambitions, as family opposition to his racing was intense. Only after years of debate did his mother relent, which meant that Bruno missed out on kart racing. Instead, he had to learn his craft in cars, starting with British Formula BMW in 2004. Then it was on to Formula Three, and Bruno's speed in 2005 was improved upon the following year as he ranked third for Raikkonen Robertson Racing. Moving to GP2, Bruno had a win in 2007 at Barcelona, and he then finished as runner-up to Giorgio Pantano in 2008. No doors to an F1 ride opened to him, even with the obvious draw of the Senna name, and so he had to keep himself busy by racing in sportscars for the ORECA Team. Then, with three new teams entering Formula One in 2010, he found a drive with one of these, HRT, lost the ride for 2011, but joined Renault when it dropped Nick Heidfeld, before landing his chance with Williams.

TRACK NOTES

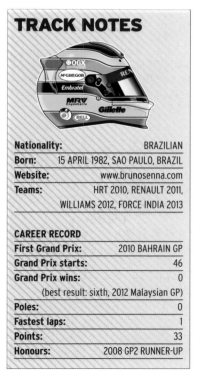

Nationality:	BRAZILIAN
Born:	15 APRIL 1982, SAO PAULO, BRAZIL
Website:	www.brunosenna.com
Teams:	HRT 2010, RENAULT 2011,
	WILLIAMS 2012, FORCE INDIA 2013

CAREER RECORD	
First Grand Prix:	2010 BAHRAIN GP
Grand Prix starts:	46
Grand Prix wins:	0
(best result: sixth, 2012 Malaysian GP)	
Poles:	0
Fastest laps:	1
Points:	33
Honours:	2008 GP2 RUNNER-UP

* unconfirmed at time of going to press.

WILLIAMS

Williams was back among the winners last year when Pastor Maldonado triumphed in Spain, and this was followed up by further flashes of brilliance, so there's no reason why this once-great team can't rise back up the rankings again.

Pastor Maldonado gave Williams its first win since 2004 last year but the team needs him to score on a more regular basis in 2013.

Nobody the length of the Formula One pit lane could begrudge Sir Frank Williams his rare moment of joy last May when not only did one of his cars lead the Spanish GP, but the usually over-dramatic Pastor Maldonado held it all together under extreme pressure from Fernando Alonso, as the local hero pressed for victory in front of his home fans, and was still in front when they took the chequered flag. This was the reward that Sir Frank and his team needed after some trying recent campaigns and the setback of losing works engines at the end of 2009 when Toyota pulled out. Fortunately, Williams restored its historic partnership with Renault last year and the benefits were immediate. This was their first win together since Jacques Villeneuve triumphed in the Luxembourg GP at the Nurburgring in his 1997 title-winning season.

There's a perception, probably correct, that Formula One is in good health when its long-established teams are winning or at least running at the front of the field,

much as is the case in the leading national football leagues around the world, as casual onlookers tend to think that something is amiss when victory goes to a team or club of whom they've never heard. It remains to be seen whether Williams can make it all the way back to the top to challenge McLaren and Ferrari on a regular basis as

KEY MOMENTS AND KEY PEOPLE

TEAM HISTORY

Sir Frank Williams raced in Formula Three but didn't have the money to advance, so he ran cars for others, achieving notable success with Piers Courage until his death. His breakthrough was forming this F1 team with Patrick Head in 1977, and Sir Frank's drive and Patrick's engineering genius combined to produce a first win in 1979, a title in 1980 with Alan Jones and two more in that decade before Nigel Mansell, Alain Prost, Damon Hill and Jacques Villeneuve were helped to the top. Since the late 1990s, the team has been beneath its best.

TOTO WOLFF

It was the success of his private equity company that enabled Toto to buy a share of the team at the end of 2009, but he has racing in his blood, having competed in Formula Ford in his native Austria before focusing on business. By the end of last century, he was racing again, in GTs, and then he started a driver management company. Although he raced again, finishing runner-up in the 2006 Austrian Rally Championship, these days it's business first for Toto.

2012 DRIVERS & RESULTS

Driver	Nationality	Races	Wins	Pts	Pos
Pastor Maldonado	Venezuelan	20	1	45	15th
Bruno Senna	Brazilian	20	0	31	16th

it used to, but the sport would certainly be all the stronger for it if a team founded and still run by a dyed-in-the-wool racer was winning regularly again.

Technical director Mike Coughlan has every reason to be proud of his efforts, as they translated directly into the most effective Williams in years, making his return from being banned from Formula One all the sweeter. Made to stand on the sidelines for two years after being charged with industrial espionage while working for McLaren, he combined extremely effectively with chief operations engineer Mark Gillan to produce a car that was clearly a step forward from its predecessors. Indeed, many felt that last year's Williams FW34 was worthy of more points than its drivers could deliver. Maldonado's occasionally over-robust approach resulted in several wasted opportunities, starting with last year's opening round in Australia, when he drove brilliantly to be running sixth, set to score more points than Williams collected in the entire 2011 World Championship, but then crashed out of the race on the final lap. Fortunately the Venezuelan was able to atone for this later in the spring. Better still, team-mate Bruno Senna – forming a poignant link to the team's fleeting time with his late uncle Ayrton in 1994 – raced to sixth place next time out in Malaysia and so set the ball rolling in a season in which

the points flowed for Williams, at least occasionally, after a dire 2011 in which they picked up just five.

Maldonado's place in the team for 2013 was kept safe by that win and other sparkling drives, as well as the large budget he brings from Venezuela. Senna, though, knew that he had the team's third driver, Valtteri Bottas, to contend with, and the Finn produced a series of exceedingly promising drives in Friday morning practice, winning him many fans on the team's technical side. Bottas was then given the nod for 2013.

One matter that must be sorted, according to Senna, is the team's DRS, which the Brazilian said lagged behind the systems used by rival teams in 2012, especially Mercedes with its double DRS arrangement, costing him and Maldonado some of the extra straight-line speed that it should afford to facilitate overtaking.

FOR THE RECORD

Country of origin:	England
Team base:	Grove, England
Telephone:	(44) 01235 777700
Website:	www.williamsf1.com
Active in Formula One:	From 1972
Grands Prix contested:	643
Wins:	114
Pole positions:	127
Fastest laps:	131

THE TEAM

Team principal:	Sir Frank Williams
Co-founder:	Patrick Head
Executive director:	Toto Wolff
Chief executive officer:	Alex Burns
Technical director:	Mike Coughlan
Chief designer:	Ed Wood
Head of vehicle dynamics:	Rob Gearing
Team manager:	Dickie Stanford
Test driver:	TBA
Development driver:	Susie Wolff
Chassis:	Williams FW35
Engine:	Renault V8
Tyres:	Pirelli

"We'll be looking to build on 2012 and produce a car that can finish in the points consistently at a wide range of circuits and challenge for podiums as well."
Sir Frank Williams

Mike Coughlan (right) has made great progress putting Williams back where it should be.

PASTOR MALDONADO

Pastor used to be seen as a fast driver, but one who cracked under pressure, and then he drove the perfect race to hold off Fernando Alonso in Spain last year to take his maiden victory. However, there were also accidents and incidents.

As a driver Pastor continues to be a work in progress. Yet his place in Formula One is safe, backed as he is by considerable sponsorship from his native Venezuela. The money, you see, more than makes up for Pastor's down days.

Amazingly, no corner had really been turned by Pastor last May, as his win at the Circuit de Catalunya didn't propel him on to a higher level - after that he failed to score at the next nine grands prix before landing eighth place in the Japanese GP at Suzuka. It wasn't even as though the Williams FW34 wasn't competitive enough to do so, as team-mate Bruno Senna managed to score five times across those nine races.

Of course, Williams needs money to make its way back up the order, but it needs a driver to be consistent to help it in this. A cameo of Pastor's failing on this count was seen in the first race of the 2012 season, when he crashed out on the final lap at Melbourne, when lying in sixth place. Those lost eight points were more than Williams had collected in all of 2011.

Still, Hugo Chavez winning another term as president of Venezuela last October

Pastor must make fewer mistakes if he is to turn his talent into points.

cemented Pastor's place with Williams for another year at least, as Chavez is happy for PDVSA - the state-owned gas and oil group - to write cheques for as much as $55m per year to the team. Pastor will have to start delivering on a far more regular basis, though, for the team to see him as a long-term option, because the team's budget isn't defined only by incoming sponsorship but also by its annual ranking. The gap between the eighth it finished and the seventh it might have achieved is a cool £3.4m, the sort of money that can hire more design and engineering clout.

Feted in Venezuela as the country's first grand prix winner and leading sporting superstar, Pastor may not always listen to advice. However, if he does and applies himself, boosts his concentration and hones his judgement, he could yet become a top F1 driver. If he gets in trouble with the officials this year as many times as he did last, though, he'll be seen as damaged goods.

TRACK NOTES

Nationality:	VENEZUELAN
Born:	9 MARCH 1985, MARACAY, VENEZUELA
Website:	www.pastormaldonado.com
Teams:	WILLIAMS 2011-13

CAREER RECORD	
First Grand Prix:	2011 AUSTRALIAN GP
Grand Prix starts:	39
Grand Prix wins:	1
	2012 Spanish GP
Poles:	1
Fastest laps:	0
Points:	46
Honours:	2010 GP2 CHAMPION, 2004 ITALIAN FORMULA RENAULT CHAMPION, 2003 ITALIAN FORMULA RENAULT WINTER CHAMPION

A LONG CLIMB TO THE TOP

Some drivers appear to advance from karting to Formula One in little more than a couple of years, but not Pastor. After kart racing at home in Venezuela, he started his car racing career in Europe in 2003 at the age of 18, basing himself in Italy to race Formula Renault around Europe. Having won the Italian title in 2004, he raced in World Series with Renault in 2005, but had his first taste of F1 with a test for Minardi. In 2006 Pastor continued to race in the World Series and ranked third. Advancing to GP2 in 2007, he won at Monaco, but it would take three more years, driving for three more teams, before he landed the title - with six wins for Rapax - at which point he was ready to proceed to Formula One. Then, armed with a hefty budget from Venezuelan companies, after eight years in the training categories he landed a ride with Williams for 2011 and managed to rein in his previously accident-strewn style to score a point at Spa-Francorchamps.

VALTTERI BOTTAS

It's unusual for a test driver to step up to a plum racing seat in Formula One, especially if they haven't raced for a year, but this 23-year-old Finn is seen as something special and perhaps the driver to propel Williams forward.

It's widely acknowledged that Williams underachieved last year, with its drivers reckoned not to have gathered the championship points of which the FW34 was capable, leaving the team eighth overall rather than higher. As a result, Bruno Senna was dropped and Valtteri, known as Vale, was promoted from the team's testing role, as team chief Sir Frank Williams considers that his speed and application will yield greater results.

In these days of next to no F1 testing, it's usually hard to compare test drivers with those occupying the race seats. However, Vale went out in the Friday morning practice session in place of Senna in 15 of last year's 20 grands prix. He was invariably as fast as or faster than the team's lead driver, Pastor Maldonado, leading Williams to describe him as "quite simply one of the most talented young racing drivers I have come across".

If Vale carries this speed into 2013 and then shows that he has lost none of the racecraft that led him to win several championships on the way up from karting, then Maldonado will be kept on his toes.

Valtteri is rated very highly and knows the team well from his test driving duties.

The team needs its drivers to take any points that are on offer, and Maldonado simply wasn't doing this, getting fines and penalties alongside rather too many retirements. However, the Venezuelan stays on as he brings the bulk of the team's finance.

Taking Vale over Senna, though, shows that Williams has decided that running two pay drivers is not the way to go if this once-great team is to get back into the thick of the action. That the Finn knows the team and the way that it works is another advantage, along with his dedication to his career. Vale has chosen to live in Oxford so that he can be close to the team headquarters.

Vale comes across as a determined, no-nonsense individual, which is just how Williams likes its racers, as it has ever since nuggety Australian Alan Jones turned them from also-rans to champions in 1980. He knows this is his big chance and few believe that he will fail to grasp it with both hands.

TRACK NOTES

Nationality:	FINNISH
Born:	28 AUGUST 1989, NASTOLA, FINLAND
Website:	www.bottasvaltteri.com
Teams:	WILLIAMS 2013

CAREER RECORD

First Grand Prix:	2013 AUSTRALIAN GP
Grand Prix starts:	0
Grand Prix wins:	0
Poles:	0
Fastest laps:	0
Points:	0
Honours:	2011 GP3 CHAMPION, 2009 & 2010 FORMULA THREE MASTERS WINNER, 2008 EUROPEAN & NORTHERN EUROPEAN FORMULA RENAULT CHAMPION, 2005 VIKING TROPHY KART WINNER

GROOMED BY WILLIAMS SINCE 2010

Having raced karts since the age of six, Vale won the Viking Trophy in 2005 and competed in the World Championship in 2006. He advanced to car racing in 2007 and won the European championship title in his second year of Formula Renault in 2008, as well as winning the lesser NEC Formula Renault series. Racing in Formula Three in 2009, he ranked third in the European championship, a ranking he retained in 2010, again with ART Grand Prix, the highlight of each season being victory in the Formula Three Masters invitation race at Zandvoort. That year also marked the start of his relationship with Williams. He then served as the team's test and reserve driver through 2011, which was another great year for him on the track as he won the inaugural FIA GP3 championship for Lotus ART, with his closest competition coming from team-mate James Calado. Although he had no race ride last year, he kept competition sharp alongside his test driving duties by competing in triathlons.

Pastor Maldonado's Venezuelan backers helped Williams move forward in 2012. This year, they need to finish in the points at every outing.

SCUDERIA TORO ROSSO

A year on from forcing change by dropping both of its drivers, Toro Rosso is facing further readjustment for 2013 as it has a new technical director and must, at the least, hope to be snapping around the foot of the top 10 at every grand prix.

Daniel Ricciardo (above) and Jean-Eric Vergne are being given a second chance as Toro Rosso tries to hang on to its rival midfield teams.

The principal factor that needs to be considered when assessing this team's chances for the season ahead is that long-standing technical director Giorgio Ascanelli has been replaced for 2013. James Key, formerly of Sauber and before that Jordan, then Spyker, then Force India, took over late last August after six months on gardening leave from the Swiss team, during which time he kept himself busy by being involved with the Lotus sportscar team in the FIA World Endurance Championship. As a result of the hiatus before he started work with the team, this year's car, the Ferrari-powered Toro Rosso STR8, will most likely not be as good as the one he will produce to comply with the new regulations for 2014. Still, that's the peril of changing your design leader, but this new appointment is a clear indication that what is effectively the Red Bull second team is looking to raise its game. This has to be good news for all involved, making the future campaigns look less and less like the ones entered into with little hope even of points when the team was impoverished and raced as Minardi up until 2005.

The team continues to be based at Faenza in Italy and still has predominantly Italian personnel, save for Austrians, team principal Franz Tost, and team advisor

KEY MOMENTS AND KEY PEOPLE

TEAM HISTORY

This team started life as Minardi, racing with some success in Formula Two before graduating to Formula One in 1985. Always one of the tail-end teams as it raced on a small budget, it was the team with which many drivers made their grand prix debut, including Alessandro Nannini, Mark Webber and Fernando Alonso. Dietrich Mateschitz of Red Bull fame then bought the team for 2006 and injected money to bring it on, and two years later Sebastian Vettel gave the team its first win at Monza.

JAMES KEY

Signed to replace Giorgio Ascanelli for 2013, James was sponsored through university by Lotus and worked on its GT programme in 1996. His first taste of F1 was in 1998, when he joined Jordan, rising from data engineer to senior race engineer by 2002 and to technical director by 2005. After staying on as the team became Spyker, then Force India, he left in 2010 to be Sauber's technical director before moving on to Toro Rosso last September.

2012 DRIVERS & RESULTS

Driver	Nationality	Races	Wins	Pts	Pos
Jean-Eric Vergne	French	20	0	16	17th
Daniel Ricciardo	Australian	20	0	10	18th

Helmut Marko. Key will be supported in the designing of the STR8 by chief designer Luca Furbatto and chief aerodynamicist Nicolo Petrucci, and they will hope that not only can their drivers score first time out, as Daniel Ricciardo managed with ninth place in Melbourne last March, but that this form can be maintained.

Last year's all-new driver pairing of Ricciardo and Jean-Eric Vergne brought just 11 grands prix's worth of F1 racing experience between them, but both raced well through 2012, snaffling points whenever any of the drivers of the more highly ranked teams faltered. The Belgian GP was a high-water mark, as both drivers scored, showing the merits not only of the car but of employing drivers who can boast the British Formula Three title on their career CV. It is true that they were helped by Romain Grosjean eliminating himself, Fernando Alonso and Lewis Hamilton at the first corner on the opening lap, but points count however they are gathered. They scored when they could, but were frequently a few places outside the top 10 finishers, so came away empty-handed, thus making it hard for the team to boost its ranking in the constructors' championship, and it ended up languishing ninth overall. Overall, they displayed probably more promise in their first season than Toro Rosso's previous driver pairing of Jaime Alguersuari and Sebastien Buemi. What will define their

second season together is whether they can drive well enough and consistently enough to make higher-ranked teams want to take them on to greater things. The original plan was that Toro Rosso would develop drivers to pass up to Red Bull Racing, as it did with Sebastian Vettel, but the teams' cars were closer together then, in fact all but identical, whereas now they are a world apart, making the next step less obvious.

The team does need to advance, though, as it spent 2012 in that no-man's-land between the established midfield teams and the three teams that were new in 2010, Caterham, Marussia and HRT, i.e. in ninth place out of the 12 teams and some way back from challenging for eighth place in the constructors' championship and the greatly increased travel money from Formula One Management that this would bring.

FOR THE RECORD

Country of origin:	Italy
Team base:	Faenza, Italy
Telephone:	(39) 546 696111
Website:	www.scuderiatororosso.com
Active in Formula One:	As Minardi 1995-2005; as Toro Rosso since 2006
Grands Prix contested:	469
Wins:	1
Pole positions:	0
Fastest laps:	0

THE TEAM

Team owner:	Dietrich Mateschitz
Team principal:	Franz Tost
Technical director:	James Key
Team manager:	Gianfranco Fantuzzi
Chief designer:	Luca Furbatto
Chief aerodynamicist:	Nicolo Petrucci
Chief engineer:	Laurent Mekies
Test driver:	TBA
Chassis:	Toro Rosso STR8
Engine:	Ferrari V8
Tyres:	Pirelli

Helmut Marko (left) and Franz Tost are hard to please but seem impressed with their drivers.

"Our late-season improvement in form wasn't enough to change our ninth place, but it was a good way to end as the 2013 regulations aren't very different to the ones we had."

Franz Tost

JEAN-ERIC VERGNE

A solid first season in Formula One earned Jean-Eric a second season with Toro Rosso, and French Formula One fans will be hoping that his obvious talent will enable him to work his way up the grid in 2013.

A glance at Jean-Eric's career record shows that he is a driver who tends to be either champion or at the very least runner-up rather than an also-ran. Finishing just one place outside the points on his F1 debut in Melbourne underlined this. However, improving on that second time out to finish eighth at Sepang really made Formula One people sit up and pay attention to what "JEV" was up to. Thanks to two more eighth-place finishes, at Spa-Francorchamps and Yeongam, the Italian team elected last November to keep him on, along with team-mate Daniel Ricciardo, as they had shown more speed than the drivers they replaced, Jaime Alguersuari and Sebastien Buemi. It was good to see hire 'em, fire 'em Red Bull keeping faith with these drivers, both of whom they have nurtured pretty much from their karting days, rather than hanging them out to dry, as they have done to so many of their predecessors.

Team principal Franz Tost said towards the end of last season that he had been impressed by the maturity shown by JEV in working with the engineers, as well as by his racecraft on the track, which isn't always guaranteed in a drivers' rookie year.

Jean-Eric comes back for a second year after a good first season.

What JEV must aspire to in the season ahead is performances like his highlight of last year, his eighth place in the Korean GP. This came from 16th on the grid, and the fact that he finished only 15 seconds behind Romain Grosjean's Lotus shows just how well he went. That he also held off Lewis Hamilton's McLaren in the closing stages demonstrated his ever-improving racecraft.

To achieve greater results in 2013, he must not only pray for a more competitive and consistent car but also work on improving his speed in qualifying, a department in which he was clearly inferior to Ricciardo. What he must avoid is the sort of lapse of concentration that he suffered in India when he slammed into Michael Schumacher's Mercedes at the start.

TRACK NOTES

Nationality:	FRENCH
Born:	25 APRIL 1990, PONTOISE, FRANCE
Website:	www.jeanericvergne.com
Teams:	TORO ROSSO 2012-13

CAREER RECORD

First Grand Prix:	2012 AUSTRALIAN GP
Grand Prix starts:	20
Grand Prix wins:	0 (best result: eighth, 2012 Malaysian GP, Belgian GP, Korean GP)
Poles:	0
Fastest laps:	0
Points:	16
Honours:	2011 FORMULA RENAULT 3.5 RUNNER-UP, 2010 BRITISH FORMULA THREE CHAMPION, 2009 EUROPEAN FORMULA RENAULT RUNNER-UP & WESTERN EUROPE RUNNER-UP, 2008 FRENCH FORMULA RENAULT CHAMPION, 2007 FRENCH FORMULA CAMPUS CHAMPION, 2001 FRENCH CADET KART CHAMPION

A RAPID ASCENT TO FORMULA ONE

Jean-Eric was French cadet kart champion in 2001 and was a front-runner in various other national series as he raced through his teenage years. Moving up to Formula Renault in 2007, Jean-Eric landed the French Formula Campus title at his first attempt. The next two years were spent winning races but no title in European Formula Renault. It was what happened in 2010, though, that really marked him out as a future star. He hit the British F3 championship like a storm and won no fewer than 13 races with Carlin to dominate the series. Late in the year he also tried Formula Renault 3.5, winning at Silverstone, which was good preparation for graduating to this more powerful series in 2011, when he won four rounds but was pipped to the title by Robert Wickens. Thanks to his Red Bull backing, Jean-Eric had test outings with the Scuderia Toro Rosso and Red Bull Racing, giving him F1 experience to carry into 2012, when he was signed to race for Toro Rosso.

DANIEL RICCIARDO

He was never challenging for race wins or even podium finishes, but this young Australian produced an impressive run of results for Toro Rosso last year and cemented his reputation as one of Formula One's new guard.

Bearing in mind that Daniel only landed his deal to move from HRT to Scuderia Toro Rosso late in the close season, when most of the rides were filled for 2012, he has every reason to be delighted that this promotion to a more competitive team went ahead.

Daniel kicked off his 2012 season with ninth place at his home grand prix for his first points, something of which he could only have dreamed during his half-season with HRT in 2011. This was no flash in the pan, however, and Daniel developed an impressive ability to bring the car home. When the STR7 found a comparative burst of speed in the second half of the season, he took full advantage with a run of three ninth-place finishes and a 10th from the five grands prix in the sequence that started at Spa-Francorchamps and continued to Yeongam, showing that he has what it takes to deliver at a higher level with a more competitive team.

Daniel is one of the few participants in Red Bull's driver scholarship scheme to have made it to Formula One, and yet he looks all but certain to stay on the

Daniel is looking to continue impressing the bosses in his second full year of F1.

sport's most high-profile stage. While others have been cast aside by former F1 racer Helmut Marko, Daniel appears to have the necessary speed, allied to an unflappable nature. The burning question,

of course, is how he will fare with a team that operates further up the grid and so demands more from its drivers in the development of the car. Only time will tell, but what he must do in the season ahead is to continue to add racecraft to his patient yet effective approach.

All that drivers in Daniel's situation can do is to focus, listen and learn at all times and make no mistakes, or at least learn from any that they do make. This is because they need to prove again and again that they're ready to fill any race seat vacancy with the top teams, as any achievement in a grand prix counts for more than one in a lesser formula.

TRACK NOTES

Nationality:	AUSTRALIAN
Born:	1 JULY 1989, PERTH, AUSTRALIA
Website:	www.danielricciardo.com
Teams:	HRT 2011, TORO ROSSO 2012-13

CAREER RECORD

First Grand Prix:	2011 BRITISH GP
Grand Prix starts:	31
Grand Prix wins:	0 (best result: ninth, 2012 Australian, Belgian, Singapore, Korean GPs)
Poles:	0
Fastest laps:	0
Points:	10
Honours:	2010 FORMULA RENAULT 3.5 RUNNER-UP, 2009 BRITISH FORMULA THREE CHAMPION, 2008 EUROPEAN FORMULA RENAULT RUNNER-UP & WESTERN EUROPE CHAMPION

RACING AND A LOT OF AIR MILES

The biggest problem for the Ricciardo family when Daniel started to shine in karting was that they come from Perth, thousands of miles away from the rest of the Australian circuits, which limited the number of rounds he could contest. A brief spell in Formula Ford followed in 2005, when he was 16, but it turned out to be just as easy to fly to compete in Asian Formula BMW, in which he ranked third before heading for Formula Renault in Europe in 2007. Runner-up to Valtteri Bottas in the European series in 2008, Daniel moved on to British Formula Three and impressed with Carlin Motorsport by winning the title at his first attempt. Racing in Formula Renault 3.5 in 2010, he won four rounds and ended the year as runner-up, having been pipped to the title at the final round. The plan was to continue in 2011, but Daniel's path took a different turn when his long-time backers Red Bull placed him in Formula One with HRT after the team dropped Narain Karthikeyan midway through the season.

CATERHAM F1 TEAM

If progress in Formula One was guaranteed by ambition and dedication, then Tony Fernandes's team would have advanced to the midfield by now, but finding those fractions of a second needed to make the leap is proving harder than expected.

Now in its fourth year in F1, this is a team that had expected more and that must find some extra pace to match the midfield teams.

Malaysian airline magnate and entrepreneur Tony Fernandes didn't make his fortune by not trying things, and his restless energy is clear to all as he strives to propel his F1 team up the order. Take his purchase of Caterham Cars. This wasn't just in order to take charge of this excellent company that builds some of the world's most thrilling and involving sportscars, but to land a famous brand name that he could use for his team following the loss of the right to call it Team Lotus, as he had through 2010 and 2011.

Yet, after three years of trying, upward progress from its established position as the third team from the bottom of the pile is proving as elusive as ever. Indeed, although in-season modifications and developments generally make the team's cars go faster, notably the aero package that it introduced at the British GP last July, their rivals are also improving at the same rate, leaving no change in the status quo and everyone extremely frustrated.

One positive development for the Caterham F1 team was its transfer last year to a new base, as it moved across the country from Hingham in Norfolk to occupy the old Arrows base at Leafield in Oxfordshire. As well as being a superior technical facility, it has the solid-gold advantage of being located right in the

KEY MOMENTS AND KEY PEOPLE

TEAM HISTORY

This is one of a trio of new teams admitted to the World Championship in 2010. Created by Malaysian entrepreneur Tony Fernandes, it started life carrying the Lotus name, which it used courtesy of James Hunt's brother David, who had bought it when the original team closed in 1994. Based originally in Hingham, with its administrative side run from an office in Kuala Lumpur, the team moved from Norfolk to the heart of England's motorsport crescent last year.

MARK SMITH

The team's technical director graduated in mechanical engineering, then worked for the March Group before moving to Reynard in 1989, working on its F3000 car. A year later, Mark became a design engineer for Jordan, becoming the team's joint chief designer in 1999. A move to Renault as chief designer followed in 2001, before Mark moved on to Red Bull Racing, serving as technical director from 2005 to 2007. He went to Force India as design director in late 2008, and joined Lotus/Caterham in mid-2010.

2012 DRIVERS & RESULTS

Driver	Nationality	Races	Wins	Pts	Pos
Heikki Kovalainen	Finnish	20	0	0	22
Vitaly Petrov	Russian	20	0	0	19

FOR THE RECORD

Country of origin:	England
Team base:	Leafield, England
Telephone:	(44) 01953 851411
Website:	www.caterhamf1.com
Active in Formula One:	From 2010
Grands Prix contested:	58
Wins:	0
Pole positions:	0
Fastest laps:	0

THE TEAM

Team owner:	Tony Fernandes
Team principal:	Cyril Abiteboul
Chief executive officer:	Riad Asmat
General manager:	Mia Sharizman
Technical director:	Mark Smith
Performance director:	John Iley
Chief designer:	Lewis Butler
Head of R&D:	Elliot Dason-Barber
Team manager:	Graham Watson
Chief engineer:	Gianluca Pisanello
Test driver:	TBA
Chassis:	Caterham CT02
Engine:	Renault V8
Tyres:	Pirelli

heart of England's motorsport crescent that runs from Northampton around London to Woking in Surrey. As such, not only are technical director Mark Smith and performance director John Iley closer to all of the specialist motorsport suppliers and their facilities, but now they might be able to entice star performers in other F1 teams' technical departments to join them, all of which is essential if the team is to advance. In the past some designers and engineers have shown unwillingness to uproot their families and move away from motorsport's version of Silicon Valley, California's centre of excellence for the computer industry, thus hampering the team. Now that this has been addressed, it will be intriguing to see who joins Smith, Iley and chief designer Lewis Butler in the coming seasons.

One new appointment that will certainly give the team some extra expertise is that of Cyril Abiteboul, Caterham's new team principal. The Frenchman, who arrived in September from Renault Sport, where he had been deputy managing director of its F1 division, was brought in to take responsibility for all the team's on-track and off-track activities. However, he was then handed the reins for the team last November when Fernandes and Kamarudin Meranun decided to step back to concentrate on AirAsia and the group's other businesses, thus making him the team principal.

On the driving front, Heikki Kovalainen did a notably good job last year, while Vitaly Petrov shone on occasion, most notably at Spa-Francorchamps, where he finished 14th. The Russian's late-season form improved and he was the one who wrested 11th place from Marussia at the final round to earn the team 10th place in the overall rankings. However, there was a time when his promised sponsorship money from Russia appeared to lose its way before getting to the team. Dutch GP2 race winner Giedo van der Garde had a few Friday runs with the team in the closing stages of last season and made himself a strong candidate for the second seat for 2013, especially as he came armed with a healthy budget contribution, while Bruno Senna and Charles Pic were also in the mix, as they both sensed a move was in the air. In the end, Caterham F1 Team opted to keep Vitaly Petrov as a partner to Pic for the season ahead.

51

"The shareholders are committed and behind us to help us to take significant steps forward over the coming years and one day challenge for the highest honours in F1."
Cyril Abiteboul

Tony Fernandes has other business interests so he's handed over the reins to a new team principal.

VITALY PETROV*

Still hunting for a drive for 2013 when last season came to an end, Vitaly has been kept on by Caterham thanks to the promise of more backing from Russia, a country that will host a grand prix for the first time next year.

It looked for much of last year's World Championship as if Caterham would be replacing both of its drivers for this year. The sport's insiders reckoned that if either of the pair was to stay on, it was more likely to be Heikki Kovalainen than Vitaly. The Finn, after all, had given the team three years of sterling service, whereas the Russian had yet to complete his first with the team after transferring from Renault at the end of 2011. Furthermore, the sponsorship money that Vitaly had promised to bring to pay for his ride was slow in materialising. To make matters worse for the Russian, Kovalainen had very much the upper hand in qualifying.

Yet as summer turned to autumn, so Vitaly's form improved, and it reached its zenith at Interlagos. Here, with yet more misfortune befalling Kovalainen, he was the one who stepped up and finished 11th in the race, to secure the 10th place in the constructors' championship that the team needed desperately to collect vital prize money. After that, not surprisingly, the team management felt very warmly towards him. This, along with the promise of more roubles from Vitaly's Russian

Vitaly raced hard and well late last year to retain his seat for a second season.

backers for 2013, helped him to edge ahead of Kovalainen in the competition to be retained to act as the experienced hand alongside Charles Pic, who is bringing both his talent and also money across from Marussia Racing.

With a year to go before Russia hosts its first grand prix at Sochi, on its Black Sea coastline, the country needs one of its own drivers to be developing at the sport's cutting edge. It is vital to the future of Formula One there that Vitaly is not only present but putting in decent performances. How high he can be placed in grands prix this year remains to be seen, as he failed to score a point in any of last year's 20 rounds - certainly not as high as in the heady days of 2011, when he was up at the sharp end of the field with Renault. However, it is true that points are not to be expected with Caterham, just hoped for - but even a single point could provide a springboard for the team and help guarantee some of its 2014 budget.

TRACK NOTES

Nationality:	RUSSIAN
Born:	8 SEPTEMBER 1984, VYBORG, RUSSIA
Website:	www.vitalypetrov.ru
Teams:	RENAULT 2010-11, CATERHAM 2012-13

CAREER RECORD

First Grand Prix:	2010 BAHRAIN GP
Grand Prix starts:	57
Grand Prix wins:	0
	(best result: third, 2011 Australian GP)
Poles:	0
Fastest laps:	1
Points:	64
Honours:	2009 GP2 RUNNER-UP,
	2005 RUSSIAN FORMULA 1600 CHAMPION &
	RUSSIAN LADA REVOLUTION CHAMPION,
	2002 LADA CUP CHAMPION

AN UNTRODDEN ROUTE TO GLORY

As Russia's first and only F1 racer to date, it's hardly surprising that Vitaly has taken a route untrodden by his rivals. He made his car racing debut in small saloons, winning the Russian Lada Cup at his second attempt in 2002. It was only after this that he tried single-seaters and spent a couple of years racing in the European Formula Renault series. Then, short of money, he returned to Russia in 2005 and won a national title in both single-seaters and saloons. Intent on progressing towards Formula One, Vitaly found his way back on to the conventional ladder to the top, placing third in the Italian Formula 3000 series. Concentrating on GP2 in 2007, he won a race that season, then another in 2008, before two wins in 2009 earned him second-place ranking behind Nico Hulkenberg. This was enough to land him his F1 break with Renault for 2010, his best result for the team being third in Australia in 2011 before he moved to Caterham.

* unconfirmed at time of going to press.

CHARLES PIC

Charles had an excellent rookie season with Marussia Racing last year and displayed not only the raw speed his CV suggested he possessed but an ability to learn as he went. He should benefit from his move to Caterham.

Here is a driver who in his first year of Formula One did everything required of him and more. As the season advanced, the now 23-year-old Frenchman not only became a match for his experienced Marussia Racing team-mate Timo Glock, but sometimes ran ahead of him. Thus he laid to rest the rent-a-driver tag with which he had been saddled. Yes, Charles comes from a wealthy family, but he has enough speed to warrant his place at racing's top table.

For this year, anxious to climb up the race order, Charles has moved across to the Caterham F1 Team. If the status quo prevails, this will elevate Charles only by one row of the grid, but there's hope that the Malaysian-owned but England-based team will continue its progress and at least be snapping at the rump of the midfield. He should certainly enjoy the Renault horsepower, finding it a step up from what he had from Cosworth last year.

It will be fascinating to see how Charles advances when he arrives at the circuits outside Europe that he saw for the first time last year. With the benefit of this experience, he can be expected to go better still.

Charles was 2012's most impressive rookie but he'll have to get to know his new team.

His best result last year was 12th, achieved in the final round in Brazil, when he lost the battle for 11th place with Caterham's Vitaly Petrov and so consigned Marsussia Racing to 11th place in the constructors' rankings and his team for this year to the more lucrative 10th place. And that, barring unusual races such as the Singapore GP, in which Glock collected a 12th place, was about as high as Marussia could have expected to finish in these days of commendable mechanical reliability.

As quick learner, Charles will discover something else in the year ahead, which is that a driver is cut some slack in his maiden season of F1 but from then on is expected to deliver, race in, race out – making this a key season. What is essential for Charles's continued progress is having a more experienced team-mate from whom to learn, much as he benefited from Timo Glock's knowledge last year.

TRACK NOTES

Nationality:	FRENCH
Born:	15 FEBRUARY 1990, MONTELIMAR, FRANCE
Website:	www.charlespic.com
Teams:	MARUSSIA 2012, CATERHAM 2013

CAREER RECORD

First Grand Prix:	2012 AUSTRALIAN GP
Grand Prix starts:	20
Grand Prix wins:	0
	(best result: 12th, 2012 Brazilian GP)
Poles:	0
Fastest laps:	0
Points:	0
Honours:	2005 ITALIAN JUNIOR KART RUNNER-UP

A RECIPIENT OF EXCELLENT ADVICE

Charles had the good fortune to be born into a family that loves its racing. His father's transport company had backed future F1 racers Eric Bernard and Olivier Panis in Formula 3000, and it was Bernard who offered Charles a kart ride on his 12th birthday. This led to the junior French kart title two years later, in 2004, and Bernard's advice helped Charles and younger brother Arthur advance through Formula Campus and Formula Renault. In 2008 Charles stepped up to Formula Renault 3.5 and ranked sixth, then third in 2009, winning at Silverstone and the Nurburgring. At the end of that year, he contested the GP2 Asia series and won in Bahrain, before a full GP2 campaign in 2010 that started with a win in Barcelona but produced no more, leaving him 10th. When he returned for a second attempt in 2011, Panis – winner of the 1996 Monaco GP – was appointed as his coach, to prepare him for Formula One, and Charles responded by winning twice to rank fourth, while Romain Grosjean dominated.

MARUSSIA F1 TEAM

Marussia made progress last year and is bound to make some more in the season ahead, but despite closing the time deficit to the leading teams it still finds itself fighting to move up the order, while points remain out of its reach.

Marussia struggled without KERS in 2012 but their biggest setback was falling to 11th place, which cost them millions in lost prize money.

Last year's Marussia MR01 was notable for being the first car entered in the World Championship by this team that had not been built wholly using computational fluid dynamics (CFD). That it was more competitive than its two predecessors might tell a story, and the fact that this year's Marussia, the MR02, will also have been designed and produced in the more traditional way, using wind tunnels and all manner of other technical aids, is proof that the team considers that its original technical director Nick Wirth might have been too quick to embrace all-CFD design.

The MR01 was produced by chief designer John McQuilliam, with help from Rob Taylor and chief aerodynamicist Richard Taylor and engineering input from Mark Herd. Yet, guiding them along the path was an extra, very valuable layer of assistance. This came from McLaren with the provision of aerodynamic advice as well as an invitation to use McLaren's wind tunnel in Woking to assess their workings. When a team is in its formative years, all assistance is most welcome, if only to prevent the team's design outfit from heading up an expensive and time-consuming dead end. Helping this all to run smoothly, former Benetton and Renault executive director of engineering

KEY MOMENTS AND KEY PEOPLE

TEAM HISTORY

The team known as Marussia F1 Team started as Virgin Racing when it entered the World Championship in 2010. This was set up on a team that grew out of successful Formula Renault and Formula Three team Manor Motorsport, run by John Booth. Originally based near Sheffield, it subsequently moved south to Banbury to be closer to the suppliers and expertise in the heart of England. Timo Glock has been the backbone of its driving force, supported by Lucas di Grassi, Jerome d'Ambrosio and then Charles Pic.

GRAEME LOWDON

After graduating in mechanical engineering, Graeme was working in Switzerland when he became involved in a sponsorship deal for an Indycar team, and this was his way into the sport. After setting up his own Formula Renault team, Eiger Racing, in 1996, he raced against Manor Motorsport for several years before joining them as commercial manager in 2000. He was later involved in helping the team step up to Formula One in 2010, when it provided the base on which Virgin Racing, now Marussia F1, was built.

2012 DRIVERS & RESULTS

Driver	Nationality	Races	Wins	Pts	Pos
Timo Glock	German	20	0	0	20th
Charles Pic	French	20	0	0	21st

Pat Symonds had already taken a look at how the team worked in the new base at Banbury that it moved into from its original base in Dinnington in Yorkshire to enable those below him to work more freely and accurately.

Although the eventual results achieved by drivers Timo Glock and Charles Pic matched or even exceeded expectations, the team suffered the embarrassment of not having its car ready for pre-season testing. It had failed the mandatory crash test and so didn't get to go testing for the first time until it arrived in Melbourne in March. That this followed on from the team's 2010 car being built with a fuel tank that was too small to run a grand prix non-stop, as became required, was unfortunate to say the least.

Luckily, both cars managed to be classified as finishers in the opening round, and their finishing record was fair after that. Glock used his years of F1 experience to help bring the car on, but it was first-year F1 racer Pic who tended to excite as he exceeded expectations and laid to rest the fact that his family simply bought his ride. This is now seen as an outright benefit rather than a partial encumbrance.

After Glock collected a brace of 14th-place finishes and Pic a pair of 15th places, the team's highlight last year came when Glock raced to 12th place on Singapore's Marina Bay street circuit. Although this must have felt good for Glock, it has to be remembered that he had finished rather higher here before, notably in second place in 2009 when he raced for Toyota.

Then, in the final round in Brazil, Pic ran 11th until six laps from the end before being pushed back to 12th when he was too cautious and Vitaly Petrov passed him. It was a costly mistake, as it dropped the team to 11th overall.

The cars continue to be Cosworth-powered, and Glock has agreed to go on leading on the track. When it became clear that Pic might take his money and head to a better-placed team rather than stay, British GP2 racer Max Chilton approached the team with a sizeable budget of around £9.25m courtesy of his father's AON insurance company. Chilton had prior experience of the team, having driven an MR01 in the mid-season young driver tests at Silverstone. Indonesian driver Rio Haryanto also had a run and may become part of the team.

FOR THE RECORD

Country of origin:	England
Team base:	Banbury, England
Telephone:	(44) 01909 517250
Website:	www.marussiaf1team.com
Active in Formula One:	From 2010
Grands Prix contested:	58
Wins:	0
Pole positions:	0
Fastest laps:	0

THE TEAM

Team principal:	John Booth
Chief executive officer:	Andy Webb
Technical consultant:	Pat Symonds
Chief engineer:	Dave Greenwood
Sporting director & president:	Graeme Lowdon
Chief designer:	John McQuilliam
Deputy design chief:	Rob Taylor
Chief aerodynamicist:	Richard Taylor
Team manager:	Dave O'Neill
Test driver:	TBA
Chassis:	Marussia MR02
Engine:	Cosworth V8
Tyres:	Pirelli

"Last year, the gap between our fastest lap and the winner's was 4.5 per cent, but in the closing stages of the season we had reduced that to 2.5 per cent, even without KERS."
John Booth

Straight-talking technical consultant Pat Symonds is looking for gains in the team's performance.

TIMO GLOCK

There has been little clear progress for Marussia, but Timo is back for a fourth year with the team in the hope that they will be able to move from the back of the grid, providing good continuity for its technical team.

It's hard to know what satisfaction this serious German racer gets from driving around at the tail of the field. After all, the 2013 season is more than nine years on from his F1 debut, when he marked himself out as one to watch by finishing in an impressive seventh place, one place ahead of his far more experienced Jordan team-mate Nick Heidfeld, but he is in almost no danger of doing so again as the focus at Marussia is unlikely to shift from doing its utmost to ensure that at the very least it doesn't finish last.

As even the greatest effort expended for a backmarking team is all but invisible, it's not as though his great drives in uncompetitive machinery are suddenly going to propel Timo to a drive with even a midfield team. His chance for that has long since evaporated, as younger and possibly faster drivers arrive each year and make all the right noises about being able to grasp any driver openings that occur.

Last year was Timo's third difficult campaign for the team, and Timo suffered the indignity of his rookie team-mate Charles Pic outpacing him on more than one occasion, especially as the season

Timo remains for a fourth year but must be wondering when progress will come.

went on. Certainly, it was Timo who collected the team's best finish, 12th place, in Singapore, until Pic matched it in the final round in Brazil, but this wily drive was the exception rather than the rule. The three years that had passed

since he finished second on the same circuit with Toyota must have felt like a very long time.

If the team can find superior form from this year's MR02, its second car conceived by regular methods rather than through the sole use of computational fluid dynamics (CFD), then perhaps Timo might pick off Caterham's drivers in the races, but the midfield battle will probably still appear to be taking place a very long way ahead of him. So, another trying season lies ahead, in which he will have to make the most of his years of experience and the very least he must hope for is to keep his team-mate behind him.

TRACK NOTES

Nationality:	GERMAN
Born: 18 MARCH 1982, LINDENFELS, GERMANY	
Website:	www.timoglock.de
Teams:	JORDAN 2004, TOYOTA 2008-09, VIRGIN/MARUSSIA 2010-13

CAREER RECORD	
First Grand Prix:	2004 CANADIAN GP
Grand Prix starts:	91
Grand Prix wins:	0
(best result: second, 2008 Hungarian GP, 2009 Singapore GP)	
Poles:	0
Fastest laps:	1
Points:	51
Honours:	2007 GP2 CHAMPION, 2001 GERMAN FORMULA BMW CHAMPION, 2000 GERMAN FORMULA BMW JUNIOR CHAMPION

SECOND TIME AROUND

On paper the early stages of Timo's racing career look like textbook stuff, as he won the German Formula BMW Junior title in 2000, then the German Formula BMW title the following year. In Formula Three, though, after a strong rookie campaign in which he ranked third in the German series, his momentum faltered in 2003 and Timo could rank only fifth in the German series as Ryan Briscoe became champion. However, his sponsors landed him an F1 ride midway through 2004 when the Jordan dropped Giorgio Pantano. Although he finished seventh on his debut, there was no ride for 2005, so Timo raced in Indycars for Rocketsports Racing and ranked an impressive eighth overall. Looking to return to Formula One, though, he raced in GP2 in 2006, going on to win the title in 2007. Then, for two years, he was back in F1 with Toyota, for whom he twice finished second. The team shut at the end of 2009, and since then Timo has raced for Virgin, now Marussia.

MAX CHILTON

Having run as a third driver for Marussia late last year, GP2 race winner Max identified this tail-end team as his way into a Formula One race seat and then used his substantial family backing to secure the ride.

Make no mistake, Max is a very rapid driver. Of course, as a driver who has not won a title in single-seaters, there will always be the question as to whether he would have made it to Formula One had he not been able to call on his family's immense wealth, earned from the insurance industry. But he now has a chance to prove himself.

Of course, driving for Marussia Racing, Max will be doing well to qualify anywhere other than the final row of the grid now that fellow tail-ender HRT has shut up shop. However, what will mark the 21-year-old English driver out is whether he can perform to the car's maximum potential in the races, making his tyres last, nailing his pit stops when called in and not losing too much time when having to go off the racing line to allow the leading drivers to lap him. That alone will be a new experience that is counterintuitive in so many ways, but it's something that all drivers for the less competitive teams must face.

Furthermore, the step up from being run by a 10-man team in GP2 to being run by five times that number in Formula One

Max is set to discover how much of a jump it is from test driver to race driver.

is gargantuan and demands a whole new level of maturity and focus. Fortunately, in Timo Glock he has a proven and experienced team-mate and it will be vital for Max to look, listen and learn. Being

a grand prix driver involves far more than simply being able to lap fast, and he will also have to demonstrate that he understands the car and the circuits well enough to contribute to debriefs. Luckily for Max, he has some F1 mileage behind him, having performed the Friday morning practice duties for Marussia Racing in Abu Dhabi last year, where he was not disgraced by comparison to Glock, lapping within one second of the German's pace.

Then, of course, there is the vastly increased amount of PR activity in which he will have to engage, making each grand prix meeting as much of an endurance session when he's out of the car as when he's in it. One thing that will come across, though, is that Max loves his racing and is an extremely personable character who will be happy to talk but would rather let his driving do the talking.

SPEED AND EXPERIENCE

Max followed his older brother Tom into racing, stepping up from karts to racing cars at the age of 14 to compete in T-Cars, a base-level silhouette saloon car series for teenagers. He was runner-up in his second season, then stepped up to single-seaters in 2007, bypassing Formula Ford or Formula Renault to contest the British Formula Three Championship with Arena International. In 2008, driving for Hitech Racing, he was far more competitive, but he didn't take his first win until his third year in the category when he ranked fourth overall for Carlin Motorsport as rookie team-mate Daniel Ricciardo dominated. Next came GP2, Formula One's feeder category, where he spent the next three years, improving from 25th overall with Ocean Racing Technology in 2010 and 20th with Carlin in 2011 to fourth overall, again with Carlin, in 2012, just behind this year's Sauber rookie Esteban Gutierrez, thanks to winning at the Hungaroring from pole position and then adding a further win on the Singapore street circuit.

TRACK NOTES

Nationality:	BRITISH
Born:	21 APRIL 1991, REIGATE, ENGLAND
Website:	www.maxchilton.com
Teams:	MARUSSIA 2013

CAREER RECORD	
First Grand Prix:	2013 AUSTRALIAN GP
Grand Prix starts:	0
Grand Prix wins:	0
Poles:	0
Fastest laps:	0
Points:	0
Honours:	2006 T CARS CHAMPION

Kimi Raikkonen pays tribute to the late 1976 World Champion James Hunt during a qualifying session at Monaco last year.

TALKING POINT: RENAULT IS THE POWER BEHIND THE CHAMPIONS

Renault won the first grand prix in 1906 and has made several bids for F1 glory, but it has almost always come when powering cars entered by others.

It was a huge leap from that race on a road circuit around Le Mans in 1906, when Ferenc Szisz was triumphant, to Renault's modern-day grand prix racing debut at Silverstone in 1977. Yet, despite pioneering turbocharged engines in Formula One, and coming very close in 1983 thanks to Alain Prost's efforts, Renault never managed to become the champion team until it took over an established British team in the 21st century.

There were moments of promise under the guidance of Jean Sage, with Jean-Pierre Jabouille setting the ball rolling and René Arnoux pushing Prost hard on occasion. Yet, this most French of teams had no titles to call its own when it closed its doors at the end of 1985.

It was at this moment that Renault made a decision that would yield dividends: it would continue developing its engines for other teams to use. This was wise, as it would be able to take some credit should they or their drivers end the year on top, but would not have to take stick if they should fail.

Lotus had been running Renault engines since 1983 and was joined by Ligier in 1984 and then by Tyrrell in 1985. Ayrton Senna was its most successful driver in 1986, racing for Lotus. Then there were two years on the sidelines before Renault bounced back as an engine supplier with Williams, and Thierry Boutsen and Riccardo Patrese helped it rank second behind the McLarens. Then, after pushing the Honda-powered McLarens close in 1991, Renault and Williams struck gold together in 1992

when Nigel Mansell dominated to become champion, helping Renault to its first title. Their margin of victory together was even greater in 1993 when Prost finally won a title with Renault power. Williams and Renault made it three constructors' titles in a row in 1994, but this success was blighted by Senna's death at Imola.

In 1995, Williams ended up being beaten by a team with the same engine, Benetton, which had switched from Ford power as Michael Schumacher landed his second title in succession. Benetton lost ground in 1996, with Damon Hill taking the title for Williams ahead of team-mate Jacques Villeneuve, while Schumacher fell to third overall. The French-Canadian landed the title in his second season, 1997, and so Renault had a share in six straight constructors' titles, making for some excellent publicity.

Mercedes became the winning engine in 1998, with McLaren, after which Ferrari finally found its feet again to dominate through until the end of 2004. Renault engines kept a presence with Benetton before taking the team over and renaming it Renault for 2002. This second Renault F1 team was based in England and so had no connection to the one that ran from 1977 to 1985. Wins didn't come straight away, but Fernando Alonso scored Renault's first victory in Hungary in 2003 before taking it to title glory in 2005, edging out McLaren. He landed the drivers' title too and repeated the feat in 2006 for another title double.

Then, in 2007, the team "fell off a cliff",

scoring only a quarter of Ferrari's points after Alonso left for McLaren. However, Red Bull Racing started using Renault engines and began to get up to speed. Alonso's return to the team made little impact, as by then it was a team in decline and its form fell away so badly that it ranked only eighth in 2009, when Red Bull started winning through Sebastian Vettel and Mark Webber. Second only to Brawn GP and Jenson Button that year, Vettel, Red Bull and Renault were champions in 2010 before repeating the result in even more dominant fashion in 2011 and 2012.

Renault were thankful for this success with Red Bull as the team spent 2009 reeling from the fall-out from Alonso's win at Singapore that led to "Crashgate" after team-mate Nelson Piquet Jr claimed that he'd been asked to crash to bring out the safety car and thus facilitate Alonso's success. With team principal Flavio Briatore and engineering director Pat Symonds fired, the team was taken over by Genii Capital for 2010. Its great hope was the ever-improving form of Robert Kubica, but he was injured in a rallying accident and the team struggled in 2011, after which it was rebadged as Lotus and all connection bar the engines was removed, showing yet again that Renault's greatest successes in F1 tend to be with other teams.

Right: Alain Prost led from pole position at Monaco for Renault in 1983 but had to settle for third place in a year that promised more than it delivered.

Left: Renault's first F1 appearance was at the 1977 British GP, with Jean-Pierre Jabouille qualifying 21st, then retiring.

Below: Williams dominated in 1992 with Renault power, with lead driver Nigel Mansell collecting nine wins in 16 rounds to become a clear world champion.

TALKING POINT: FORMULA ONE SEEKS A FIXED HOME IN THE USA

The United States GP is one of Formula One's wandering races, and its continued quest to find a home has now resulted in two on the annual calendar, with a GP in New Jersey joining the one in Austin in 2014.

The USA has such a packed sporting schedule for its most popular sports – basketball, baseball, American football, ice hockey and NASCAR stock car racing – that it can easily do without Formula One. However, the reverse is not true, as F1 certainly needs the USA if it is to be the most international sport of all.

Tracking the course of the United States GP since it was first part of the World Championship is truly dizzying, for it has crossed that huge country pretty much from south to north and from west to east since the inaugural race held at Sebring, Florida, in 1959. The following year the race moved thousands of miles away to the opposite coast, to Riverside in California, then back east to Watkins Glen, New York State, in 1961. This should have been a triumphant homecoming for Phil Hill, who had just been crowned as America's first World Champion, but Ferrari chose not to attend. Fortunately, the race found a great home at Watkins Glen and remained there until 1980, as part of an autumn double-header with the Canadian GP just over the border at Mosport Park in Ontario. After 20 years, however, the circuit was deemed not just unsafe and perhaps too remote, but also too grungy, with its infield swamp always something to be avoided.

Back across the continent in California, there was already an alternative grand prix event, the US GP West, which was held on a temporary street circuit in Long Beach. This ran from 1976 to 1983, with great crowds turning out to watch the USA's only other World Champion, Mario Andretti, by which time Formula One had been courted by a couple of other suitors.

Firstly, there was a race in Las Vegas, in the car park of the Caesar's Palace casino, but this failed to lure the public away from the gaming halls and so lasted only from 1981 to 1982.

The other city that tried to make the race its own was Detroit. This was fitting, as it's the centre of the American automotive industry, home to Ford, Chrysler and General Motors, and "Motown" needed some glamour as the Japanese manufacturers started to cut into its profits. The race stayed there from 1982 until 1988, with Ayrton Senna winning the last three in a row. However, Detroit was not a great circuit, its 90-degree corners and bumpy surface winning few fans.

By then, Dallas had also hosted a race, in 1984, but the conditions were meltingly hot and the track surface simply wouldn't stay down, making every lap a new adventure for the drivers. The Fair Park street circuit never saw Formula One again.

What it really needed was a fast, flowing road circuit to show the cars at their best, rather than in the point-and-squirt street circuits where their average lap speeds were so slow, but both Mid-Ohio and Road America were too far from the metropolises, and so it was to yet another street circuit that the US GP turned next. This time it moved to Phoenix in the Arizona desert. It may have been a fast-growing city, but few attended its races between 1989 and 1991.

Then, it seemed that Formula One and the USA had gone their separate ways, much to the disappointment of the legions of American F1 fans. In 2000, however, Formula One finally returned,

to the Indianapolis Motor Speedway. Revered as the home of the Indy 500, it had actually hosted 10 rounds of the World Championship before, from 1950 until 1959, but these were in fact the Indy 500 rather than a US GP, and it was only after the arrangement ceased that the F1 teams started to enter cars in the Indy 500 in pursuit of its considerable winner's prize. The F1 race was held from 2000 to 2007 on a circuit laid out on part of the banking and around the infield, but then the USA found itself without a grand prix once more.

Now, with the Circuit of the Americas in Austin proving to be the first North American track since Watkins Glen at which the F1 cars really stretch their legs as they should, the sport and the country has finally got it right. Add in the street circuit in New Jersey from 2014 and the USA might learn to love Formula One at last.

Right: Formula One ran at Indianapolis from 2000 until 2007, using the banking for part of the lap. It drew good crowds but it never really felt like the race's natural home.

Above: Andretti's successes in Europe, such as winning at Zolder in 1978 ahead of Lotus team-mate Peterson and Ferrari's Reutemann, helped him become the USA's second F1 champion.

Below: The first United States GP was held at Sebring in 1959, with Bruce McLaren winning in a Cooper.

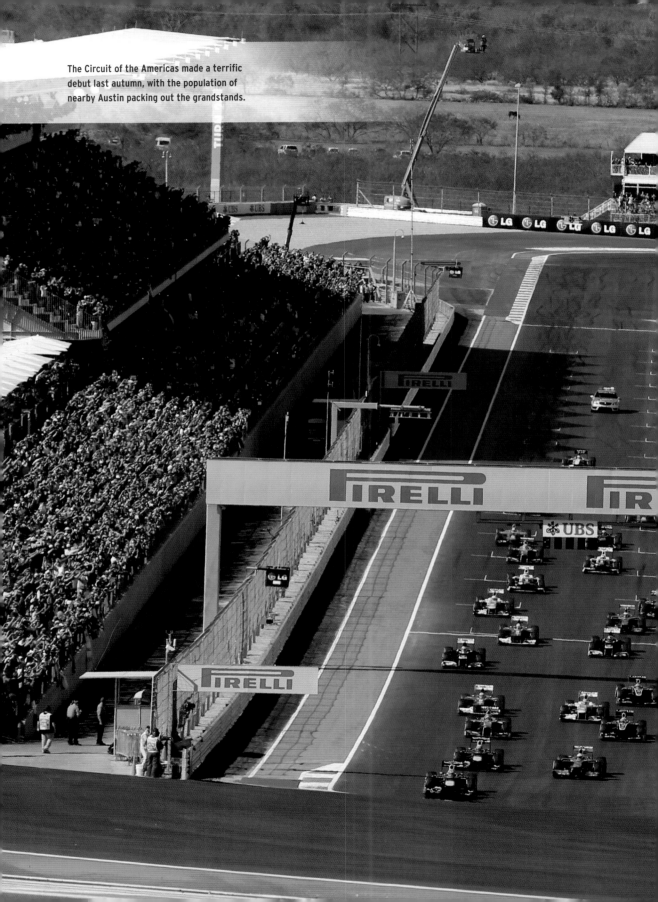

The Circuit of the Americas made a terrific debut last autumn, with the population of nearby Austin packing out the grandstands.

KNOW THE TRACKS 2013

After the welcome debut of a new circuit in the USA last autumn, there's the possibility of one returning this year in the shape of the Red Bull Ring (formerly the A1-Ring), which replaces the race that was going to be held in New Jersey. The New Jersey event will now make its bow in 2014. The European circuits continue to feel the pinch financially and their predominance goes on dwindling as Asian markets continue to provide revenue and Russia lines up for its first grand prix next year.

The early years of the 21st century have witnessed considerable change to the make-up of the Formula One World Championship. There has been at least one addition every year since 2008, and that year there were two, as both Valencia and Singapore signed up. The new races have been spread around the world, from Spain to Singapore to Abu Dhabi to South Korea to India and to the USA, has only strengthened the sport's global appeal.

Entering the Russian arena in 2014 will take that on a stage further. These are indeed exciting times for F1 and its fans.

Some have asked where this might stop, or even when, as the line of potential new host nations surely has to dry up, with the global economy still struggling to work its way out of the recession. However, discussions are taking place about the championship trail being extended to as many as 23 races

year, so perhaps not all of the European races will have to be discarded to make way for them.

The pattern of the front end of the season is familiar, the first four races taking place in Australia, South-East Asia and then the Middle East. The year's first race in Europe is in Spain as usual. As before, Monaco is next, followed by a trip across the pond to the Canadian GP.

The British GP has been pushed forward a week to the end of June, and there was discussion about the possibility of the French GP being revived and inserted into the slot after this, either at Magny-Cours or Paul Ricard, but this came to nothing. So, after races in Germany - with the Nurburgring only able to take its place in its rotation with Hockenheim after a rescue package was put together by local government - and Hungary, F1 folk get a much-needed summer break, with four weeks between the race at the Hungaroring and the next one, at Spa-Francorchamps.

Although almost all new races are being added at the expense of an old one, the postponement of the planned new race on a street circuit in New Jersey until 2014 has left Formula One Management considering whether to take a grand prix back to the A1-Ring for the first time since 2003 in the slot between the German and Hungarian GPs in July, to keep the number of races at 20.

After the Italian GP, the teams have to pack again and set off on a gruelling tail end to the season with seven races in 10 weeks. Bouncing around the East, from Singapore to Yeongam to Suzuka and then back west again via the Indian and Abu Dhabi GPs, the team personnel ought to be able to drop back home to Europe for clean clothes before crossing the Atlantic for a double-headed finale that starts in Austin, Texas, and ends at Interlagos.

The World Championship is a mammoth trek these days, but the globalisation of the sport keeps the drivers and team personnel aware of where they are, because a grand prix in, say, South Korea will always produce a very different atmosphere from that experienced at traditional venues like Monza or Silverstone, where the fans have been attending races for generations. Converting new fans is another matter, most especially in countries where there's no history of any form of motor sport. The best way to draw in fans is to have a local hero competing. So bear that in mind when you look ahead to these new races, and check out which drivers in the junior international single-seater formulae might fit the description over the next few years, with the USA's Alexander Rossi on the brink of an F1 ride and a host of Russians hoping to be the one who draws the attention when Sochi hosts its first grand prix.

MELBOURNE

There was protest about a grand prix being held in Melbourne before its debut in 1996, but Albert Park has settled down into one of the staples of the Formula One calendar.

Before Formula One came to Melbourne, Albert Park was a dusty park around a lake in one of the city's inner suburbs. Yet, with the construction of the temporary circuit for annual use, the park was upgraded and the hotels, bars and restaurants filled up.

The Australian GP is more than just a money-spinner, as it adds to Melbourne's reputation as one of the world's top sports-mad cities, alongside world-class tennis and cricket which are also held there, all blessed with packed grandstands that add to the vibrancy of these events.

The circuit is not an exciting stretch of tarmac in its own right, as it offers little in the way of passing opportunities. However,

it's made exciting by the fact that this race is normally the opening race of the championship, so it offers the first realistic chance to see who is going fast and which new partnerships are gelling well.

The first corner often offers drama on the opening lap as too many cars fight to occupy too little space. Then, for those who didn't manage a passing manoeuvre there, Turn 3 is an even sharper right-hander with plenty of run-off and so offers a second chance for a driver to make a dive up the inside. Throw in the usual sunshine, though, and Melbourne gives F1 fans a colourful setting for their beloved sport to burst back into life.

"I love racing at home, but the hardest bit is the attention, so time management isn't always easy. You have to treat it like any other grand prix." **Mark Webber**

68

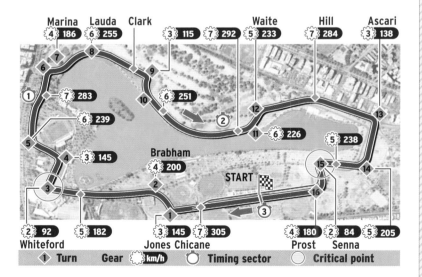

| 1 | Turn | Gear | km/h | Timing sector | Critical point |

2012 POLE TIME: **HAMILTON (McLAREN)**, 1M24.922S, 139.681MPH /224.795KPH
2012 WINNER'S AVERAGE SPEED: **121.783MPH/195.911KPH**

2012 FASTEST LAP: **BUTTON (McLAREN)**, 1M29.187S, 133.006MPH/214.053KPH
LAP RECORD: **M. SCHUMACHER (FERRARI)**, 1M24.125S, 141.016MPH/226.944KPH, 2004

INSIDE TRACK
AUSTRALIAN GRAND PRIX

Date:	**17 March**
Circuit name:	**Albert Park**
Circuit length:	**3.295 miles/5.300km**
Number of laps:	**58**
Email:	**enquiries@grandprix.com.au**
Website:	**www.grandprix.com.au**

PREVIOUS WINNERS	
2003	**David Coulthard** McLAREN
2004	**Michael Schumacher** FERRARI
2005	**Giancarlo Fisichella** RENAULT
2006	**Fernando Alonso** RENAULT
2007	**Kimi Räikkönen** FERRARI
2008	**Lewis Hamilton** McLAREN
2009	**Jenson Button** BRAWN
2010	**Jenson Button** McLAREN
2011	**Sebastian Vettel** RED BULL
2012	**Jenson Button** McLAREN

First race: The first time Melbourne hosted the Australian GP, in 1996, almost produced a huge turn-up for the books as Jacques Villeneuve came close to being only the second driver ever to win on his World Championship debut, and thus match the feat of Ferrari's Giancarlo Baghetti in the 1961 French GP. As it was, the French-Canadian's oil pressure started to drop with only a few laps to run, and his Williams team-mate Damon Hill motored by for victory.

First corner: Turn 1 is a corner that has claimed more scalps than most, as it narrows at the turn-in point and so often puts one driver into the path of another.

Greatest local hero: Jack Brabham is the most titled Australian F1 driver, with three World Championships to his name. However, he was from near Sydney and the greatest driver from Melbourne was Alan Jones, World Champion for Williams in 1980, and son of Stan, who won the Australian GP at Longford in 1959 in its non-championship days.

Do you remember when? Martin Brundle got airborne into Turn 3 on lap 1 in Albert Park's inaugural Australian GP in 1996 after Olivier Panis was forced to brake hard and David Coulthard swerved into his path.

SEPANG

Not all circuits offer many places to overtake, but Sepang does. It also comes with the possibility of a tropical rainstorm that can turn the course of a race with a sudden, intense flurry.

While Malaysia's soaring heat and energy-sapping humidity will always be a concern for drivers, they all love heading to Sepang because it's a circuit that offers them a real challenge and the chance to do some proper racing.

It remains the best of the many modern Hermann Tilke-designed circuits, offering not only a wonderful flow to its lap but three very realistic spots for overtaking per lap, which is three more than at certain other circuits visited by the World Championship. These three spots are at the first corner or even between there and Turn 2 as the drivers reposition themselves for the tight left that follows, then going up the rise to the sharp right at Turn 4, and lastly at the end of the long back straight feeding into the final corner, a hairpin. A generous width of circuit helps in each of these locations. The hairpin at Turn 9, with its flat entry into an uphill exit, is another place where drivers can pass if they've had a good enough run through Turns 7 and 8.

Better still, Sepang is a circuit with some really testing corners, the prime example being the run through Turns 5 and 6 where sharp, high-speed changes of direction are required. Further around the lap, drivers also need some bravado to attack the sequence of Turns 12 and 13, fast corners on undulating terrain.

"Sepang is about feeling the flow. The track is big, fast and wide, so it's easy to hit top speed and carry it through the 15 corners."

Lewis Hamilton

INSIDE TRACK
MALAYSIAN GRAND PRIX

Date:	**24 March**
Circuit name:	**Sepang Circuit**
Circuit length:	**3.444 miles/5.542km**
Number of laps:	**56**
Email:	**inquiries@sepangcircuit.com.my**
Website:	**www.malaysiangp.com.my**

PREVIOUS WINNERS	
2003	**Kimi Raïkkönen** McLAREN
2004	**Michael Schumacher** FERRARI
2005	**Fernando Alonso** RENAULT
2006	**Giancarlo Fisichella** RENAULT
2007	**Fernando Alonso** McLAREN
2008	**Kimi Raïkkönen** FERRARI
2009	**Jenson Button** BRAWN
2010	**Sebastian Vettel** RED BULL
2011	**Sebastian Vettel** RED BULL
2012	**Fernando Alonso** FERRARI

First race: A broken leg at the British GP ended any hopes Michael Schumacher had of winning the world title in 1999, but he arrived for Malaysia's first grand prix looking to assist team-mate Eddie Irvine's bid to land the title ahead of Mika Hakkinen. Schumacher led, then let Irvine through and kept Hakkinen back to give Irvine a four-point lead going into the final round.

First corner: Turn 1 is among Formula One's best for overtaking. It's a hairpin at the end of a long straight, down which drivers can set up their move by using KERS and DRS. Also they can take a number of lines both in and out of the corner, as the exit feeds almost straight into Turn 2.

Greatest local hero: Alex Yoong, Malaysia's only F1 driver, came to Formula One late in 2001 with Minardi before running a full season in 2002. The former water-skiing star earned more plaudits when he won for the Malaysian team in A1GP in 2006 and 2007.

Do you remember when? It was almost dark when the race was declared in 2009. A storm had left cars aquaplaning off and brought out the red flag. Then, after a long wait for the storm to dissipate, time ran out as darkness began to fall, leaving Jenson Button as the winner.

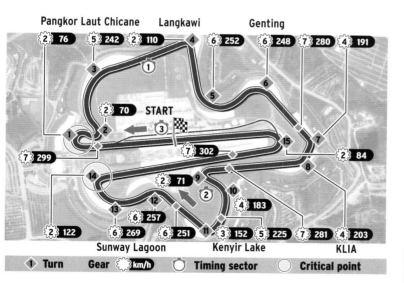

Pangkor Laut Chicane — Langkawi — Genting

| 2 | 76 | 5 | 242 | 2 | 110 | 4 | | 6 | 252 | 6 | 248 | 7 | 280 | 4 | 191 |

| 2 | 70 | START |

| 7 | 299 | | 7 | 302 | | 2 | 84 |

| 2 | 71 | 9 |

| 4 | 183 |

| 2 | 122 | 6 | 269 | 6 | 251 | 11 | 3 | 152 | 5 | 225 | 7 | 281 | 4 | 203 |

| 6 | 257 |

Sunway Lagoon — Kenyir Lake — KLIA

◆ Turn   Gear   ✺ km/h   ○ Timing sector   ◯ Critical point

2012 POLE TIME: HAMILTON (McLAREN), 1M36.219S, 128.856MPH/207.374KPH
2012 WINNER'S AVERAGE SPEED: 70.199MPH/112.975KPH

2012 FASTEST LAP: RAIKKONEN (LOTUS), 1M40.722S, 123.110MPH/198.127KPH
LAP RECORD: MONTOYA (WILLIAMS), 1M34.223S, 131.991MPH/212.419KPH, 2004

SHANGHAI

Formula One still hasn't caught on in China in the way that the teams and sponsors had hoped that it would. Perhaps all it will take to fill the grandstands is a Chinese driver.

Expectations were high when Formula One broke into the Chinese market in 2004. Then, it really was F1's brave new world. However, the race organisers have never managed to fill the grandstands around the Shanghai International Circuit, and now, after nine grands prix, they have taken to covering the empty seats with large advertising banners.

For all that, though, this circuit still offers something different from the F1 mix. First off, it's vast, with facilities so large that they dwarf anything anywhere else on the calendar. Secondly, it offers both a true challenge to the drivers and the opportunity for plenty of overtaking, both down the 1,170m back straight and past the

pit exit on to Turn 1. With DRS and KERS both offering extra oomph for the chasing driver, overtaking action is all but assured.

The sheer scale of the place has a habit of making the cars look as though they are not travelling as fast as they really are, but watching them tackle the fast sweepers behind the paddock, Turns 7 and 8, tells your brain otherwise, and a driver's level of confidence in his car's handling is more plain to see here than anywhere else.

One counterbalance to the circuit's on-track offerings is that it still lacks atmosphere, and this can be exacerbated by the smog that generally hangs over the place, giving everything a grey air.

"It's a very good, modern circuit. The first two sectors are pretty technical, there are some interesting combinations of corners and you need a good, responsive car." **Jenson Button**

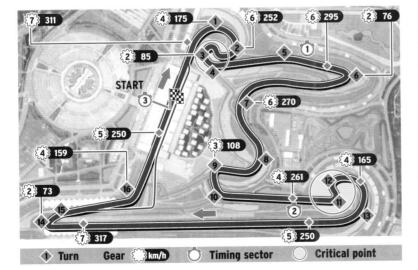

| ◆ Turn | Gear | km/h | ○ Timing sector | ○ Critical point |

2012 POLE TIME: **ROSBERG (MERCEDES), 1M35.121S, 128.300MPH/206.479KPH**
2012 WINNER'S AVERAGE SPEED: **117.922MPH/189.777KPH**

2012 FASTEST LAP: **KOBAYASHI (SAUBER), 1M39.960S, 121.984MPH/196.315KPH**
LAP RECORD: **M. SCHUMACHER (FERRARI), 1M32.238S, 132.202MPH/212.759KPH, 2004**

INSIDE TRACK
CHINESE GRAND PRIX

Date:	**14 April**
Circuit name:	**Shanghai International Circuit**
Circuit length:	**3.390 miles/5.450km**
Number of laps:	**56**
Email:	**f1@china-sss.com**
Website:	**www.f1china.com.cn**

PREVIOUS WINNERS

2004	**Rubens Barrichello** FERRARI
2005	**Fernando Alonso** RENAULT
2006	**Michael Schumacher** FERRARI
2007	**Kimi Raïkkönen** FERRARI
2008	**Lewis Hamilton** McLAREN
2009	**Sebastian Vettel** RED BULL
2010	**Jenson Button** McLAREN
2011	**Lewis Hamilton** McLAREN
2012	**Nico Rosberg** MERCEDES

First race: F1 team personnel were amazed by the scale of the facilities on their first visit in 2004 and Ferrari had most reason to smile as Rubens Barrichello took victory.

First corner: Approached down a long, wide straight, this right-hander is far from easy as it not only angles uphill as it turns right, but also feeds into Turn 2, which, in turn, feeds into Turn 3, making an attacking driver choose between trying to grab the inside line or staying wide and hopefully out of trouble to maybe get the inside line as the track drops away again for Turn 3.

Greatest local hero: Thus far, both Ho-Pin Tung and "Frankie" Cheng have tested F1 cars without landing a race seat, while Ma Qing Hua matched their feat when he tried an HRT at Silverstone last July. In time, there will surely be a Chinese driver landing a full-time ride.

Do you remember when? Lewis Hamilton was looking good to take the F1 title in his rookie season, 2007, but he came unstuck in Shanghai. Hamilton had led and was struggling on worn tyres when Ferrari's Kimi Raikkonen passed him. Then, having decided to pit for fresh rubber, as the points for second would still help his championship cause, he ran wide and became beached in a gravel trap at pit entry.

SAKHIR

Back on the calendar last year after the teams were persuaded that political unrest was under control, Bahrain offers a very different image of the Middle East from that of nearby Abu Dhabi.

After the cancellation of the race in 2011 because of anti-government street protests in the capital Manama, the 2012 Bahrain GP was only given the go-ahead at the last moment, and somewhat controversially at that. Now its long-term place on the World Championship roster remains a matter of debate, especially as the teams would prefer to drop a few events to make way for upcoming ones such as the Russian GP, scheduled for 2014.

The desert circuit has yet to win many friends. The drivers are not enthusiastic about it, nor does it seem to have caught the imagination of the local populace, with grandstands far from full.

Split into two distinct parts, the circuit moves away from the watered section around the pits to a "desert" section as it exits Turn 2. What follows is a selection of corners, fast, medium and slow, across a scrappy, rocky landscape, with the esses between Turns 5 and 7 the highlight. There is a decent straight out of Turn 13, but Turn 14 is too tight for drivers to maximise the use of their KERS when chasing before coming on to the grass-bordered start/finish straight.

In one way, though, the track is certainly a challenge to the drivers, because they know that a gust of wind could suddenly leave a coating of sand on their line around a corner and thus make it interesting.

INSIDE TRACK
BAHRAIN GRAND PRIX

Date:	**21 April**
Circuit name:	**Bahrain International Circuit**
Circuit length:	**3.363 miles/5.412km**
Number of laps:	**57**
Email:	**info@bic.com.bh**
Website:	**www.bahraingp.com.bh**

PREVIOUS WINNERS

2004	**Michael Schumacher** FERRARI
2005	**Fernando Alonso** RENAULT
2006	**Fernando Alonso** RENAULT
2007	**Felipe Massa** FERRARI
2008	**Felipe Massa** FERRARI
2009	**Jenson Button** BRAWN
2010	**Fernando Alonso** FERRARI
2012	**Sebastian Vettel** RED BULL

First race: Formula One's first race in the Middle East was held in 2004. The dusty, rocky backdrop at Sakhir couldn't have been more different from the lush, sylvan setting of Spa-Francorchamps or the vertiginous and narrow streets of Monaco. The race was all about Ferrari, with Michael Schumacher and Rubens Barrichello dominating as both Williams and McLaren wilted and left the way clear for Jenson Button to finish third for BAR.

First corner: With no history of racing to use, the corners are not named after people or places, but simply numbered. Turn 1 is the most likely place for overtaking as this right-hand hairpin comes at the end of the circuit's longest straight.

Greatest local hero: One might have thought that by now, nine years after the Bahrain International Circuit opened for racing, one of its aspiring stars would have started to impress on the international stage, looking to break into Formula One, but none has, with Salman Al Khalifa having turned to sportscars and Hamad Al Fardan having stopped racing.

Do you remember when? The circuit was used with a different layout in 2010, with an extra loop adding 887 metres and seven corners to its lap. This wasn't adjudged to have added anything to the spectacle and so was dropped before the following year.

> "Sakhir is one of the typical modern circuits. It doesn't have any really challenging corners and you can push hard most of the lap, particularly over the kerbs." **Heikki Kovalainen**

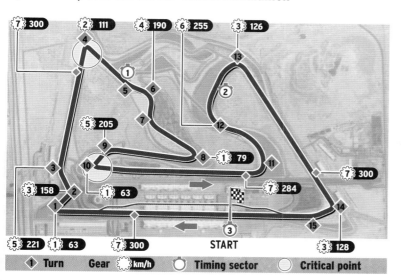

Turn   Gear   km/h   Timing sector   Critical point

2012 POLE TIME: VETTEL (RED BULL),
1M32.422S, 130.995MPH/210.816KPH
2012 WINNER'S AVERAGE SPEED:
120.733MPH/194.301KPH

2012 FASTEST LAP: VETTEL (RED BULL),
1M36.379S, 125.611MPH/202.152KPH
LAP RECORD: M. SCHUMACHER (FERRARI),
1M30.252S, 134.262MPH/216.074KPH, 2004

BARCELONA

As long as Fernando Alonso remains in Formula One, this circuit on the outskirts of Barcelona will be packed with Asturian flags, adding colour to an otherwise less than special venue.

Spain finally looked to be taking Formula One seriously in 1991 when it moved its grand prix here. There was still no home driver to cheer on, as Alonso was only just starting his kart racing career, but the new facility was a cut above anywhere their grand prix had been held before.

With its mixture of every sort of corner, fast, medium and slow, and with gradient thrown in to add to the interest, the venue soon became popular with the teams for testing. However, it has seldom offered much in the way of exciting racing.

The lap starts with the best bit, a downward-sloping straight into a 90-degree right, offering drivers the chance to attack on the inside or even on the outside if they feel brave. The next chance for passing comes if drivers manage a rapid run over the crest through Turn 9 and so carry more speed down the infield straight to Turn 10. After that, the lap tends to offer follow-my-leader processions, with the left/right chicane at Turn 14 scuppering the chances that drivers used to have to get into the slipstream of the car they were chasing to gain a tow past the pits down to Turn 1. Williams racer Pastor Maldonado used this to his advantage last year to hold off Alonso's Ferrari for his first win.

> "It's a very enjoyable circuit, technical but still quick with Turns 3 and 9 a real test. It's also hard to set the car up, as there are high-, medium- and low-speed corners." **Pastor Maldonado**

INSIDE TRACK
SPANISH GRAND PRIX

Date:	**12 May**
Circuit name:	**Circuit de Catalunya**
Circuit length:	**2.892 miles/4.654km**
Number of laps:	**66**
Telephone:	**(34) 935 719700**
Website:	**www.circuitcat.com**

PREVIOUS WINNERS

2003	**Michael Schumacher** FERRARI
2004	**Michael Schumacher** FERRARI
2005	**Kimi Raikkonen** McLAREN
2006	**Fernando Alonso** RENAULT
2007	**Felipe Massa** FERRARI
2008	**Kimi Raikkonen** FERRARI
2009	**Jenson Button** BRAWN
2010	**Mark Webber** RED BULL
2011	**Sebastian Vettel** RED BULL
2012	**Pastor Maldonado** WILLIAMS

First race: The Circuit de Catalunya made its debut in 1991, and spectators were treated to a wonderful battle between Nigel Mansell and Ayrton Senna before Mansell went on to win and Senna fell to fifth after a spin.

First corner: Turn 1 is the most likely scene for overtaking around the lap of this circuit where it's famously hard to pass. It's approached down the circuit's longest straight and it allows any driver who managed to catch a tow or use their KERS and DRS to good effect to gain the extra momentum to pull off a passing move.

Greatest local hero: Until Fernando Alonso arrived, Spain had delivered little. Alfonso de Portago had shown verve in the 1950s; Emilio de Villota tried but failed in the 1970s; and then Pedro de la Rosa was not in the best machinery in the 1990s. So, with Spanish motorcyclists winning titles galore, it's not surprising that two-wheeled sport was preferred and that the grandstands only filled after Alonso started winning from 2003.

Do you remember when? Mika Hakkinen had victory in the bag in 2001, leading Michael Schumacher comfortably with only a lap to go before being halted by clutch failure, which allowed the Ferrari driver to cruise past to win.

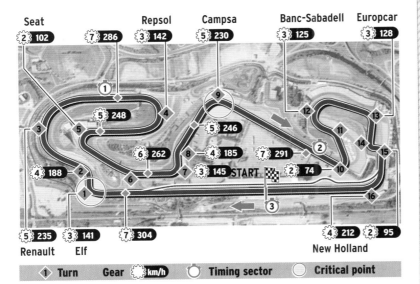

Seat — 2 102
Repsol — 7 286
Campsa — 3 142
5 230
Banc-Sabadell — 3 125
Europcar — 3 128

1
5 248
4
9
12
13
3
5
5 246
11
14
15
6 262
8
4 185
7 291
2
4 188
2
7
3 145 START
2 74
10
6
1
3
16

5 235
3 141
7 304
4 212
2 95

Renault   Elf
New Holland

◆ **Turn**   ⚙ **Gear**   ❄ **km/h**   ⭕ **Timing sector**   ⭕ **Critical point**

2012 POLE TIME: **MALDONADO (WILLIAMS)**, 1M22.285S, 126.547MPH/203.658KPH
2012 WINNER'S AVERAGE SPEED: **115.474MPH/185.837KPH**

2012 FASTEST LAP: **GROSJEAN (LOTUS)**, 1M26.250S, 120.729MPH/194.295KPH
LAP RECORD: **RAIKKONEN (FERRARI)**, 1M21.670S, 127.500MPH/205.192KPH, 2008

MONACO

No circuit is more synonymous with Formula One than Monaco, yet it could be said that its shape and its restrictions make it unsuitable for hosting a grand prix in the first place.

To the fans, Monaco is many things, from colourful to glamorous to exciting. To the teams, it's let down by a lack of space and an overabundance of celebrities getting in their way, while its race meeting goes on a day longer than normal, starting on the Thursday. The team sponsors, on the other hand, wouldn't wish to be without it, and that is why it's stayed on the World Championship calendar since 1950.

Monaco is different in almost every way. For starters, its start/finish straight is more of a curve than a straight. Its pits, although enlarged, are by far the smallest that teams have to endure. The paddock isn't next to the pits, and during the race the crew can cross to it only by a footbridge.

Its corners, from the first twist, at Ste Devote, to Casino Square, to the dive down past Mirabeau to the waterfront, to the run through the tunnel, to the blast past the yachts before Tabac and later the oh so slow hairpin at the penultimate corner, La Rascasse, are so different that they could only be at Monaco. It's not fast or even tiring for the drivers, as their gearboxes have long been semi-automatic, but even without much overtaking it's a very special place to go racing, and F1 would be the poorer without it.

"Monaco is a hugely challenging track, to the extent that you're not really racing other people: it's you against the track and you get away with nothing." **Mark Webber**

INSIDE TRACK
MONACO GRAND PRIX

Date:	**26 May**
Circuit name:	**Monte Carlo Circuit**
Circuit length:	**2.075 miles/3.339km**
Number of laps:	**78**
Email:	**info@acm.mc**
Website:	**www.acm.mc**

PREVIOUS WINNERS		
2003	**Juan Pablo Montoya**	WILLIAMS
2004	**Jarno Trulli**	RENAULT
2005	**Kimi Raikkonen**	McLAREN
2006	**Fernando Alonso**	RENAULT
2007	**Fernando Alonso**	McLAREN
2008	**Lewis Hamilton**	McLAREN
2009	**Jenson Button**	BRAWN
2010	**Mark Webber**	RED BULL
2011	**Sebastian Vettel**	RED BULL
2012	**Mark Webber**	RED BULL

First race: The first Monaco GP was held in 1929, with the win going to British Bugatti racer "W. Williams". However, the first one to be part of the World Championship was in 1950 and Juan Manuel Fangio won that for Alfa Romeo by a lap from Ferrari's Alberto Ascari, having got away at the end of the opening lap when the circuit was all but blocked by crashed cars and debris.

First corner: Taken in isolation, Ste Devote is far from the toughest corner in Formula One, being just a gentle right-hander with an uphill exit. But at the start of the grand prix, with its blind entry and lack of width, and a full field of drivers looking to move up a place or two, it can be a minefield.

Greatest local hero: Louis Chiron remains the most successful F1 driver to have hailed from the principality, finishing third there in 1950. These days, though, Monaco can at least claim to be the home of half of the drivers on the grid, thanks to its fine weather and, more importantly, its generous tax laws.

Do you remember when? There was a Monaco GP that no one seemed to want to win. This was in 1982, with a flurry of leaders in the final four laps before Riccardo Patrese recovered from a spin to take the win for Brabham.

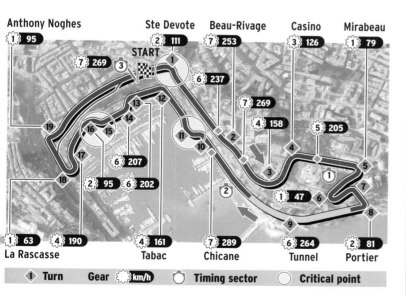

Anthony Noghes 1 95
7 269 3
Ste Devote 2 111
START 1
6 237
Beau-Rivage 7 253
7 269
4 158
Casino 3 126
5 205
Mirabeau 1 79
13 12
14
19 16 15
17
18 2 95 6 202
6 207
11
10
2
3
4
1
5
7
6 1 47
8
9
1 63 4 190
La Rascasse
4 161
Tabac
7 289
Chicane
6 264
Tunnel
2 81
Portier

◆ Turn   Gear   km/h   ○ Timing sector   ○ Critical point

2012 POLE TIME: WEBBER (RED BULL), 1M14.381S, 100.429MPH/161.625KPH
2012 WINNER'S AVERAGE SPEED: 91.535MPH/147.312KPH

2012 FASTEST LAP: PEREZ (SAUBER), 1M17.296S, 96.658MPH/155.556KPH
LAP RECORD: M. SCHUMACHER (FERRARI), 1M14.439S, 100.373MPH/161.535KPH, 2004

MONTREAL

The Circuit Gilles Villeneuve is not only a spectacular place to watch racing but also one that always seems to supply a grand prix packed with drama. Long may that continue.

Here is a circuit that appears to be made more of water than of land as it sits on a narrow island on the St Lawrence River, with the rowing lake used for the 1976 Olympics behind the pits and another lake behind the grandstands on the opposite side of the start/finish straight.

Opened in 1978, after Mosport Park had become unsafe for Formula One, this circuit just across the river from downtown Montreal was given a dream start when local hero Gilles Villeneuve won for Ferrari. That guaranteed the grandstands would be packed for subsequent years and they have remained so to this day, despite there

not having been a Canadian F1 driver since Gilles's son Jacques quit Formula One at the end of the 2006 season.

The lap starts with a tightening left that causes all sorts of constrictions on the opening lap, but then it gains some flow out of Coin Senna. Running through the back section, largely out of sight of the fans, the course is sinuous but offers little in the way of overtaking opportunities until the cars arrive at L'Epingle. The best chance of all, though, comes at the end of the main straight down to the final esse. Get the exit to this wrong, though, and a concrete wall is there to seal a driver's retirement.

"The circuit is super-fast in places, which means it requires finesse and precision, but you can also end up racing wheel to wheel at 200mph, which is an incredible sensation." **Lewis Hamilton**

74

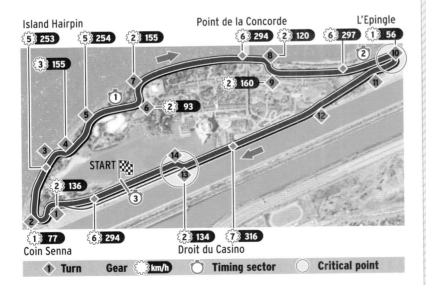

Coin Senna
Island Hairpin
Point de la Concorde
L'Epingle
Droit du Casino

| ⚙ Turn | Gear | km/h | Timing sector | Critical point |

2012 POLE TIME: **VETTEL (RED BULL),**
1M13.784S, 132.224MPH/212.794KPH
2012 WINNER'S AVERAGE SPEED:
123.048MPH/198.027KPH

2012 FASTEST LAP: **VETTEL (RED BULL),**
1M15.752S, 128.778MPH/207.248KPH
LAP RECORD: **BARRICHELLO (FERRARI),**
1M13.622S, 132.511MPH/213.256KPH, 2004

INSIDE TRACK

CANADIAN GRAND PRIX

Date:	9 June
Circuit name:	Circuit Gilles Villeneuve
Circuit length:	2.710 miles/4.361km
Number of laps:	70
Email:	info@circuitgillesvilleneuve.ca
Website:	www.circuitgillesvilleneuve.ca

PREVIOUS WINNERS

2002	**Michael Schumacher** FERRARI
2003	**Michael Schumacher** FERRARI
2004	**Michael Schumacher** FERRARI
2005	**Kimi Raikkonen** McLAREN
2006	**Fernando Alonso** RENAULT
2007	**Lewis Hamilton** McLAREN
2008	**Robert Kubica** BMW SAUBER
2010	**Lewis Hamilton** McLAREN
2011	**Jenson Button** McLAREN
2012	**Lewis Hamilton** McLAREN

First race: The first time Canada hosted a round of the World Championship was in 1967 at Mosport Park, with victory going to Jack Brabham. However, the first time the grand prix was held on this circuit in Montreal, in 1978, was an infinitely more memorable event as Gilles Villeneuve triumphed for Ferrari.

First corner: As the first corner is really a simple kink, people tend to treat the tight left that follows as the first corner. On the opening lap this is inevitably the scene of place-changing and the occasional spin or off-track excursion, with drivers immediately having to try to claim their line for the next corner, Virage Senna.

Greatest local hero: Jacques Villeneuve is the only Canadian driver to have become World Champion, but even though he won the title in 1997 in only his second year of Formula One, his exploits for Williams were overshadowed by those of his flamboyant father, Gilles, with Ferrari.

Do you remember when? Lewis Hamilton scored his breakthrough win here in 2007. This was the seventh round of his rookie season with McLaren and he led pretty much all of the way from pole, even keeping his cool through two restarts after safety car periods.

SILVERSTONE

Formula One and Silverstone go back all the way to the opening round of the inaugural World Championship in 1950, but it's safe to say that the circuit is very different today.

While the Silverstone circuit used in 1950 was mainly laid out around the perimeter roads of a former Second World War airfield, today's layout has deviated somewhat from that and sprouted state-of-the-art facilities at last to complement its historical values.

The lap has started for the past two years on the stretch of track between Club and Abbey rather than between Woodcote and Copse, and the infield section added recently makes the drivers dive through a fast right flick before it snakes through three slow corners and then feeds them on to a longish straight down to Brooklands.

The second half of the lap is unchanged, with the Becketts sweepers still the most testing part of the lap and the dash down the Hangar straight to Stowe still one of F1's great sights.

The crowds are always enormous – on all three days, unlike some venues – and, as most of the F1 teams are British and so bring their factory-bound staff along, the atmosphere makes it feel like an extra-special race. Unfortunately the 2012 event was made trying for Silverstone by the record duration of rain in the lead-up, resulting in car parks that were more like swamps, but the organisers did all they could to minimise the inconvenience.

> "It's the track that makes you really appreciate what an F1 car is capable of, especially the aerodynamic grip through the quick corners and the change of direction." **Paul di Resta**

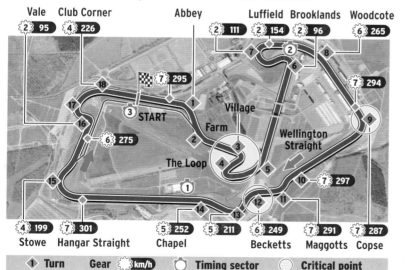

Vale Club Corner Abbey Luffield Brooklands Woodcote
2 95 4 226 2 111 2 154 2 96 6 265
7
18 7 295 7 294
17
3 START 1 9
16 Village
6 275 Farm Wellington Straight
The Loop 2
3
15 4
5 10 7 297
1
12 11
14 13
4 199 7 301 5 252 5 211 6 249 7 291 7 287
Stowe Hangar Straight Chapel Becketts Maggotts Copse

1 Turn   Gear   km/h   ○ Timing sector   ○ Critical point

2012 POLE TIME: **ALONSO (FERRARI),** 1M51.746S, 117.878MPH/189.707KPH
2012 WINNER'S AVERAGE SPEED: **134.006MPH/215.662KPH**

2012 FASTEST LAP: **RAIKKONEN (LOTUS),** 1M34.661S, 139.210MPH/224.037KPH
LAP RECORD: **ALONSO (FERRARI), 1M30.874S, 145.011MPH/233.373KPH, 2011**

INSIDE TRACK
BRITISH GRAND PRIX

Date:	**30 June**
Circuit name:	**Silverstone**
Circuit length:	**3.659 miles/5.900km**
Number of laps:	**52**
Email:	**sales@silverstone-circuit.co.uk**
Website:	**www.silverstone-circuit.co.uk**

PREVIOUS WINNERS

2003	**Rubens Barrichello** FERRARI
2004	**Michael Schumacher** FERRARI
2005	**Juan Pablo Montoya** McLAREN
2006	**Fernando Alonso** RENAULT
2007	**Kimi Raikkonen** FERRARI
2008	**Lewis Hamilton** McLAREN
2009	**Sebastian Vettel** RED BULL
2010	**Mark Webber** RED BULL
2011	**Fernando Alonso** FERRARI
2012	**Mark Webber** RED BULL

First race: Transformed from wartime airfield into a circuit in 1948, Silverstone hosted a grand prix that year, won by Luigi Villoresi for Maserati. Two years later, it was the venue for the first-ever round of the World Championship and it was the turn of rival Italian constructor Alfa Romeo.

First corner: Abbey became the circuit's first corner in 2011. The previous year its new layout had already made it a fast right flick into a new infield loop rather than a left-hand chicane, but that was before the new pits were opened. So it was in 2011 that Abbey replaced Copse as the first turn and, mercifully, it hasn't proved to be a Turn 1 pinchpoint.

Greatest local hero: British fans are strident in their support, but refreshingly open to backing drivers of all nationalities. That said, Nigel Mansell remains probably the most revered, for his heroics in the late 1980s in particular, while current support seems to be split between Lewis Hamilton and Jenson Button.

Do you remember when? A sudden, intense rain shower hit Silverstone during the 1975 British GP. While the circuit was still bone dry at the pits, over on the far side it was drenched, and car after car rotated off the track into the catch fencing at Stowe.

NURBURGRING

Back on the calendar in 2013 after missing a year because of its alternation with Hockenheim, the Nurburgring nearly didn't make it this time – bankruptcy was looming before the local government stepped in.

It seems crazy that a country as economically powerful as Germany struggles to host a grand prix, but that has been the situation of late, exacerbated by the annual race being shared between the Nurburgring and Hockenheim, which is a far from ideal business model.

What has made life so difficult for the Nurburgring is that it undertook a comprehensive redevelopment project, including a theme park and fun fair, which put it into financial difficulties.

The circuit itself remains unchanged, with the start of the lap the most exciting part. It offers a wide entry into a tight right-hander, presenting many possible lines both into and out of the corner, which makes it exceptionally busy on the opening lap as drivers simultaneously attempt to pass those ahead of them and keep others behind.

The circuit has good flow both down the hill to Dunlop Kehre and then again back up to Michelin Kurve, with the dip from Bit Kurve and the rise to the NGK-Schikane offering a wholly different feel, especially with its backdrop of the old, 14-mile Nordschleife circuit snaking away into the trees, hinting at the circuit's fabulous history.

One factor that can add spice to any race at the Nurburgring is rain, which is a possibility at any time of the year in the Eifel mountains.

76

> "There's so much history around this amazing track, especially for Mercedes-Benz, with great drivers from the past having had such successful times on the Nurburgring." **Nico Rosberg**

INSIDE TRACK
GERMAN GRAND PRIX

Date:	7 July
Circuit name:	Nurburgring
Circuit length:	3.199 miles/5.148km
Number of laps:	60
Email:	info@nuerburgring.de
Website:	www.nuerburgring.de

PREVIOUS WINNERS		
2000*	Michael Schumacher	FERRARI
2001*	Michael Schumacher	FERRARI
2002*	Rubens Barrichello	FERRARI
2003*	Ralf Schumacher	WILLIAMS
2004*	Michael Schumacher	FERRARI
2005*	Fernando Alonso	RENAULT
2006*	Michael Schumacher	FERRARI
2007*	Fernando Alonso	McLAREN
2009	Mark Webber	RED BULL
2011	Lewis Hamilton	McLAREN

* As the European GP

First race: The Nurburgring was Germany's showpiece circuit after it was built in 1926, and the 14.167-mile circuit hosted the German GP for the first time the following year, but this was for sportscars, with Otto Merz winning for Mercedes-Benz. Its first World Championship grand prix came in 1951, and Alberto Ascari triumphed for Ferrari.

First corner: Changed markedly for 2002, the first corner, the Castrol S, is no longer a fast esse, but a hairpin that feeds the cars into an additional loop. Wide on entry, it allows drivers a choice of lines and, on the opening lap, space to try to stay out of trouble.

Greatest local hero: When a country possesses a seven-time World Champion, the identity of their greatest driver is obvious: Michael Schumacher. What's more, he was born not far away in Kerpen.

Do you remember when? Stewart Grand Prix won only one grand prix, but the way that it achieved this famous victory here in 1999 was a remarkable story. Johnny Herbert had started only 14th, but he worked his way forward and was in position to profit from changing conditions by guessing the weather variations right. Team-mate Rubens Barrichello finished third.

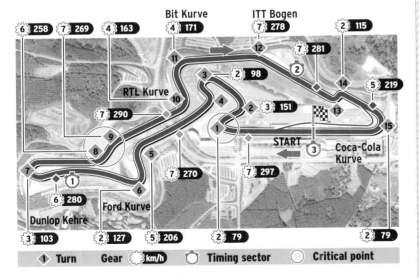

| ① Turn | Gear | ✿ km/h | ⏲ Timing sector | ◯ Critical point |

2011 POLE TIME: **WEBBER (RED BULL),** 1M30.079S, 127.728MPH/205.558KPH
2011 WINNER'S AVERAGE SPEED: **118.004MPH/189.909KPH**

2011 FASTEST LAP: **HAMILTON (McLAREN),** 1M34.302S, 122.115MPH/196.525KPH
LAP RECORD: **M. SCHUMACHER (FERRARI),** 1M29.468S, 128.721MPH/207.157KPH, 2004

Sebastian Vettel powers his Red Bull past the grandstands during qualifying for his home grand prix at the Nurburgring in 2011.

HUNGARORING

To look at, the Hungaroring is a thing of beauty, a bucking stretch of blacktop draped across a valley, with fans thronging the grandstands, but sadly it offers next to no overtaking.

No one knew what to expect when Formula One ventured to Hungary in 1986, as it was taking the world's most capitalist sport to a communist country. Things were a bit rough around the edges, but the circuit more than met expectations, if only for the fact that it drew in 200,000 spectators on race day.

Now, 27 years on, the Hungaroring is part of Formula One's furniture, with a fixed position as the race after the German GP. Yet one has to ask whether what it has to offer is enough in 2013, because the circuit layout is so restrictive, with its predominance of tight corners, that overtaking is very difficult and processional races abound.

What the circuit really needs is some reprofiling to provide it with a longer straight, perhaps out of Turn 2, preferably ending in a tight corner so as to permit some passing moves. The drivers enjoy their laps there, especially the twisting stretch across the far side of the valley from Turn 5 to Turn 11, but that is no longer enough. Throw in the usually hot and humid conditions, and many of them find it a long afternoon of looking at a rival's exhaust pipes, as Kimi Raikkonen found in 2007, when he followed Lewis Hamilton's McLaren all afternoon – as he did again in the 2012 race.

> "The Hungaroring is very challenging. It's like a street circuit but on a normal track because of the many tight and twisty turns and not so many straights." **Nico Rosberg**

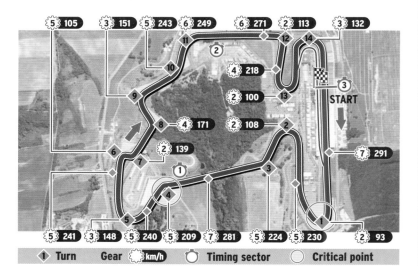

♦ **Turn**   **Gear** ⟨km/h⟩   ○ **Timing sector**   ○ **Critical point**

2012 POLE TIME: **HAMILTON (McLAREN),** 1M20.953S, 120.915MPH/194.594KPH
2012 WINNER'S AVERAGE SPEED: **111.468MPH/179.390KPH**

2012 FASTEST LAP: **VETTEL (RED BULL),** 1M24.136S, 116.478MPH/187.454KPH
LAP RECORD: **M. SCHUMACHER (FERRARI),** 1M19.071S, 123.828MPH/199.282KPH, 2004

INSIDE TRACK
HUNGARIAN GRAND PRIX

Date:	**28 July**
Circuit name:	**Hungaroring**
Circuit length:	**2.722 miles/4.381km**
Number of laps:	**70**
Email:	**office@hungaroring.hu**
Website:	**www.hungaroring.hu**

PREVIOUS WINNERS

2003	**Fernando Alonso** RENAULT
2004	**Michael Schumacher** FERRARI
2005	**Kimi Raikkonen** McLAREN
2006	**Jenson Button** HONDA
2007	**Lewis Hamilton** McLAREN
2008	**Heikki Kovalainen** McLAREN
2009	**Lewis Hamilton** McLAREN
2010	**Mark Webber** RED BULL
2011	**Jenson Button** McLAREN
2012	**Lewis Hamilton** McLAREN

First race: The teams didn't know what to expect when they saw the track for the first time in 1986. Ayrton Senna took pole for Lotus but had to settle for second place behind Nelson Piquet in the superior Honda-powered Williams, with all others a lap or more behind.

First corner: Turn 1 is approached on a sloping straight that drops from the startline. It offers attacking drivers the chance to make a bid on either the inside (preferable) or the outside, and positioning for Turn 2 can also yield a pass on lap 1, when cars run two or three abreast.

Greatest local hero: Zsolt Baumgartner is the only Hungarian driver to have raced in the World Championship. However, his time with Jordan in 2003 was short, his record less than glorious. Instead, the accolade should go to Ferenc Szisz, who holds the honour of winning the first-ever grand prix. This was the 1906 French GP on a 64-mile circuit around Le Mans, and his Renault won by 32 minutes after 12 hours of racing.

Do you remember when? Jenson Button scored his breakthrough F1 victory here in 2006. It came on his 113th grand prix outing and he mastered wet conditions to also give Honda its first win since John Surtees triumphed in the 1967 Italian GP.

SPA-FRANCORCHAMPS

This is a rare circuit that emanates greatness from every angle. It's scenic and high-speed, offering places for overtaking and a real challenge. It's where Formula One is seen at its very best.

Spa-Francorchamps contains everything that a great circuit should have, with testing corners all over the varied terrain, beautiful scenery and a rich history. Some people will point out that it often rains at Spa, but that's about the only criticism you'll hear of the place, for it's formidable in almost all other aspects. Anyhow, the rain has frequently added to the spectacle, giving the race story another twist.

What stands out, though, is that the circuit is one that stretches not just the drivers but their cars too. The drop and then sharp, twisting rise that is Eau Rouge is taken in sixth gear, drivers changing almost immediately up to seventh as they crest the brow at Raidillon.

A good exit from here is essential, as the following straight that goes on up the hill to Les Combes stretches away to the point that drivers hit more than 200mph before having to break heavily. The dive downhill from Malmedy to Pouhon is epic, and the blast up again through Blanchimont at 190mph makes you realise how F1 drivers really earn their keep as the track carves its way up through the trees.

Because of this character and challenge, Spa-Francorchamps is the antidote to some of the less special new circuits. F1 fans should rejoice that it now has a deal to host the Belgian GP through until 2015.

"Spa is the greatest racing circuit in the world. You can't get the same sort of feeling anywhere else. It's great to race with a modern racing car at a proper circuit." **Kimi Raikkonen**

INSIDE TRACK
BELGIAN GRAND PRIX

Date:	25 August
Circuit name:	Spa-Francorchamps
Circuit length:	4.352 miles/7.004km
Number of laps:	44
Email:	secretariat@spa-francorchamps.be
Website:	www.spa-francorchamps.be

PREVIOUS WINNERS

2001	**Michael Schumacher** FERRARI
2002	**Michael Schumacher** FERRARI
2004	**Kimi Raikkonen** McLAREN
2005	**Kimi Raikkonen** McLAREN
2007	**Kimi Raikkonen** FERRARI
2008	**Felipe Massa** FERRARI
2009	**Kimi Raikkonen** FERRARI
2010	**Lewis Hamilton** McLAREN
2011	**Sebastian Vettel** RED BULL
2012	**Jenson Button** McLAREN

First race: Opened in 1924, Spa-Francorchamps held the Belgian GP in 1925 and Louis Chiron won in a Bugatti. Its first World Championship round came in 1950 when Juan Manuel Fangio triumphed for Alfa Romeo around the full 14.12-mile circuit. Team-mate Giuseppe Farina had run with him but retired.

First corner: Eau Rouge used to be the first corner, but since the pits were moved to just after Bus Stop in 1984 it has been La Source. This uphill right-hand hairpin is known as a place of guaranteed incident, both at the turn in and on the exit as cars jostle to get on the power for the descent that follows.

Greatest local hero: Thierry Boutsen was a race winner in the late 1980s and early 1990s, but the greatest Belgian racing driver is undoubtedly Jacky Ickx. Not only did Ickx win grands prix for Ferrari and Brabham, and finish as runner-up in the drivers' championship in 1969 and 1970, but he won the Le Mans 24 Hours on six occasions, a record broken only recently by Tom Kristensen.

Do you remember when?: Close on half the field was caught up in a massed collision just after the start in 1998 when David Coulthard ran wide out of La Source and triggered chaos. A dozen cars were involved, causing the race to be stopped.

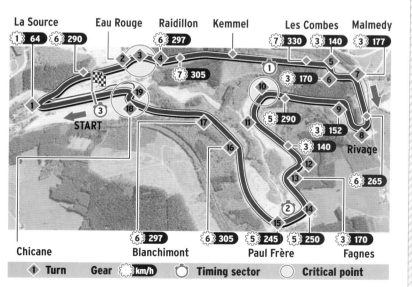

La Source	Eau Rouge	Raidillon	Kemmel	Les Combes	Malmedy

START

Rivage

Chicane		Blanchimont	Paul Frère			Fagnes

◆ **Turn**   **Gear** ⬡km/h   ○ **Timing sector**   ◯ **Critical point**

**2012 POLE TIME: HAMILTON (McLAREN),
1M20.953S, 120.915MPH/194.594KPH**
**2012 WINNER'S AVERAGE SPEED:
111.468MPH/179.390KPH**

**2012 FASTEST LAP: VETTEL (RED BULL),
1M24.136S, 116.478MPH/187.454KPH**
LAP RECORD: M. SCHUMACHER (FERRARI),
1M19.071S, 123.828MPH/199.282KPH, 2004

MONZA

In these days of ever more modern circuits being used around the world to host grands prix, this ancient venue provides a welcome and important link with the sport's magnificent past.

It's the size of the trees framing the Monza circuit that tell you this isn't one of the recent, made-to-measure circuits. The trees are huge and have obviously been here a very long time. Indeed, they were here before the circuit was built in 1922, as this was a royal park, and still is.

Although the banked circuit has fallen into a state of disrepair and chicanes were inserted at three points around the lap in the early 1970s to reduce extravagant speeds, Monza still very much feels like Monza, showing continuity in its circuit shape and even in its buildings, since the main grandstand opposite the pits and the old scoring tower both remain.

The circuit does have bottlenecks at the chicanes, most especially the first one, but the drivers have learned now to live with those, albeit with the odd stumble on the opening lap when the cars are bunched together. Fans love watching drivers accelerate hard out of Variante Ascari, slipstream the car ahead and then fan out in an attempt to make a passing move into Curva Parabolica, the long, long fourth-gear corner that completes the lap.

With the flag-waving *tifosi* always out in force, Monza still really matters, as it has such an obvious tie to its past, both for those supporting Ferrari and for others. It is a place to be cherished.

> "You're flat-out for almost the entire lap, so you need the engine to be powerful at the top end as any gain is worth a considerable amount of time." **Sebastian Vettel**

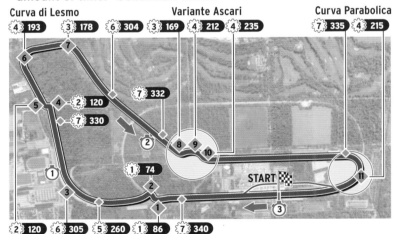

Curva di Lesmo | 4 193 | 3 178 | 6 304 | 3 169 | 4 212 | 4 235 — **Variante Ascari** | 7 335 | 4 215 — **Curva Parabolica**

7 332

4 2 120

7 330

START

2 120 | 6 305 | 5 260 | 1 86 | 7 340
Roggia **Curva Biassono** **Variante del Rettifilio** **Rettifilio Tribune**

◆ Turn   Gear km/h   Timing sector   ◯ Critical point

2012 POLE TIME: HAMILTON (McLAREN), 1M24.010S, 154.250MPH/248.241KPH
2012 WINNER'S AVERAGE SPEED: 143.501MPH/230.943KPH

2012 FASTEST LAP: ROSBERG (MERCEDES), 1M27.239S, 148.540MPH/239.053KPH
LAP RECORD: BARRICHELLO (FERRARI), 1M21.046S, 159.909MPH/257.349KPH, 2004

INSIDE TRACK
ITALIAN GRAND PRIX

Date:	8 September
Circuit name:	Monza Circuit
Circuit length:	3.600 miles/5.793km
Number of laps:	53
Email:	infoautodromo@monzanet.it
Website:	www.monzanet.it

PREVIOUS WINNERS	
2003	**Michael Schumacher** FERRARI
2004	**Rubens Barrichello** FERRARI
2005	**Juan Pablo Montoya** McLAREN
2006	**Michael Schumacher** FERRARI
2007	**Fernando Alonso** McLAREN
2008	**Sebastian Vettel** TORO ROSSO
2009	**Rubens Barrichello** BRAWN
2010	**Fernando Alonso** FERRARI
2011	**Sebastian Vettel** RED BULL
2012	**Lewis Hamilon** McLAREN

First race: Monza first hosted the Italian GP in 1922, but not a round of the World Championship until its inaugural season in 1950. Then, with Alfa Romeo dominant, victory was taken by Giuseppe Farina as he raced to the first world crown.

First corner: The Variante del Rettifilio didn't exist until 1972, when this frequently altered chicane was inserted to break up the packs of slipstreaming cars. There's a low-speed first part, turning sharp right, before a less angled second part turning left.

Greatest local hero: Italy's glory is centred on the 1950s and, amazingly, Alberto Ascari – World Champion in 1952 and 1953 – remains their only champion since Farina in 1950.

Do you remember when? Jim Clark produced the most astonishing comeback drive in 1967 yet was denied victory in the dying moments. He'd been beaten away from pole by Dan Gurney, took the lead on lap 3 and then overcame a challenge by Jack Brabham. But a puncture on lap 13 forced a pit stop, and this cost him a whole lap. Amazingly, he made up all the time he lost and took the lead again with eight laps to go, only to slow at the start of the last lap with a fuel problem, which let Honda's John Surtees and Brabham by.

MARINA BAY

The home of Formula One's first night race is a place that gives the World Championship an extra dimension, taking racing right into the heart of this vibrant and cosmopolitan city.

When the World Championship landed its first grand prix in Singapore for 2008, it was clear that the race would be a great addition to the World Championship, but it has since delivered more than anyone expected.

The city backdrop, especially when evening turns into night and the lights of the office blocks illuminate the shapes of the cityscape, really gives the venue a vibrant identity, so it's not surprising that the TV directors, camera crews and photographers love it. The teams and drivers love it too, and not only because they are just a short ride from their hotels and the city's array of restaurants.

A common downfall of street circuits is a lack of decent straights, but the Marina Bay circuit has enough of these to allow drivers to think that they have got a chance of overtaking, especially into corners such as Turn 7 after the kinked run from Turn 5, and into Turn 14 too, with Turn 1 offering probably the best chance of all.

The races thus far have turned up few surprises since Fernando Alonso's tainted win in 2008 (see sidebar), but the night shots add drama and the walls that enclose the entire course claim a victim or two every year, not that the passengers on the buses that travel across the bridges over the circuit always notice.

"Most of the braking zones are approached at very high speed, and the walls are never far away. Factor in the heat and humidity and it's very challenging." **Lewis Hamilton**

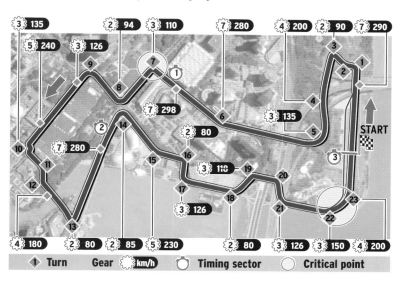

Turn   **Gear**   **km/h**   ⏱ **Timing sector**   ○ **Critical point**

2012 POLE TIME: **HAMILTON (McLAREN)**, 1M46.362S, 106.692MPH/171.704KPH
2012 WINNER'S AVERAGE SPEED: 92.611MPH/149.043KPH

2012 FASTEST LAP: **HULKENBERG (FORCE INDIA)**, 1M51.033S, 102.203MPH/164.480KPH
LAP RECORD: **RAIKKONEN (FERRARI)**, 1M45.599S, 107.358MPH/172.776KPH, 2008

INSIDE TRACK
SINGAPORE GRAND PRIX

Date:	22 September
Circuit name:	Marina Bay Circuit
Circuit length:	3.152 miles/5.073km
Number of laps:	61
Email:	info@singaporegp.sg
Website:	www.singaporegp.sg

PREVIOUS WINNERS	
2008	**Fernando Alonso** RENAULT
2009	**Lewis Hamilton** McLAREN
2010	**Fernando Alonso** FERRARI
2011	**Sebastian Vettel** RED BULL
2012	**Sebastian Vettel** RED BULL

First race: The inaugural Singapore GP in 2008 is sadly remembered for an act of underhand teamwork that contravened the rules of sportsmanship. Fernando Alonso had started 15th for Renault and failed to progress far up the order when the team called him in to make an early first pit stop. Then team-mate Nelson Piquet Jr crashed and brought out the safety car. Alonso's rivals were finally allowed to stop when the safety car withdrew, elevating him to fifth, and when notably Felipe Massa and Nico Rosberg had problems, he rose from there to win. A year after the race, Piquet Jr said that he had been instructed to crash.

First corner: Turn 1 is a 90-degree left into a chicane, which makes overtaking on the opening lap fraught with danger. At full racing speed on subsequent laps, passing is possible under braking, especially if a driver has got a good enough run through Turns 22 and 23 to get a tow.

Greatest local hero: Like so many countries that have been granted grands prix recently, there's not yet a driver from Singapore who has raced in Formula One. Unlike many, Singapore has long had a racing scene, but this was mainly contested by expats.

Do you remember when? Felipe Massa was in with a chance of winning the first Singapore GP in 2008, but at his first pit stop he was signalled via a light on his steering wheel to leave before the fuel hose had been withdrawn, and he drove off with it still attached, knocking down two of his pit crew.

YEONGAM

This Korean circuit is one that will only get better with age as the bumps are flattened out and the surrounding infrastructure of this ambitious complex is gradually completed.

When the plans were first shown for the Yeongam circuit, the outline included an incredible, almost space-age city in its midst. Work continues apace, but the overall plans are far from being realised. Luckily, the circuit was fully complete when the teams made their first repeat visit in 2011, and it really is a track that offers something different.

Indeed, the circuit itself is one with considerable potential to excite, most notably due to the tight Turn 1/Turn 2 complex that feeds the cars on to Formula One's longest straight. In the grands prix held there to date, it has offered great slipstreaming with DRS, and drivers have hit 190mph or so

before throwing out the anchors to scrub off 140mph so that they can take the right-hand hairpin at its conclusion. Not everybody will get this right, but fortunately there is space for the over-ambitious to rectify their errors without hitting anything, unless they tag the car they are attempting to pass, as shown by Kamui Kobayashi when he hit Jenson Button and Nico Rosberg there in 2011.

Another section of interest is towards the end of the unusual anticlockwise lap, where Turns 14 to 18 really make the drivers work to be fast while keeping their cars from hitting the barriers. When rain falls, as it often does in autumn, the challenge is all the greater.

"At the end of the fastest part of the circuit comes the slowest corner, an overtaking possibility but a difficult one, slowing from 190mph to 50." **Mark Webber**

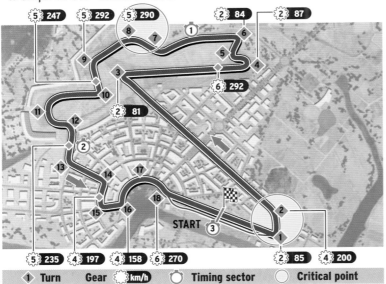

| ◆ Turn | Gear | km/h | ○ Timing sector | ○ Critical point |

2012 POLE TIME: WEBBER (RED BULL),
1M37.242S, 129.166MPH/207.873KPH
2012 WINNER'S AVERAGE SPEED:
119.265MPH/191.939KPH

2012 FASTEST LAP: WEBBER (RED BULL),
1M42.037S, 123.096MPH/198.104KPH
LAP RECORD: **VETTEL (RED BULL),**
1M39.605S, 126.101MPH/202.941KPH, 2011

INSIDE TRACK
KOREAN GRAND PRIX

Date:	6 October
Circuit name:	Korea International Circuit
Circuit length:	3.489 miles/5.615km
Number of laps:	57
Email:	N/A
Website:	www.koreangp.kr

PREVIOUS WINNERS		
2010	**Fernando Alonso** FERRARI
2011	**Sebastian Vettel** RED BULL
2012	**Sebastian Vettel** RED BULL

First race: The finishing touches were still being applied to the circuit when the World Championship road show splashed its way into Yeongam for the first time in 2010. Then, unfortunately, there was the rain, lots of it. In fact, it was so wet that the inaugural Korean GP was started with the drivers circulating behind the safety car for three laps, after which it was adjudged too wet to continue. An hour later, they tried again, and when the cars were finally released by the safety car after 17 laps, Sebastian Vettel looked all set to record the first win here, but his Red Bull's engine failed and so Fernando Alonso took over the lead and won the day for Ferrari.

First corner: Turn 1 is a sharp left that feeds almost directly into a gentle left. What's important here is not just to try and dive down the inside of any car ahead but to be sure of being in the right position to carry as much speed as possible on to the immensely long straight that runs for 0.74 miles up to Turn 3.

Greatest local hero: There have not been any Korean drivers in F1 yet, while the best on the international racing scene is Keisuke Kunimoto, who has Korean heritage but races under the Japanese flag.

Do you remember when? Vitaly Petrov got it all wrong during an overtaking move in the 2011 Korean GP and took out Michael Schumacher. The Russian Renault driver had been fighting with Fernando Alonso after a pit stop and became so fixated on the Spaniard's Ferrari that he locked up into Turn 3 and clouted Schumacher's Mercedes.

SUZUKA

Some circuits are a test of both man and machine, but this Japanese gem really tips the balance towards the man, as it's incredibly technical yet requires considerable bravery to lap fast.

The only drivers who don't look forward to racing at the home of the Japanese GP are those who know that their car will offer them little grip. Without this vital part of their arsenal, they will struggle here however valiant and precise they may be. Furthermore, they will know whether they will be competitive very early in the lap, when they have rounded the first two bends and are faced with the "S" Curves. If their car won't turn in to these uphill esses, they can say goodbye to any real chance of scoring points.

For those enjoying good handling allied with a healthy dose of horsepower, the lap offers great treats, such as being able to run quickly through the Degner Curve and carry momentum under the flyover towards the hairpin. Then they ought also to be able to get the power down early through Spoon Curve to power down the longest straight past the famous and fearsome 130R. If this is done well, their rivals will have no chance of making a move.

Suzuka is a track like no other, with the amusement park outside the final corner so close that it's almost surreal, although those present have eyes only for F1 folk on grand prix weekend, whether from the Ferris wheel, from the kerbside as the drivers arrive, or simply from the grandstands.

"Suzuka is really enjoyable to drive if you get in the right rhythm. The 'S' Curves, three, four, five, six and seven, are my favourites." **Kamui Kobayashi**

INSIDE TRACK
JAPANESE GRAND PRIX

Date:	13 October
Circuit name:	Suzuka
Circuit length:	3.608 miles/5.806km
Number of laps:	53
Email:	info@suzukacircuit.com.jp
Website:	www.suzukacircuit.co.jp

PREVIOUS WINNERS	
2001	**Michael Schumacher** FERRARI
2002	**Michael Schumacher** FERRARI
2003	**Rubens Barrichello** FERRARI
2004	**Michael Schumacher** FERRARI
2005	**Kimi Raikkonen** McLAREN
2006	**Fernando Alonso** RENAULT
2009	**Sebastian Vettel** RED BULL
2010	**Sebastian Vettel** RED BULL
2011	**Jenson Button** McLAREN
2012	**Sebastian Vettel** RED BULL

First race: The Japanese GP was held in 1976 and 1977 at Fuji Speedway, but it did not appear on the calendar again until 1987, which was when Suzuka took over. Ferrari's Gerhard Berger won that race after Alain Prost's McLaren picked up a puncture.

First corner: Turn 1 is tricky and narrow, with its downhill entry adding to the difficulty as it's taken in sixth. Also, Turn 2, a much tighter right, is arrived at seconds later, and positioning is everything for this if a driver is to get the acceleration needed for the uphill stretch that follows.

Greatest local hero: There has still not been a Japanese F1 winner, although Aguri Suzuki and Kamui Kobayashi have got to experience the view down from the Suzuka podium.

Do you remember when? Mika Hakkinen took victory at Suzuka in 1998 to clinch the first of his two F1 titles. It had been set up to be a tough scrap with title rival Michael Schumacher, but the German stalled his pole-sitting Ferrari and later suffered a blow-out to cede the honours to the Finn. After arriving back at *parc fermé*, delirious with delight, Mika went running down the track waving to the crowd before he could be rounded up for the podium ceremony.

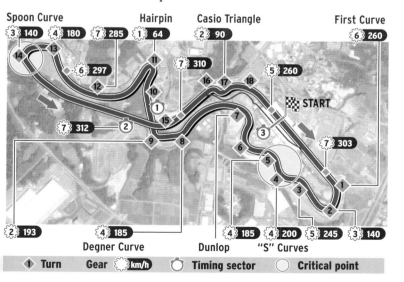

Spoon Curve — Hairpin — Casio Triangle — First Curve

Degner Curve — Dunlop — "S" Curves

◆ Turn   Gear   km/h   ○ Timing sector   ○ Critical point

2012 POLE TIME: **VETTEL (RED BULL)**, 1M30.839S, 142.998MPH/230.134KPH
2012 WINNER'S AVERAGE SPEED: 128.890MPH/207.429KPH

2012 FASTEST LAP: **VETTEL (RED BULL)**, 1M35.774S, 135.630MPH/218.276KPH
LAP RECORD: **RAIKKONEN (MCLAREN)**, 1M31.540S, 141.904MPH/228.373KPH, 2005

BUDDH INTERNATIONAL

India's circuit impressed when it made its debut in 2011 as it not only won its race to be completed on time but also provided the drivers with both serious challenges and overtaking opportunities.

It's safe to say that it was an almighty rush to get the Buddh International Circuit completed in time for its first Indian GP at the end of the 2011 World Championship, and there were power cuts as well as other inconveniences, but the raw ingredients for a memorable race weekend were clearly all present.

Indeed, the key to the circuit's appeal is its considerable use of gradient, with only Spa-Francorchamps offering more vertical gain. The climb from Turn 2 up to Turn 3 is the first sign of this, and the kick-up at the end of the back straight into Turn 4 is the next. However, the most spectacular point

is the crest at Turn 10 before the track dives down again out of Turn 11.

The inaugural race in 2011 was watched by a good-sized crowd, auguring well for the future of the event in this sports-mad country. What will add further to its success is when an Indian driver, perhaps Narain Karthikeyan or an up-and-coming star, can land a ride with a competitive team and really give the crowd something to shout about.

Second time around, in 2012, everything ran more smoothly at this venue and Vettel made it two wins in succession by leading every lap as he and team-mate Mark Webber dominated the race.

"I never thought that India would be able to host a grand prix during my career, so it was hard not to be overwhelmed around the first few laps." **Narain Karthikeyan**

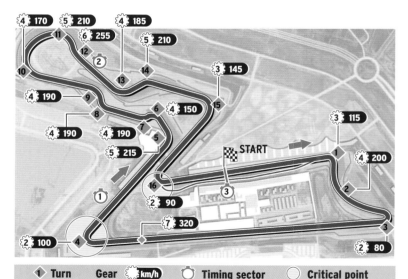

◆ **Turn**   **Gear** 🏁 **km/h**   ○ **Timing sector**   ○ **Critical point**

2012 POLE TIME: **VETTEL (RED BULL)**, 1M25.283S, 134.426MPH/216.338KPH
2012 WINNER'S AVERAGE SPEED: 125.630MPH/202.183KPH

2012 FASTEST LAP: **BUTTON (McLAREN)**, 1M28.203S, 129.976MPH/209.176KPH
LAP RECORD: **VETTEL (RED BULL)**, 1M27.249S, 131.387MPH/211.463KPH, 2011

INSIDE TRACK

INDIAN GRAND PRIX

Date:	27 October
Circuit name:	**Buddh International Circuit**
Circuit length:	**3.190 miles/5.134km**
Number of laps:	**61**
Email:	**jaypee.sports@jalindia.co/in**
Website:	**www.jaypeesports.com**

PREVIOUS WINNERS		
2011	**Sebastian Vettel**	RED BULL
2012	**Sebastian Vettel**	RED BULL

First race: Sebastian Vettel was always likely to win India's first World Championship round at the end of 2011 as he'd won 10 of the season's 16 grands prix up to that point for Red Bull Racing. The German ace qualified on pole and led every lap. He had to push all the way, though, as Jenson Button was making his tyres work better in his McLaren and closed in at the end of each stint.

First corner: This right-hander at the foot of the grandstands is an overtaking prospect in its own right, but on the opening lap it takes on greater significance as drivers have an extra requirement to be on the right side of the track to try a passing move into Turn 3.

Greatest Indian driver: There's a choice thus far of just two Indian F1 drivers: Narain Karthikeyan and Karun Chandhok. The former was the country's first F1 racer, with Jordan in 2005; then Chandhok raced for HRT in 2010 and tested for Lotus the following year when Karthikeyan returned to race for HRT. Karthikeyan's five points for fourth place at the 2005 United States GP remain the country's only points to date.

Do you remember when? Lewis Hamilton and Felipe Massa had a history of clashing throughout 2011 and added their sixth contact of the year at that first Indian GP. Their clash came at Turn 15, when Hamilton dived up the inside of the Brazilian in an attempt to take fifth place, the Brazilian turned in and they collided. This earned the Ferrari driver a drive-through penalty and later his suspension collapsed, tipping him out of the race.

YAS MARINA

Although Formula One has been coming to Abu Dhabi's Yas Marina circuit since 2009, it still feels like a step into the future thanks to its extravagant architecture.

One of the most wonderful facets of Formula One until the 1980s was that each circuit was distinctive. That changed through the 1990s and particularly the early years of the 21st century with the advent of a new generation of circuits, with huge gravel traps pushing the fans and scenery ever further from the action. Thankfully, the Yas Marina circuit changed all this when it broke cover in 2009, as it was the first of Hermann Tilke's circuits since Sepang to have a strong identity of its own. After all, any circuit that is draped with wacky architecture that even straddles the track, adorns itself with a marina and lines itself up against a Ferrari-related theme park is bound to look different. That every facility

for the teams and spectators is cutting edge is testament to Abu Dhabi's desire to impress with its almost unimaginable oil wealth.

The one concern about Yas Marina is that, so far, the most spectacular aspect of races there has been their starting time, as day turns to twilight, rather than the on-track action. While the racing has been close, there has been a shortage of overtaking. Turns 2, 3 and 4 offer a good display of the F1 cars' direction-changing ability, but the long straights down to Turn 8 and Turn 11 have yet to provide as much passing as people had expected, although last year's race was a marked improvement.

"It's incredibly satisfying to hook together a good run through the marina sector." Lewis Hamilton

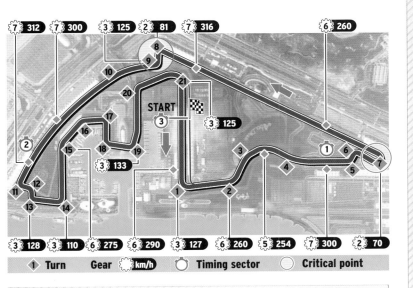

2012 POLE TIME: HAMILTON (McLAREN), 1M40.630S, 123.461MPH/198.692KPH
2012 WINNER'S AVERAGE SPEED: 107.421MPH/172.878KPH

2012 FASTEST LAP: VETTEL (RED BULL), 1M43.964S, 119.502MPH/192.320KPH
LAP RECORD: VETTEL (RED BULL), 1M40.279S, 131.387MPH/211.463KPH, 2009

INSIDE TRACK
ABU DHABI GRAND PRIX

Date:	**3 November**
Circuit name:	**Yas Marina Circuit**
Circuit length:	**3.451 miles/5.554km**
Number of laps:	**56**
Email:	
customerservice@yasmarinacircuit.com	
Website:	**www.yasmarinacircuit.com**

PREVIOUS WINNERS

2009	**Sebastian Vettel** RED BULL
2010	**Sebastian Vettel** RED BULL
2011	**Lewis Hamilton** McLAREN
2012	**Kimi Raikkonen** LOTUS

First race: The F1 regulars were still stunned by the opulence and cutting-edge facilities at Yas Marina when Lewis Hamilton lined up on pole position for the first race here in 2009. However, it was Sebastian Vettel who went home happiest as he took over a lead that he was to keep when a brake problem slowed Hamilton's McLaren, going on to head home Mark Webber for a Red Bull Racing one-two.

First corner: Turn 1, a tight left of more than 90 degrees, can be a daunting prospect on the opening lap when the cars are jostling for position as a pack. Further into the race, though, it tends not to be seen by drivers as a place to overtake. Turn 1 also has the unusual feature of a pit exit that runs through a tunnel, so that cars leaving the pits rejoin the track on the other side.

Greatest local hero: There has not been, as yet, a driver from Abu Dhabi who has shone on the international racing scene. One problem is that racing is still relatively new here, and locals are just as likely to look to the drag racing events held on the back straight for their entertainment.

Do you remember when? Michael Schumacher nearly lost his head at Yas Marina in 2010. This dramatic near miss came at Turn 6 on the opening lap when the seven-time World Champion spun his Mercedes and Vitantonio Liuzzi had no way of avoiding the silver car with his Force India and rode up over its nose – but fortunately not over Michael's head. Both were eliminated on the spot.

AUSTIN

It was shown in 2011 by India's Buddh International that new circuits can have gradient, and Austin's Circuit of the Americas has followed suit, offering a distinctive, photogenic and truly challenging circuit.

Everyone knows that a modern racing circuit can't be as intimate as the ones of old, as safety requirements dictate that gravel beds must be in place, which means that the spectators are kept further back from the action. However, adding gradient to the track's course not only makes it more fun for the drivers but also enables the fans to see more of the lap and so feel more in touch. The inclines make for great TV angles too, and this is why the Circuit of the Americas looked so impressive on its debut in November 2012.

From the outset, the lap was designed to include corners like those considered the the best corners from the great circuits

of the world, and designer Hermann Tilke has included both a stretch of esses like the famous ones at Suzuka between Turns 3 and 6, and a long downhill run from the lofty hairpin at Turn 11 to a sharp right, for the lap's premier overtaking spot.

Austin immediately became popular with the teams as it is such a lovely city to visit and forms, along with Brazil, a perfect pair of races to round out the season. The crowd last November was huge and it's now up to the American fans to support not one grand prix but two, with New Jersey joining the roster in 2014, but it's a large enough country to do just that.

"It's an awesome circuit. It's good fun to drive and there is a nice variation of corners which gives us a good rhythm to the track."
Nico Hulkenberg

86

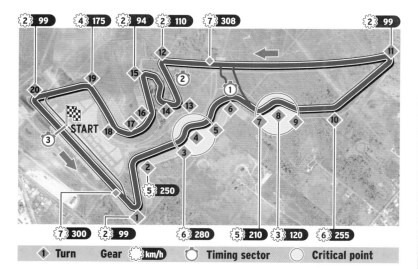

Turn ◆   Gear ⚙   km/h ○   Timing sector ○   Critical point

2012 POLE TIME: **VETTEL (RED BULL),**
1M35.657S, 128.921MPH/207.478KPH
2012 WINNER'S AVERAGE SPEED:
119.869MPH/192.911KPH

2012 FASTEST LAP: **VETTEL (RED BULL),**
1M39.347S, 124.132MPH/199.772KPH
LAP RECORD: **VETTEL (RED BULL), 1M39.347S,**
124.132MPH/199.772KPH, 2012

INSIDE TRACK
UNITED STATES GRAND PRIX

Date:	**17 November**
Circuit name:	**Circuit of the Americas**
Circuit length:	**3.400 miles/5.472km**
Number of laps:	**56**
Email:	**info@circuitoftheamericas.com**
Website:	**www.circuitoftheamericas.com**

PREVIOUS WINNERS
2012   **Lewis Hamilton** McLAREN

First race: The Circuit of the Americas' inaugural grand prix last November was a wonderful start with Lewis Hamilton hunting down Sebastian Vettel's Red Bull, pulling off an ace passing move into Turn 12 and motoring on to his final victory for McLaren.

First corner: Braking into a gradient is the key at Turn 1, as the track rises 40 metres from the level pit straight before doubling left and back down the slope again. Those who get it wrong will have a great view but a lousy lap time.

Greatest local hero: Texans are proud of their distinct character, and two of America's F1 drivers have hailed from the Lone Star State: Carroll Shelby and Jim Hall. The former peaked with fourth place in a Scuderia Centro Sud Maserati in the 1958 Italian GP before going on to win the following year's Le Mans 24 Hours and later creating the AC Cobra. The latter's best was fifth, at the Nurburgring for British Racing Partnership in 1963, but he was probably a little quicker. Hall later went on to run his own team in Indycars. Shelby died in 2012, sadly just too soon to witness Texas having its first grand prix.

Do you remember when? The United States of America last changed venue for its grand prix in 2000 when it headed to the Indianapolis Motor Speedway, home of the Indy 500. The F1 cars raced on only part of the banked oval used by the Indycar racers, and in the opposite direction, with much of their lap twisting around a special circuit on the infield. Victory in this went to Michael Schumacher for Ferrari ahead of team-mate Rubens Barrichello.

INTERLAGOS

For years there has been talk about Interlagos receiving a facelift, even a new pit complex, but it remains unchanged, meaning woeful facilities though still a great track packed with wonderful fans.

As it stands, Interlagos remains a marvellous circuit for racing, with its sweeping corners draped over sloping terrain, falling away from the grandstands at the pit exit end of the start/finish straight, pitching down to its lowest point at Descida do Lago, rising up again to Ferradura before running down, up and down again to the point where the drivers can finally accelerate flat out from Junçao all the way to the first corner, which is absolutely the place to pull off a passing move. The entry to Desicda do Lago is another overtaking point.

What makes the circuit so special is the atmosphere, which crackles with passion.

The fans love their racing and have had drivers of their own to cheer on since Emerson Fittipaldi blazed a trail for Brazil in the early 1970s, followed by Carlos Pace, after whom the circuit is named, Nelson Piquet, their absolute favourite Ayrton Senna, and then Rubens Barrichello.

The circuit's development plans are centred on building a new pit and paddock complex on the straight between Curva do Sol and Descida do Lago. There have been changes suggested for the circuit too, with a kink to the right planned to take the cars around the lake before rejoining the current layout on the climb back up the hill, but nothing has been agreed.

"The long left turns put an extreme burden on our neck muscles because of the centrifugal forces created by driving anti-clockwise."
Sebastian Vettel

INSIDE TRACK
BRAZILIAN GRAND PRIX

Date:	24 November
Circuit name:	Autodromo Jose Carlos Pace Interlagos
Circuit length:	2.667 miles/4.292km
Number of laps:	71
Email:	info@gpbrazil.com
Website:	www.gpbrazil.com

PREVIOUS WINNERS

2003	Giancarlo Fisichella	JORDAN
2004	Juan Pablo Montoya	WILLIAMS
2005	Juan Pablo Montoya	McLAREN
2006	Felipe Massa	FERRARI
2007	Kimi Raikkonen	FERRARI
2008	Felipe Massa	FERRARI
2009	Mark Webber	RED BULL
2010	Sebastian Vettel	RED BULL
2011	Mark Webber	RED BULL
2012	Jenson Button	McLAREN

First race: Interlagos hosted a non-championship race in 1972, won by Carlos Reutemann, but its World Championship bow produced a home winner in 1973 when Emerson Fittipaldi outsprinted pole-sitting Lotus team-mate Ronnie Peterson and led every lap.

First corner: Known as the Senna "S", this is a vicious corner. The exit is blind at turn-in, and the camber throws drivers towards the outside just as they want to line up their entry into the right-hander at the foot of the incline.

Greatest local hero: Emerson Fittipaldi was born almost within sight of Interlagos, and compatriot Rubens Barrichello spent much of his childhood overlooking the circuit. However, there can be no doubt that the best Brazilian to have raced in Formula One was a fellow Paulista: Ayrton Senna. He raced here only five times, winning in 1991 and 1993, but the first of these was a special race as it gave him his first home win in eight attempts.

Do you remember when? Eddie Irvine triggered a four-car accident in 1994 when he put Jos Verstappen's Benetton on to the grass at Descida do Lago. He was given a one-race ban that was extended to three races when he appealed against the decision.

Senna "S" — [3] 106
[7] 320 — START — [3]
Subida dos Boxes — [7] 309 — [2] 76 — [6] 276 — Junçao — [3] 130
[7] 72 — [5] 220
[15]
[8] — [14]
[10]
[2] 104 — [9] — [2] 72
[5] 231 — [6] — [5] 235 — [11] — [2] — [13]
[5] 218 — [12]
[6] 293 — [5]
[1] — [4]
[3] 166 — [5] 257 — [7] 280 — [7] 323 — [4] 154 — [5] 251
Curva do Sol — Reta Oposta — Descida do Lago

◆ Turn   Gear ⚙ km/h   ○ Timing sector   ◯ Critical point

2012 POLE TIME: **HAMILTON (McLAREN),** 1M12.458S, 133.028MPH/214.088KPH
2012 WINNER'S AVERAGE SPEED: 108.229MPH/174.178KPH

2012 FASTEST LAP: **HAMILTON (McLAREN),** 1M18.069S, 123.467MPH/198.701KPH
LAP RECORD: **MONTOYA (WILLIAMS),** 1M11.473S, 134.837MPH/217.000KPH, 2004

There are other street circuits, but Monaco's draw is unique and unmatched, with the spectacle of F1 cars blasting around the harbour having changed remarkably little over the decades.

REVIEW OF THE 2012 SEASON

The 2012 World Championship was exciting and unpredictable. From confusion in the early races as the teams struggled to understand the new Pirelli tyres, Sebastian Vettel emerged as a key player, with Fernando Alonso working wonders in a less competitive Ferrari. Six other drivers won races, but this duo went to the final race still fighting before Vettel did just enough to make it three titles in a row.

Sebastian Vettel couldn't quite believe it as he parked after last November's season-closing Brazilian GP, but he had just become not only the youngest triple Formula One Champion but also the third driver to win three titles in succession. With the other two being Juan Manuel Fangio and Michael Schumacher, he is in very lofty company.

Thus it was fitting that one of the first people to congratulate him was Schumacher, parking up after his final grand prix. The mantle has been passed on.

The 2012 World Championship was a season that took a long while to settle down, even the top teams seemingly perplexed as to why their cars were on the pace at some races yet not at others. The list of winners – Jenson Button, then Fernando Alonso (just ahead of Sauber's Sergio Perez), then Nico Rosberg, then Vettel, then Pastor Maldonado, then Mark Webber, then Lewis Hamilton – shows how no one driver took control of proceedings until Alonso became the first double winner when he won on the Valencia street circuit.

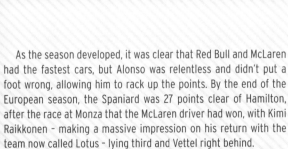

As the season developed, it was clear that Red Bull and McLaren had the fastest cars, but Alonso was relentless and didn't put a foot wrong, allowing him to rack up the points. By the end of the European season, the Spaniard was 27 points clear of Hamilton, after the race at Monza that the McLaren driver had won, with Kimi Raikkonen - making a massive impression on his return with the team now called Lotus - lying third and Vettel right behind.

Hamilton's title hopes then faltered when his car failed as he was heading for victory in Singapore, and so started a run of four wins in succession for Vettel, and Alonso could only pray as the German slashed his points lead and then moved ahead.

Yet, despite not having won since the German GP in July, Alonso stayed in the title battle until that final round, where he came within a whisker of being the newest triple F1 champion instead of Vettel. It was an incredible end to an enthralling season. Had the dice fallen only slightly differently, McLaren might have helped Hamilton to a second title before his departure to Mercedes. However, car failures and early-season pit-stop glitches for both him and Button cost them dear.

At Red Bull Racing, Webber added two wins to Vettel's five, and their combined efforts gave the team its third straight constructors' title. Ferrari seemed at first to be a one-driver team as Felipe Massa couldn't get anywhere near Alonso for pace but, as people talked of who would replace the Brazilian for 2013, he gradually picked

up speed. By season's end, he was all but matching Alonso, thus marking his return to form after the head injuries he suffered in Hungary in 2009.

Beyond these top three teams, three other teams won races, but only one was consistently near the ultimate pace. This was the team that was renamed as Lotus for 2012, but had been Renault in 2011 and can trace its history back to Toleman before its blossoming as Benetton. Raikkonen and team-mate Romain Grosjean showed good speed and the Finn was as consistent as Alonso, achieving every point the car would permit and peaking with a flawless win in Abu Dhabi. Grosjean was fast but had too many collisions.

The other winning teams were Mercedes and Williams. For Mercedes, the season started well, with Rosberg's win in China its first, but after others followed its double-DRS concept, it faded away. Williams's victory in Barcelona came from an inspired drive by Maldonado, but neither he nor Bruno Senna scored regularly. Two second places for Sauber's Sergio Perez marked him out as a rising talent, which is why McLaren has signed him.

For the tail-end teams, Caterham eventually won the scrap at the final round to pip Marussia, while HRT didn't have the backing to do anything but bring up the rear.

The biggest success of the year, though, was probably the US GP at the Circuit of the Americas in Texas, as it offered a great race on a wonderful circuit in front of packed grandstands.

AUSTRALIAN GP

The 2012 opener was a riveting race. McLaren's Jenson Button was first to the flag, having coped better than the rest with wear and tear on the car that was higher than anticipated. Sebastian Vettel came home second and a disconsolate Lewis Hamilton was third.

The degree to which each team had successfully interpreted the new rules was shown by the starting positions. Lewis Hamilton headed Button for an all-McLaren front row, ensuring that elegance headed the step-nosed horrors that filled the grid. Red Bull Racing's slide from its 2011 position of dominance was made clear when its better qualifier in Melbourne, Mark Webber, was only fast enough for fifth place. That Romain Grosjean, entered by the Lotus team that had previously been Renault, was third and Michael Schumacher fourth for Mercedes was further evidence of how the formbook had been reset. Reigning World Champion Sebastian Vettel could qualify only sixth, a fraction ahead of Nico Rosberg in the other Mercedes, with Williams returning to form as Pastor Maldonado lined up eighth.

A poor start by Hamilton allowed Button to grab the lead, while Grosjean fluffed an upchange and was passed not only by Schumacher but also by fast starters Rosberg and Vettel. Webber was demoted to ninth and clashed with Nico Hulkenberg's Force India at Turn 1, putting the German out of the race, while Bruno Senna's Williams was pitched skywards.

Button edged clear of Hamilton. Yet, with a grippier than expected track enabling the cars to lap fast, teams realised that they might not have enough fuel to run the whole race at their optimum lap times, and the McLaren drivers were told to back off as early as lap 8. By then, Grosjean had been forced into retirement when Maldonado clouted him and Vettel had produced the move of the race when he passed Rosberg for third around the outside at Turn 9, also on lap 2. Schumacher was next in Vettel's sights and he was given the place on lap 6 when the seven-time World Champion arrived too fast at Turn 1 and spun. Transmission problems would sideline Schumacher, leaving Vettel free to close in on the already backed-off McLarens. He had no answer to Button's mastery of the conditions,

Jenson Button mastered tyre wear and fuel consumption issues better than his rivals.

MELBOURNE ROUND 1

DATE: **18 MARCH 2012**

Laps: **58** • Distance: **191.117 miles/307.574km** • Weather: **Warm & sunny**

Pos	Driver	Team	Result	Stops	Qualifying Time	Grid
1	**Jenson Button**	McLaren	1h34m09.565s	2	1m25.074s	2
2	**Sebastian Vettel**	Red Bull	1h34m11.704s	2	1m25.668s	6
3	**Lewis Hamilton**	McLaren	1h34m13.640s	2	1m24.922s	1
4	**Mark Webber**	Red Bull	1h34m14.112s	2	1m25.561s	5
5	**Fernando Alonso**	Ferrari	1h34m31.130s	2	1m26.494s	12
6	**Kamui Kobayashi**	Sauber	1h34m46.331s	2	1m26.590s	13
7	**Kimi Raikkonen**	Lotus	1h34m47.579s	2	1m27.758s	17
8	**Sergio Perez**	Sauber	1h34m49.023s	1	No time	22*
9	**Daniel Ricciardo**	Toro Rosso	1h34m49.121s	3	No time	10
10	**Paul di Resta**	Force India	1h34m49.302s	2	1m27.086s	15
11	**Jean-Eric Vergne**	Toro Rosso	1h34m49.413s	2	1m26.429s	11
12	**Nico Rosberg**	Mercedes	1h35m07.207s	2	1m25.686s	7
13	**Pastor Maldonado**	Williams	57 laps/accident	2	1m25.908s	8
14	**Timo Glock**	Marussia	57 laps	2	1m30.923s	20
15	**Charles Pic**	Marussia	53 laps/oil pressure	3	1m31.670s	21
16	**Bruno Senna**	Williams	52 laps/accident	3	1m26.663s	14
R	**Felipe Massa**	Ferrari	46 laps/accident	3	1m27.497s	16
R	**Heiki Kovalainen**	Caterham	38 laps/suspension	3	1m28.679s	18
R	**Vitaly Petrov**	Caterham	34 laps/steering	1	1m29.018s	19
R	**Michael Schumacher**	Mercedes	10 laps/transmission	0	1m25.336s	4
R	**Romain Grosjean**	Lotus	1 lap/accident	0	1m25.302s	3
R	**Nico Hulkenberg**	Force India	0 laps/accident	0	1m26.451s	9

FASTEST LAP: BUTTON, 1M29.187S, 133.006MPH/214.053KPH ON LAP 56 • RACE LEADERS: BUTTON 1-15, 17-35, 37-58; HAMILTON 16; VETTEL 36
* 5-PLACE GRID PENALTY

but with Hamilton losing time behind Sergio Perez after his first pitstop, followed by the fortuitous deployment of the safety car, Vettel was able to make his second pitstop "for free" and emerge between the McLarens.

Fernando Alonso advanced brilliantly from 12th to fifth, while sixth would have gone to Maldonado if he had not crashed on the final lap, throwing away more points than Williams scored in the whole of the 2011 season.

92

MALAYSIAN GP

This was a great race but a strange one, as rain enlivened proceedings and the honours were contested by two mid-grid cars, with Fernando Alonso just staying ahead of Sauber's Sergio Perez to take victory at a meeting where he felt his Ferrari was far from competitive.

McLaren arrived full of optimism and claimed the front row, again with Lewis Hamilton ahead of Jenson Button. Michael Schumacher claimed his second successive row two position for Mercedes as rumblings continued about the team using a slot in its rear wing that was revealed when DRS was engaged to feed air forward to stall the front wing and make the car even sleeker. Mark Webber and Sebastian Vettel lined up fourth and fifth for Red Bull, with Romain Grosjean again outpacing his more fancied Lotus team-mate Kimi Raikkonen.

Rain arrived just before the start and it was in the spray that Grosjean and Schumacher tangled at Turn 4 as they fought over third, with Schumacher and Webber nipping past as they collided, followed by Vettel and Fernando Alonso. Two laps later, Grosjean spun out. At the end of lap 1, Perez pitted to change from intermediates to wets, as did Bruno Senna. Button and Alonso waited until lap 4 before they did the same, with Hamilton, Webber and Vettel coming in on lap 5. When they rejoined, Perez was third behind the McLarens. However, the rain intensified and the safety car came out to lead the cars around before the race was red-flagged on lap 10.

After a 50-minute delay, the race got under way again and Button was first to pit for intermediates, but came in a lap too soon. This cost him time, and then Hamilton overshot his pit, allowing Alonso to take the lead ahead of Perez, the cooler conditions suiting his Ferrari while they made the McLarens struggle. Button then damaged his nose wing on Narain Karthikeyan's HRT, after which Vettel also hit the Indian's car, to be slowed by the resultant puncture. At the front, Alonso pulled away from Perez, but the Mexican fought back later in the stint, by which time Rosberg's tyres had been consumed and he had to pit for new ones, resulting in him dropping him behind Vettel, Raikkonen and Webber.

SEPANG ROUND 2

DATE: **25 MARCH 2012**

Laps: 56 • Distance: **192.864 miles/310.385km** • Weather: **Hot & damp, then wet**

Pos	Driver	Team	Result	Stops	Qualifying Time	Grid
1	**Fernando Alonso**	Ferrari	2h44m51.812s	3	1m37.566s	8
2	**Sergio Perez**	Sauber	2h44m54.075s	3	1m37.968s	9
3	**Lewis Hamilton**	McLaren	2h45m06.403s	3	1m36.219s	1
4	**Mark Webber**	Red Bull	2h45m09.500s	3	1m36.461s	4
5	**Kimi Raikkonen**	Lotus	2h45m21.268s	3	1m36.461s	10*
6	**Bruno Senna**	Williams	2h45m29.459s	4	1m37.841s	13
7	**Paul di Resta**	Force India	2h45m36.224s	3	1m37.877s	14
8	**Jean-Eric Vergne**	Toro Rosso	2h45m38.797s	2	1m39.077s	18
9	**Nico Hulkenberg**	Force India	2h45m39.704s	3	1m37.890s	16
10	**Michael Schumacher**	Mercedes	2h45m41.808s	3	1m36.391s.	3
11	**Sebastian Vettel**	Red Bull	2h46m07.339s	4	1m36.634s	5
12	**Daniel Ricciardo**	Toro Rosso	2h46m08.640s	4	1m37.883s	15
13	**Nico Rosberg**	Mercedes	2h46m10.405s	4	1m36.664s	7
14	**Jenson Button**	McLaren	2h46m11.531s	5	1m36.368s	2
15	**Felipe Massa**	Ferrari	2h46m29.131s	4	1m37.731s	12
16	**Vitaly Petrov**	Caterham	55 laps	3	1m39.567s	19
17	**Timo Glock**	Marussia	55 laps	3	1m40.903s	20
18	**Heikki Kovalainen**	Caterham	55 laps	4	1m39.306s	24*
19	**Pastor Maldonado**	Williams	54 laps/engine	4	1m37.589s	11
20	**Charles Pic**	Marussia	54 laps	3	1m41.250s	21
21	**Narain Karthikeyan**	HRT	54 laps	2	1m43.655s	23
22	**Pedro de la Rosa**	HRT	54 laps	2	1m42.914s	22
R	**Kamui Kobayashi**	Sauber	46 laps/brakes	3	1m38.069s	17
R	**Romain Grosjean**	Lotus	3 laps/spun off	0	1m36.658s	6

FASTEST LAP: RAIKKONEN, 1M40.722S, 123.110MPH/198.127KPH ON LAP 53 • RACE LEADERS: HAMILTON 1-13; PEREZ, 14-15, 40-41; ALONSO, 16-39, 42-56 • * 5-PLACE GRID PENALTY

Fernando Alonso resisted a stern challenge from Sergio Perez to take an unexpected win.

When Alonso made his final tyre change, Perez wanted to pit too, but Sauber kept him out for a further lap. Then, once on to a new set of dry-weather tyres, he started coming back at Alonso. With six laps to go, as he was shaping up to pass, Perez slid wide at Turn 13. Second place was fantastic, but it could so easily have been first.

CHINESE GP

Mercedes racer Nico Rosberg took his maiden grand prix win at last, at his 111th attempt, but he was made to fight all the way by McLaren's Jenson Button, who might have won the race had it not been for a botched final pit stop.

This was a great grand prix, with some epic racing and, at the end of it all, 1982 World Champion Keke Rosberg had a giant smile on his face as his son Nico had finally reaped the reward that his talents had deserved. For Mercedes GP, too, there was relief that it had achieved its first victory. Although the team is related only by name to the works team of old, the win was the first for Mercedes since the Italian GP in 1955.

Mercedes filled the front row, Rosberg ahead of Michael Schumacher, who lined up where Lewis Hamilton's McLaren would have been, but for a five-place grid penalty for a gearbox change. Form suggested that the McLarens, starting fifth and seventh, would be faster in race trim, but a sudden drop of temperature before the start swung the advantage towards the Mercedes.

Rosberg made a great getaway at the start and Schumacher was offered no chance to pass him. Kamui Kobayashi was slow away from third on the grid in his Sauber, though, and both Kiki Raikkonen and Jenson Button passed him, with the McLaren driver then diving up the inside of the Finn at Turn 3. By Turn 6, Hamilton was also past Kobayashi, followed by Sergio Perez. What followed was a race that remained incredibly close as the use of DRS down the long back straight allowed chasing cars to stay in touch if not often to pass, and the grandstand overlooking Turn 14 was definitely the one to be occupying.

Rosberg looked supreme in the lead, with Schumacher as his buffer. McLaren elected to pit three times, and perhaps this played into Mercedes' hands, but Schumacher was soon out of the race, having been signalled to leave the pits before one of his wheels had been attached. This left Button to chase Rosberg, and chase he did, expecting to make his move in the closing laps on fresher rubber than the two-stopping Rosberg would be using. But it didn't work out that way as a pit-stop blunder left him adrift and allowed

Mercedes to the front as Nico Rosberg leads Michael Schumacher in the opening laps.

SHANGHAI ROUND 3

DATE: **15 APRIL 2012**

Laps: 56 • Distance: **189.559 miles/305.066km** • Weather: **Warm & overcast**

Pos	Driver	Team	Result	Stops	Qualifying Time	Grid
1	**Nico Rosberg**	Mercedes	1h36m26.929s	2	1m35.121s	1
2	**Jenson Button**	McLaren	1h36m47.555s	3	1m36.191s	5
3	**Lewis Hamilton**	McLaren	1h36m52.941s	3	1m35.626s	7*
4	**Mark Webber**	Red Bull	1h36m54.853s	3	1m36.290s	6
5	**Sebastian Vettel**	Red Bull	1h36m57.412s	2	1m36.031s	11
6	**Romain Grosjean**	Lotus	1h36m58.420s	2	No time	10
7	**Bruno Senna**	Williams	1h37m01.526s	2	1m36.289s	14
8	**Pastor Maldonado**	Williams	1h37m02.572s	2	1m36.283s	13
9	**Fernando Alonso**	Ferrari	1h37m04.185s	3	1m36.622s	9
10	**Kamui Kobayashi**	Sauber	1h37m05.649s	3	1m35.784s	3
11	**Sergio Perez**	Sauber	1h37m07.995s	2	1m36.524s	8
12	**Paul di Resta**	Force India	1h37m09.202s	2	1m36.317s	15
13	**Felipe Massa**	Ferrari	1h37m09.708s	2	1m36.255s	12
14	**Kimi Raikkonen**	Lotus	1h37m17.502s	2	1m35.898s	4
15	**Nico Hulkenberg**	Force India	1h37m18.142s	2	1m36.745s	16
16	**Jean-Eric Vergne**	Toro Rosso	1h37m18.685s	3	1m37.714s	24**
17	**Daniel Ricciardo**	Toro Rosso	1h37m30.085s	2	1m36.956s	17
18	**Vitaly Petrov**	Caterham	55 laps	2	1m38.677s	19
19	**Timo Glock**	Marussia	55 laps	2	1m39.282s	20
20	**Charles Pic**	Marussia	55 laps	3	1m39.717s	21
21	**Pedro de la Rosa**	HRT	55 laps	2	1m40.411s	22
22	**Narain Karthikeyan**	HRT	54 laps	2	1m41.000s	23
23	**Heikki Kovalainen**	Caterham	53 laps	4	1m38.463s	18
R	**Michael Schumacher**	Mercedes	12 laps/loose wheel	1	1m35.691s	2

FASTEST LAP: KOBAYASHI, 1M39.960S, 121.990121MPH/196.324KPH ON LAP 40 • RACE LEADERS: ROSBERG 1-13, 17-34, 40-56; PEREZ 14-16; BUTTON 35-39 • * 5-PLACE GRID PENALTY FOR GEARBOX CHANGE ** STARTED FROM PIT LANE

Rosberg to motor on to that famous first win. Hamilton completed the podium, relieved to have made it there after being delayed behind Felipe Massa following a pit stop. Fernando

Alonso might have finished third instead, but a spin when passing Pastor Maldonado cost him time and he ended up ninth, leaving Mark Webber to chase Hamilton home.

BAHRAIN GP

It was a considerable surprise to many that Sebastian Vettel, after his 11 grand prix victories in 2011, took until the fourth round to win again, and even more of a surprise that he was joined on the podium at Sakhir by the Lotus drivers.

The teams and drivers were wary when they headed to Bahrain, as the civil unrest that had led to the cancellation of the race in 2011 was simmering on. Fortunately, the event ran without a hitch, and no driver was more relieved at that than Sebastian Vettel, who really got his 2012 campaign up to speed after a mixed start to the year.

The double World Champion took pole position, but it would have gone to Nico Rosberg had not his fellow German run wide at the final corner and wrecked his lap, causing Rosberg to fall back to fifth behind Vettel, Lewis Hamilton, Mark Webber and Jenson Button.

Vettel led away from Hamilton, but what unfolded demonstrated how the teams were struggling to be consistent in 2012, as McLaren would find out. Their problem was largely down to tyres that offered a huge difference in temperature between front and back, resulting in cars that were unbalanced.

Meanwhile the Lotus drivers Kimi Raikkonen and Romain Grosjean found that their handling remained relatively unaffected, which enabled them to climb the order. Grosjean had made a sensational start, rising from seventh to fourth, just before Raikkonen worked the traffic well to go from 11th to seventh.

Vettel was untroubled at the front, Hamilton struggling for grip and Webber unable to hold off Grosjean, who passed Hamilton for second on lap 7, with Raikkonen demoting Button on that same lap, then pitting later than Alonso, Webber and Hamilton to move up to third after his first pit stop.

Hamilton's race was wrecked by blunders at two of his three pit stops and he would fall to eighth, with McLaren's bad day compounded when Button lost an already disappointing seventh place with differential failure.

Race leader Vettel was reeled in by Raikkonen, who got ahead of Grosjean after their second stops. The Finn then went after his first win since his sojourn in rallying and made a bid to pass Vettel going into Turn 1 on lap 34, but it wasn't to be as Vettel blocked it. After that, Raikkonen's tyres went off, and his moment had passed.

Webber was a distant fourth, with a damaged floor, while Rosberg led home the closely packed gaggle of di Resta, Alonso and the frustrated Hamilton.

SAKHIR ROUND 4

DATE: **22 APRIL 2012**

Laps: 57 • Distance: 191.530 miles/308.238km • Weather: **Hot & overcast**

Pos	Driver	Team	Result	Stops	Qualifying Time	Grid
1	Sebastian Vettel	Red Bull	1h35m10.990s	3	1m32.422s	1
2	Kimi Raikkonen	Lotus	1h35m14.323s	3	1m33.789s	11
3	Romain Grosjean	Lotus	1h35m21.184s	3	1m33.008s	7
4	Mark Webber	Red Bull	1h35m49.778s	3	1m32.637s	3
5	Nico Rosberg	Mercedes	1h36m06.450s	3	1m32.821s	5
6	Paul di Resta	Force India	1h36m08.533s	2	No time	10
7	Fernando Alonso	Ferrari	1h36m08.793s	3	No time	9
8	Lewis Hamilton	McLaren	1h36m09.974s	3	1m32.520s	2
9	Felipe Massa	Ferrari	1h36m15.989s	3	1m33.912s	14
10	Michael Schumacher	Mercedes	1h36m22.480s	3	1m34.865s	22*
11	Sergio Perez	Sauber	1h36m23.692s	3	1m33.394s	8
12	Nico Hulkenberg	Force India	1h36m27.529s	3	1m33.807s	13
13	Kamnui Kobayashi	Sauber	1h36m41.324s	3	1m33.806s	12
14	Jean-Eric Vergne	Toro Rosso	1h36m44.713s	3	1m35.014s	17
15	Daniel Ricciardo	Toro Rosso	56 laps	3	1m32.912s	6
16	Vitaly Petrov	Caterham	56 laps	3	1m35.823s	18
17	Heikki Kovalainen	Caterham	56 laps	4	1m36.132s	16
18	Jenson Button	McLaren	55 laps/differential	4	1m32.711s	4
19	Timo Glock	Marussia	55 laps	3	1m37.905s	23
20	Pedro de la Rosa	HRT	55 laps	3	1m37.883s	20
21	Narain Karthikeyan	HRT	55 laps	4	1m38.314s	24
R	Bruno Senna	Williams	54 laps/handling	3	1m34.017s	15
R	Pastor Maldonado	Williams	25 laps/suspension	2	No time	21*
R	Charles Pic	Marussia	24 laps/engine	1	1m37.683s	19

FASTEST LAP: VETTEL, 1M36.379S, 125.611MPH/202.152KPH ON LAP 41 • RACE LEADERS: VETTEL 1–11, 13–29, 41–57; DI RESTA 12; GROSJEAN 40 •
* 5-PLACE GRID PENALTY FOR GEARBOX CHANGE

Lotus drivers Kimi Raikkonen and Romain Grosjean joined Sebastian Vettel on the podium.

SPANISH GP

This was an extraordinary performance for it produced not only Williams's first win since 2004 but also the first win for Pastor Maldonado, and he achieved it by resisting intense pressure from double World Champion Fernando Alonso.

The Williams team had hinted at the season's opening race in Australia that it had a more competitive car than it had had for years. The result didn't come, as Pastor Maldonado crashed out of sixth place on the final lap, but it was there to be seen. Then, like every one of their rivals, their form fluctuated in this most erratic season, but changes introduced for the Spanish GP to give the car qualifying speed as well as race pace worked a treat as Maldonado ended up second fastest. This became pole position when fastest qualifier Lewis Hamilton was moved back to the last place on the grid for a fuel transgression.

Now all Maldonado had to do was get a good start and stay ahead for the remainder of the race, which wasn't something many would have predicted as his speed has always been offset by mistakes ... Yet on the Venezuelan's day of days, he held it all together and delivered a career-changing drive to become the fifth winner in the season's first five races.

Maldonado's first test came when Alonso tried to dive down the inside into Turn 1, but he sensibly ceded the corner rather than risk a collision and slotted into position behind the home crowd's favourite.

Their first stops came and went, with Alonso still leading when they returned. But Maldonado made his second stop two laps before Alonso's, and then was given a helping hand when Alonso was stuck behind Charles Pic's Marussia on his outlap. Maldonado was still ahead by four seconds when he made his final pit visit, but he now had to drive like never before, making his last set of tyres last 25 laps and also holding off Alonso, who soon closed to within one second and badly wanted a win on home ground.

Impressively, he did just that and people could only applaud a previously wayward driver for having made his tyres work to perfection.

In the final laps, as Alonso was frustrated, the Lotuses were the fastest in the race, with

Pastor Maldonado came under intense pressure from Fernando Alonso but held out to win.

CIRCUIT DE CATALUNYA ROUND 5   DATE: 13 MAY 2012

Laps: 66 • Distance: 190.825 miles/307.104km • Weather: Hot & bright

Pos	Driver	Team	Result	Stops	Qualifying Time	Grid
1	Pastor Maldonado	Williams	1h39m01.145s	3	1m22.285s	1
2	Fernando Alonso	Ferrari	1h39m12.340s	3	1m22.302s	2
3	Kimi Raikkonen	Lotus	1h39m13.029s	3	1m22.487s	4
4	Romain Grosjean	Lotus	1h39m23.944s	3	1m22.424s	3
5	Kamui Kobayashi	Sauber	1h40m13.786s	3	No time	9
6	Sebastian Vettel	Red Bull	1h40m16.721s	4	No time	7
7	Nico Rosberg	Mercedes	1h40m27.064s	3	1m23.005s	6
8	Lewis Hamilton	McLaren	1h40m27.285s	2	No time	24*
9	Jenson Button	McLaren	1h40m34.391s	3	1m22.944s	10
10	Nico Hulkenberg	Force India	65 laps	3	1m23.177s	13
11	Mark Webber	Red Bull	65 laps	3	1m22.977s	11
12	Jean-Eric Vergne	Toro Rosso	65 laps	3	1m23.265s	14
13	Daniel Ricciardo	Toro Rosso	65 laps	3	1m23.442s	15
14	Paul di Resta	Force India	65 laps	3	1m23.125s	12
15	Felipe Massa	Ferrari	65 laps	4	1m23.444s	16
16	Heikki Kovalainen	Caterham	65 laps	3	1m25.507s	19
17	Vitaly Petrov	Caterham	65 laps	3	1m25.277s	18
18	Timo Glock	Marussia	64 laps	3	1m27.032s	21
19	Pedro de la Rosa	HRT	63 laps	3	1m27.555s	22
R	Sergio Perez	Sauber	37 laps/transmission	3	1m22.533s	5
R	Charles Pic	Marussia	35 laps/halfshaft	2	1m26.582s	20
R	Narain Karthikeyan	HRT	22 laps/wheel	2	1m31.122s	23
R	Bruno Senna	Williams	12 laps/accident	0	1m24.981s	17
R	Michael Schumacher	Mercedes	12 laps/accident	1	No time	8

FASTEST LAP: GROSJEAN, 1M26.250S, 120.729MPH/194.295KPH ON LAP 53 • RACE LEADERS: ALONSO 1-9, 12-26, 42-44; MALDONADO 10-11, 27-41, 47-66; RAIKKONEN 45-46 • * EXCLUDED FROM QUALIFYING FOR A TECHNICAL INFRINGEMENT

Kimi Raikkonen closing right in on Alonso at flag fall. Team-mate Romain Grosjean finished fourth, slowed by damaging his front wing in a lap 1 clash with Sergio Perez.

With the McLarens, Red Bulls and Mercedes off the pace, Kamui Kobayashi finished a distant fifth for Sauber after passing Button and Rosberg in the final stint.

MONACO GP

The pattern of Formula One's incredible season was maintained as Mark Webber made it six winners from six races. The victory also showed how, unlike in 2011, the Australian was back to his best form and every bit the equal of his team-mate.

There could have been the headline "Michael Schumacher takes pole at Monaco", his increased speed coming from his renewed confidence and new parts that lightened the rear end of his Mercedes, but a five-place penalty meant that he knew that he would fall to sixth.

Pole position went instead to Mark Webber, with Schumacher's team-mate Nico Rosberg alongside, then Lewis Hamilton, the increasingly impressive Romain Grosjean and Fernando Alonso. Sebastian Vettel was out of sorts and qualified only ninth.

Webber led away from Rosberg and Hamilton, but not everyone got around Ste Devote without trouble. Grosjean was the one to fall first, spinning after moving across on Schumacher when Alonso dived up his inside. Kamui Kobayashi got caught out in the concertina effect as people tried to avoid hitting Grosjean – he hit Jenson Button's McLaren, getting his Sauber airborne. He would continue for a few laps, but damage to his suspension forced his retirement. Out already, though, was Pastor Maldonado. The Venezuelan hero of the Spanish GP had had to start last as he was given grid penalties totalling a 15-place drop for clashing with Sergio Perez and for having a gearbox change, and then hit Pedro de la Rosa's HRT at the first corner, taking both of them out.

What followed was a masterclass from Webber on how to control from the front, with tyre degradation so much more marked in 2012. There was also the arrival of rain a dozen laps before the finish.

Rosberg was Webber's shadow, but Ferrari appeared to make an error, as Alonso was flying when released from being delayed by Hamilton, and yet they brought him in for new tyres despite the fact that he was lapping faster even than those on new rubber. His pit stop moved him ahead of the McLaren but he reckons that if they had kept him out for a couple of laps longer, he might have got past Rosberg and even Webber too.

MONACO ROUND 6

DATE: 27 May 2012

Laps: **78** • Distance: **161.850 miles/260.473km** • Weather: **Warm, light rain later**

Pos	Driver	Team	Result	Stops	Qualifying Time	Grid
1	Mark Webber	Red Bull	1h46m06.557s	1	1m14.381s	1
2	Nico Rosberg	Mercedes	1h46m07.200s	1	1m14.448s	2
3	Fernando Alonso	Ferrari	1h46m07.504s	1	1m14.948s	5
4	Sebastian Vettel	Red Bull	1h46m07.900s	1	No time	9
5	Lewis Hamilton	McLaren	1h46m10.658s	1	1m14.583s	3
6	Felipe Massa	Ferrari	1h46m12.752s	1	1m15.049s	7
7	Paul di Resta	Force India	1h46m48.094s	1	1m15.718s	14
8	Nico Hulkenberg	Force India	1h46m49.119s	1	1m15.421s	10
9	Kimi Raikkonen	Lotus	1h46m50.593s	1	1m15.199s	8
10	Bruno Senna	Williams	1h46m51.073s	1	1m15.709s	13
11	Sergio Perez	Sauber	77 laps	2	No time	23*
12	Jean-Eric Vergne	Toro Tosso	77 laps	2	1m16.885s	16
13	Heikki Kovalainen	Caterham	77 laps	2	1m16.538s	17
14	Timo Glock	Marussia	77 laps	2	1m17.947s	19
15	Narain Karthikeyan	HRT	76 laps	2	1m19.310s	22
16	Jenson Button	McLaren	70 laps/accident	1	1m15.536s	12
R	Daniel Ricciardo	Toro Rosso	65 la ps/steering	1	1m15.878s	15
R	Charles Pic	Marussia	64 laps/electrical	1	1m18.476s	21
R	Michael Schumacher	Mercedes	63 laps/fuel pressure	1	1m14.301s	6*
R	Vitaly Petrov	Caterham	15 laps/electrical	0	1m17.404s	18
R	Kamui Kobayashi	Sauber	5 laps/accident damage	1	1m15.508s	11
R	Pedro de la Rosa	HRT	0 laps/accident damage	0	1m18.096s	20
R	Pastor Maldonado	Williams	0 laps/accident damage	0	1m15.245s	24**
R	Romain Grosjean	Lotus	0 laps/accident	0	1m14.639s	4

FASTEST LAP: PEREZ, 1M17.296S, 96.658MPH/155.556KPH ON LAP 49 • **RACE LEADERS:** WEBBER 1-28, 46-78; ALONSO 29; MASSA 30; VETTEL 31-45
* 5-PLACE GRID PENALTY ** 15-PLACE GRID PENALTY

Kamui Kobayashi's Sauber gets airborne after hitting Jenson Button's McLaren at Ste Devote.

Vettel took the lead when the others pitted. He stayed out for a further 15 laps and then came out in fourth. They then circulated in the stalemate of a six-car pack on a track with no passing points, and this is how they ran to the finish, with Webber the first of the pack to encounter rain but managing not to slip up and allow those behind to pounce.

CANADIAN GP

Lewis Hamilton must love Montreal, for he not only collected his third win here for McLaren in six years but did so with a drive of breathtaking excellence when he made a two-stop race strategy work to perfection.

With Sebastian Vettel lined up on pole position ahead of him, along with Fernando Alonso and Mark Webber right behind, Lewis Hamilton knew that he would be pitting twice but was fairly confident that they would not, and so he really needed to get the jump on the German into the first corner.

This didn't happen, though, as the Red Bull driver led away and rapidly pulled clear, with Hamilton and Alonso able to ease clear of the pack behind.

Of the front-runners, Vettel was the first to pit, on lap 16, followed two laps later by Hamilton and Webber, making Hamilton think that the Red Bulls would be two-stopping too. Alonso waited until lap 19, Romain Grosjean two laps longer. When this shook out, Hamilton led from Alonso and Vettel, having only managed to pass the Ferrari driver at the end of his out lap. Clearly employing a different tactic, Kimi Raikkonen, who had started 12th, held off from pitting, running fourth and staying there until he finally called in at the pits on lap 40, his Lotus proving again how light it is on its tyres.

Hamilton made his second stop on lap 50, but there was a delay getting his right rear wheel on, and he emerged third behind Alonso and Vettel. Now the race was on, and his startling pace on this new set of softs was more than enough to worry his rivals. Ferrari gambled on keeping Alonso out to the finish. Red Bull also realised that victory had escaped it, as Vettel wasn't far enough in front of Grosjean to pit again and emerge ahead, but with seven laps to go Vettel's tyres were so worn that he was forced to pit, falling to fifth behind not only Alonso, Hamilton and Grosjean but Sergio Perez too, the Mexican flying despite being on a one-stop run.

A lap later, Alonso was struggling for rear grip and Hamilton motored past into the lead. Alonso then plunged down the order, his gamble to one-stop having backfired, and had fallen to fifth by the end.

It's all smiles as Lewis Hamilton and third-placed Sergio Perez celebrate on the podium.

MONTREAL ROUND 7

DATE: **10 June 2012**

Laps: **70** • Distance: **189.686 miles/305.270km** • Weather: **Dry & hot**

Pos	Driver	Team	Result	Stops	Qualifying Time	Grid
1	**Lewis Hamilton**	McLaren	1h32m29.586s	2	1m14.087s	2
2	**Romain Grosjean**	Lotus	1h32m32.846s	1	1m14.645s	7
3	**Sergio Perez**	Sauber	1h32m34.846s	1	1m15.156s	15
4	**Sebastian Vettel**	Red Bull	1h32m36.881s	2	1m13.784s	1
5	**Fernando Alonso**	Ferrari	1h32m42.997s	2	1m14.151s	3
6	**Nico Rosberg**	Mercedes	1h32m43.428s	2	1m14.411s	5
7	**Mark Webber**	Red Bull	1h32m44.671s	2	1m14.346s	4
8	**Kimi Raikkonen**	Lotus	1h32m45.153s	1	1m14.734s	12
9	**Kamui Kobayashi**	Sauber	1h32m54.018s	1	1m14.688s	11
10	**Felipe Massa**	Ferrari	1h32m54.858s	2	1m14.465s	6
11	**Paul di Resta**	Force India	1h33m27.279s	2	1m14.705s	8
12	**Nico Hulkenberg**	Force India	1h33m15.822s	2	1m14.748s	13
13	**Pastor Maldonado**	Williams	1h33m16.638s	1	1m15.231s	17*
14	**Daniel Ricciardo**	Toro Rosso	1h33m34.061s	2	1m15.078s	14
15	**Jean-Eric Vergne**	Toro Rosso	69 laps	2	1m16.602s	20
16	**Jenson Button**	McLaren	69 laps	3	1m15.182s	10
17	**Bruno Senna**	Williams	69 laps	1	1m15.170s	16
18	**Heikki Kovalainen**	Caterham	69 laps	2	1m16.263s	18
19	**Vitaly Petrov**	Caterham	69 laps	2	1m16.482s	19
20	**Charles Pic**	Marussia	67 laps	1	1m18.255s	23
R	**Timo Glock**	Marussia	56 laps/suspension	1	1m17.901s	22
R	**Michael Schumacher**	Mercedes	43 laps/DRS	1	1m14.812s	9
R	**Pedro de la Rosa**	HRT	24 laps/brakes	0	1m17.492s	21
R	**Narain Karthikeyan**	HRT	22 laps/suspension	0	1m18.330s	24

FASTEST LAP: VETTEL, 1M15.752S, 128.778MPH/207.248KPH ON LAP 70 • RACE LEADERS: VETTEL 1-15; HAMILTON 16, 21-49, 64-70; ALONSO 17-19
50-63; GROSJEAN 20 • * 5-PLACE GRID PENALTY

The other McLaren driver, Jenson Button, had a horrible time, having lost running time on the Friday due to gearbox failure and qualified only 10th. He then failed to make his harder tyres work in the race and so had to pit a third time, dropping back to finish lapped and 16th, a far cry from his spectacular win here in 2010.

EUROPEAN GP

After seven winners in seven rounds, Fernando Alonso became the first double winner of the year when he thrilled his home country fans with victory in a race that had belonged to Sebastian Vettel until he was halted by alternator failure.

Spanish fans packing the grandstands would have had to be massive optimists to believe that their hero Fernando Alonso might win as he lined up 11th on the grid, but he delivered in a race that provided more incident than all the previous races here put together.

Alonso had just missed the cut for Q3, but his Ferrari appeared to have plenty of race speed, with the Spaniard enjoying a good first lap, passing Nico Rosberg, Jenson Button and Paul di Resta. At the front, pole man Sebastian Vettel led away from Lewis Hamilton, with Romain Grosjean usurping Pastor Maldonado for third at Turn 2 when the Williams driver lost momentum after a scuffle with Kimi Raikkonen in the other Lotus. Finding himself on the wrong line, Maldonado then lost a further place to Kamui Kobayashi at Turn 4.

While Vettel was running untroubled in the lead, pulling clear by roughly a second a lap, Grosjean hunted down Hamilton and on lap 10 moved his Lotus into second place at the end of the DRS zone into Turn 12.

Hamilton was the first of the front-runners to pit, on lap 13. Vettel pitted three laps later and resumed in the lead, with Grosjean coming in on the same lap and slotting back into second ahead of Hamilton. The driver who gained most in this period was Alonso, who pitted on lap 15 yet was able to rise to fourth thanks to passing Nico Hulkenberg on the track and then getting ahead of Kobayashi, Raikkonen and Maldonado when they muddled pit stops. It was clearly going to be a good day.

There was a safety car period after Jean-Eric Vergne hit Heikki Kovalainen's Caterham, slashing Vettel's comfortable lead. Then, during the seven-lap period behind it, Alonso found himself promoted to third by a pit-stop blunder that cost Hamilton time and let Raikkonen by too.

When the safety car withdrew, Alonso muscled past Grosjean at Turn 2 and, further around the lap, the crowd went wild when Vettel slowed to a halt with alternator failure

VALENCIA ROUND 8

DATE: **24 June 2012**

Laps: **57** • Distance: **191.931 miles/308.883km** • Weather: **Hot & bright**

Pos	Driver	Team	Result	Stops	Qualifying Time	Grid
1	Fernando Alonso	Ferrari	1h44m16.649s	2	1m38.707s	11
2	Kimi Raikkonen	Lotus	1h44m23.070s	2	1m38.513s	5
3	Michael Schumacher	Mercedes	1h44m29.288s	2	1m38.770s	12
4	Mark Webber	Red Bull	1h44m30.811s	2	1m40.395s	19
5	Nico Hulkenberg	Force India	1h44m36.642s	2	1m38.992s	8
6	Nico Rosberg	Mercedes	1h44m37.825s	2	1m38.623s	6
7	Paul di Resta	Force India	1h44m39.515s	1	1m38.992s	10
8	Jenson Button	McLaren	1h44m41.302s	2	1m38.801s	9
9	Sergio Perez	Sauber	1h44m44.426s	2	1m39.358s	15
10	Bruno Senna	Williams	1h44m52.610s	1	1m39.207s	14
11	Daniel Ricciardo	Toro Rosso	1h44m53.690s	2	1m40.358s	17
12	Pastor Maldonado	Williams	1h45m11.279s*	2	1m38.475s	3
13	Vitaly Petrov	Caterham	1h45m32.520s	4	1m40.457s	20
14	Heikki Kovalainen	Caterham	1h45m51.303s	2	1m40.295s	16
15	Charles Pic	Marussia	1h45m53.200s	2	1m42.675s	23
16	Felipe Massa	Ferrari	56 laps		1m38.780s	13
17	Pedro de la Rosa	HRT	56 laps	2	1m42.171s	21
18	Narain Karthikeyan	HRT	56 laps	2	1m42.527s	22
19	Lewis Hamilton	McLaren	55 laps/accident	2	1m38.410s	2
R	Romain Grosjean	Lotus	40 laps/alternator	2	1m38.505s	4
R	Sebastian Vettel	Red Bull	33 laps/alternator	2	1m38.086s	1
R	Kamui Kobayashi	Sauber	33 laps/crash damage	2	1m38.741s	7
R	Jean-Eric Vergne	Toro Rosso	26 laps/crash damage	1	1m40.203s	18
NS	Timo Glock	Marussia	0 laps/driver unwell	-	No time	-

FASTEST LAP: ROSBERG, 1M42.163S, 118.658MPH/190.962KPH ON LAP 54 • **RACE LEADERS:** VETTEL 1–33; ALONSO 34–57 • * 20S PENALTY FOR CAUSING A COLLISION

Second place from 11th would have been a good result for Alonso, then Vettel retired.

and their hero assumed the lead. It was a lead that he wasn't to lose. Life became easier still when Grosjean pulled off, also with alternator failure. Then Hamilton clashed with Maldonado with two laps to go, allowing Raikkonen to take second. Michael Schumacher also benefited from the clash and claimed the first podium of his F1 return.

The sun doesn't always shine on Formula One and qualifying
for the 2012 British GP was held in dramatically wet conditions.
This is Sebastian Vettel splashing through the Vale.

BRITISH GP

It was a wet and windy meeting, but race day remained dry, and Mark Webber chased after Fernando Alonso's Ferrari and passed him to take victory and give Red Bull Racing a boost after its disappointment at losing out to Ferrari in Valencia.

This was a topsy-turvy event, but Mark Webber wasn't complaining as he was the one who had come out on top and had done so with some determined driving that saw him catch and pass championship leader Fernando Alonso.

To say that the weather conditions were foul in qualifying is a considerable understatement, as the rain became torrential, causing a 90-minute delay in proceedings. The biggest winner in this was Alonso, who timed his runs well and so claimed pole position. Conversely, it all went wrong for Jenson Button, who failed even to get into even Q2, the result of gambling on the track drying but waiting too long and finding it wetter than before.

On race day, Alonso led away, in the dry, from Mark Webber, with Michael Schumacher third and Felipe Massa passing Sebastian Vettel for fourth. Behind them, Romain Grosjean and Paul di Resta clashed, with the Scot suffering suspension damage and the Frenchman damaging his front wing.

As long as no rain blew in, the drivers would be running two-stop races and it was Vettel who came in first as Red Bull sought to get away from the Schumacher/Massa tussle that had been delaying him.

Webber pitted before Alonso, on lap 14, then Alonso followed him in next time around. Hamilton, who had been running eighth, then led for three laps before pitting and falling back to seventh. This left Alonso leading again from Webber, with Vettel third.

At the second round of stops, the order remained the same. But, vitally, Webber was faster on his third set of tyres, a used set of hard rubber, than Alonso was on his softs. The gap came down and down. Then, on lap 48 of 52, the Australian took the lead, going past at the end of the Wellington Straight, having used his DRS to good effect. With tyres past their best, Alonso had no response. Vettel came home third, his car's handling compromised by having damaged a front wing against Massa in the

Mark Webber chased and passed Fernando Alonso's Ferrari to score his second win of 2012.

SILVERSTONE ROUND 9

DATE: **8 July 2012**

Laps: **52** • Distance: **190.262 miles/306.198km** • Weather: **Warm & sunny**

Pos	Driver	Team	Result	Stops	Qualifying Time	Grid
1	**Mark Webber**	Red Bull	1h25m11.288s	2	1m51.793s	2
2	**Fernando Alonso**	Ferrari	1h25m14.348s	2	1m51.746s	1
3	**Sebastian Vettel**	Red Bull	1h25m16.124s	2	1m52.199s	4
4	**Felipe Massa**	Ferrari	1h25m20.807s	2	1m53.065s	5
5	**Kimi Raikkonen**	Lotus	1h25m21.602s	2	1m53.290s	6
6	**Romain Grosjean**	Lotus	1h25m28.389s	2	No time	9
7	**Michael Schumacher**	Mercedes	1h25m40.441s	2	1m52.020s	3
8	**Lewis Hamilton**	McLaren	1h25m47.751s	2	1m53.543s	8
9	**Bruno Senna**	Williams	1h25m54.635s	2	1m57.426s	13
10	**Jenson Button**	McLaren	1h25m55.732s	2	1m48.044s	16
11	**Kamui Kobayashi**	Sauber	1h25m56.658s	2	1m57.071s	17*
12	**Nico Hulkenberg**	Force India	1h25m59.144s	2	1m54.382s	14*
13	**Daniel Ricciardo**	Toro Rosso	1h26m02.529s	2	1m57.132s	12
14	**Jean-Eric Vergne**	Toro Rosso	1h26m04.601s	2	1m57.719s	23**
15	**Nico Rosberg**	Mercedes	1h26m08.682s	2	1m57.108s	11
16	**Pastor Maldonado**	Williams	51 laps	2	1m53.539s	7
17	**Heikki Kovalainen**	Caterham	51 laps	2	1m49.477s	19
18	**Timo Glock**	Marussia	51 laps	2	1m51.618s	20
19	**Charles Pic**	Marussia	51 laps	2	1m54.143s	24*
20	**Pedro de la Rosa**	HRT	50 laps	1	1m52.742s	21
21	**Narain Karthikeyan**	HRT	50 laps	2	1m53.040s	22
R	**Sergio Perez**	Sauber	11 laps/accident	2	1m57.895s	15
R	**Paul di Resta**	Force India	2 laps/suspension	1	1m57.009s	10
NS	**Vitaly Petrov**	Caterham	0 laps/engine	0	1m49.027s	18

FASTEST LAP: RAIKKONEN, 1M34.661S, 139.2171MPH/224.048KPH ON LAP 50 • RACE LEADERS: ALONSO 1-15, 19-47; HAMILTON 16-18; WEBBER 48-52
• * 5-PLACE GRID PENALTY ** 10-PLACE GRID PENALTY

opening laps. The Brazilian finished five seconds back in fourth after his best run in a long time, with Raikkonen close behind in fifth. McLaren fans were disappointed, as a

decision to run Hamilton for only a seven-lap second stint didn't work and he fell to eighth, passed late in the race by Schumacher. Button could advance only to 10th place.

GERMAN GP

The start to Fernando Alonso's season had been patchy, but strong mid-season form for Ferrari was turning him into a winning machine, and the way that he controlled this race from pole showed that he was going to be hard to catch.

Fernando Alonso was able to bask in this victory, unlike the one he claimed on the championship's previous visit to Hockenheim, in 2010. On that occasion team-mate Felipe Massa had been told to move aside to let him through to win.

Alonso led away from Sebastian Vettel, with grid order being maintained behind by Michael Schumacher and Nico Hulkenberg, who had really impressed by qualifying fourth for Force India. Pastor Maldonado was pushed back to sixth on the opening lap by Jenson Button, who had been given cause for hope by modified sidepods and a new exhaust being fitted to his McLaren, then picked off Hulkenberg and Schumacher through the opening stint and would remain third after their pit stops.

Alonso's early advantage over Vettel began to be whittled down, but then, just as he was closing in at around mid-distance, Vettel was instructed to back off his KERS, which was starting to fail, leaving him practically slowest of all through the speedtrap down the curving straight to Spitzkehre.

This allowed Alonso to ease clear again and Button to close in. Button was then the first of this trio to make a second pit stop, on lap 40, with Alonso and Vettel coming in next time around. However, to Vettel's surprise and disappointment he failed to get back out before Button had flashed past, the McLaren driver having made the undercut work.

Button homed in on Alonso, but couldn't find a way past and then found that he'd exhausted his tyres, which allowed Alonso to cruise to his third victory of 2012. Vettel wanted second place back and made his move at the Spitzkehre with two laps to go. He ran around the outside of the McLaren at the hairpin and took the place, but did so only by running with all four wheels off the circuit, for which he was hit with a 20-second penalty after the race, dropping him to fifth and promoting Button, Raikkonen and Kamui Kobayashi to second, third and fourth.

HOCKENHEIM ROUND 10

DATE: 22 July 2012

Laps: 67 • Distance: 190.433 miles/306.473km • Weather: Dry & bright

Pos	Driver	Team	Result	Stops	Qualifying Time	Grid
1	Fernando Alonso	Ferrari	1h31m05.862s	2	1m40.621s	1
2	Jenson Button	McLaren	1h31m12.811s	2	1m44.113s	6
3	Kimi Raikkonen	Lotus	1h31m22.271s	2	1m45.811s	10
4	Kamui Kobayashi	Sauber	1h31m27.787s	2	1m39.985s	12
5	Sebastian Vettel	Red Bull	1h31m29.594s**	2	1m41.025s	2
6	Sergio Perez	Sauber	1h31m33.756ss	2	1m39.933s	17*
7	Michael Schumacher	Mercedes	1h31m34.832s	3	1m42.459s	3
8	Mark Webber	Red Bull	1h31m52.803s	2	1m41.496s	8*
9	Nico Hulkenberg	Force India	1h31m54.024s	3	1m43.501s	4
10	Nico Rosberg	Mercedes	1h31m54.751s	3	1m41.551s	21*
11	Paul di Resta	Force India	1h32m05.089s	2	1m44.889s	9
12	Felipe Massa	Ferrari	1h32m17.290s	3	1m40.212s	13
13	Daniel Ricciardo	Toro Rosso	1h32m22.691s	2	1m39.789s	11
14	Jean-Eric Vergne	Toro Rosso	1h32m22.827s	3	1m16.741s	15
15	Pastor Maldonado	Williams	66 laps	3	1m43.950s	5
16	Vitaly Petrov	Caterham	66 laps	3	1m18.531s	18
17	Bruno Senna	Williams	66 laps	3	1m40.752s	14
18	Romain Grosjean	Lotus	66 laps	3	1m40.754s	19*
19	Heikki Kovalainen	Caterham	65 laps	4	1m17.620s	16
20	Charles Pic	Marussia	65 laps	2	1m19.220s	20
21	Pedro de la Rosa	HRT	64 laps	2	1m19.912s	23
22	Timo Glock	Marussia	64 laps	2	1m19.291s	22
23	Narain Karthikeyan	HRT	64 laps	2	1m20.230s	24
R	Lewis Hamilton	McLaren	56 laps/handling	3	1m44.186s	7

FASTEST LAP: SCHUMACHER, 1M18.725S, 129.968MPH/209.164KPH ON LAP 57 • RACE LEADERS: ALONSO 1-17, 21-67; VETTEL 18-20 • * 5-PLACE GRID PENALTY ** 20S POST-RACE PENALTY FOR OVERTAKING OFF THE CIRCUIT

Fernando Alonso was chased by Jenson Button until the McLaren driver's tyres went off.

At a time when his tenure of the second Ferrari seat for 2013 was under increasing discussion, Massa did little to promote his case by spinning in qualifying to line up 13th, then ripping his front wing off against Daniel Ricciardo's Toro Rosso on lap 1. This dropped him to 22nd and he could only climb back to 12th.

HUNGARIAN GP

McLaren's form was really on the up in this final race before Formula One's summer recess, and Lewis Hamilton qualified on pole before racing to victory on a circuit where he has always shone, this time shadowed by the Lotus duo.

As at Monaco, where the circuit is narrow and offers next to nothing in the way of overtaking opportunities, qualifying on pole position has always been extra desirable at the Hungaroring for similar reasons.

So it was with great satisfaction that Lewis Hamilton climbed from his McLaren after qualifying, for he had not only taken pole, but he had done so by 0.403s, a considerable margin anywhere, but especially on a circuit with a lap as short as this one. Better still, the driver behind him on the grid was Lotus racer Romain Grosjean rather than points leader Fernando Alonso or either of the Red Bull Racing drivers. Indeed, Alonso was only sixth, behind Sebastian Vettel, Jenson Button and Kimi Raikkonen, with Mark Webber back in 11th.

Hamilton was so determined to lead into Turn 1 that he braked late, but still managed to negotiate the dipping right-hander in front, as a fast-starting Vettel was too busy fighting Grosjean to go down the inside. Vettel then was pushed wide and Button took no second bidding to benefit from the German's loss of momentum at the following corner. Alonso also gained a place, passing Raikkonen, who found that his Lotus's KERS was not working.

Button was called in for an early first pit stop, suggesting that the team had decided that he would be three-stopping. His rivals stayed out longer and, after they had all pitted once, Hamilton was leading from Grosjean and Button. However, Button dropped out of this group when he came in for his second stop at half-distance, falling to eighth when he rejoined. This promoted Vettel to third, but he too was planning to stop three times and dropped to sixth place when he pitted four laps later.

This left Hamilton leading the two Lotuses when they approached their second and final pit stops, nursing his tyres yet able to stay ahead of Grosjean, since passing is all but impossible here and attempting

Lewis Hamilton locks up into the first corner ahead of Sebastian Vettel and Romain Grosjean.

HUNGARORING ROUND 11

DATE: **29 JULY 2012**

Laps: **69** • Distance: **187.808 miles/302.248km** • Weather: **Hot & sunny**

Pos	Driver	Team	Result	Stops	Qualifying Time	Grid
1	**Lewis Hamilton**	McLaren	1h41m05.503s	2	1m20.953s	1
2	**Kimi Raikkonen**	Lotus	1h41m06.535s	2	1m21.730s	5
3	**Romain Grosjean**	Lotus	1h41m16.021s	2	1m21.366s	2
4	**Sebastian Vettel**	Red Bull	1h41m17.117s	3	1m21.416s	3
5	**Fernando Alonso**	Ferrari	1h41m32.156s	2	1m21.844s	6
6	**Jenson Button**	McLaren	1h41m35.746s	3	1m21.583s	4
7	**Bruno Senna**	Williams	1h41m39.402s	2	1m22.343s	9
8	**Mark Webber**	Red Bull	1h41m39.961s	3	1m21.715s	11
9	**Felipe Massa**	Ferrari	1h41m43.853s	2	1m21.900s	7
10	**Nico Rosberg**	Mercedes	1h41m56.737s	2	1m21.895s	13
11	**Nico Hulkenberg**	Force India	1h42m02.786s	2	1m22.847s	10
12	**Paul di Resta**	Force India	1h42m08.390s	2	1m21.813s	12
13	**Pastor Maldonado**	Williams	1h42m09.109s	3	1m21.939s	8
14	**Sergio Perez**	Sauber	1h42m09.997s	2	1m21.895s	14
15	**Daniel Ricciardo**	Toro Rosso	68 laps	3	1m23.250s	18
16	**Jean-Eric Vergne**	Toro Rosso	68 laps	4	1m22.380s	16
17	**Heikki Kovalainen**	Caterham	68 laps	3	1m23.576s	19
18	**Kamui Kobayashi**	Sauber	67 laps/hydraulics	2	1m22.300s	15
19	**Vitaly Petrov**	Caterham	67 laps	3	1m24.167s	20
20	**Charles Pic**	Marussia	67 laps	2	1m25.244s	21
21	**Timo Glock**	Marussia	66 laps	2	1m25.476s	22
22	**Pedro de la Rosa**	HRT	66 laps	2	1m25.916s	23
R	**Narain Karthikeyan**	HRT	60 laps/Steering	2	1m26.1786s	24
R	**Michael Schumacher**	Mercedes	58 laps/Engine	3	1m22.723s	17

FASTEST LAP: VETTEL, 1M24.136S, 116.478MPH/187.454KPH ON LAP 68 • **RACE LEADERS:** HAMILTON 1-17, 21-40, 46-69; GROSJEAN 18-19; RAIKKONEN 20, 41-45

to undercut a car ahead by pitting earlier could lead to coming back out into traffic and thus losing all benefit.

Grosjean then lost his chance of victory with a slow pit stop and was just unable to

pass the pit exit before Raikkonen emerged from his second stop, almost losing a place to Vettel as the Lotuses negotiated Turn 1 side by side. The Finn then closed in on Hamilton but simply couldn't find a way past.

BELGIAN GP

This race will always be remembered for the huge first-corner accident in which Fernando Alonso was lucky to keep his head as Romain Grosjean flew over him. This all happened behind Jenson Button, who was a serene victor, in control from restart to finish.

The images of Romain Grosjean riding over the top of Fernando Alonso's Ferrari, crossing just in front of his helmet, are scary ones. The other drivers said that enough was enough, this was an accident too far, and the Frenchman was duly banned for a race.

Starting eighth, the Lotus racer had made a good start, went outside Lewis Hamilton's McLaren, then continued to move across, forcing it towards the pit wall. They clashed and Grosjean hit Alonso's Ferrari, then both clattered into Sergio Perez's Sauber before Grosjean's Lotus hit the Ferrari again and this time rode up and over it, with Hamilton's McLaren going over Kamui Kobayashi in the other Sauber and then thumping Alonso when the Ferrari was spun around.

All of this masked a blatant jump-start by Pastor Maldonado, going from sixth to second, but he got away with this as the red flags were flown, so the drivers would have to do it all again. In fact, he'd been delayed himself by spinning out of the hairpin.

At the second time of asking, with Alonso, Grosjean, Hamilton and Perez missing, Button led away from Kimi Raikkonen, who was soon passed by Nico Hulkenberg up the hill to Les Combes. Button was able to eke out a lead and Raikkonen couldn't respond, being bottled up behind the Force India. Then Raikkonen's day got worse as his tyres lost grip and Michael Schumacher motored past him. An early pit stop confirmed that the Finn would be running a two-stop strategy, and this was great news for Button as he was planning to stop just once.

Sebastian Vettel qualified only 10th and, by dint of running a one-stop strategy like Button, he was nowhere in the early laps, then advanced as the two-stoppers pitted, to reach second place by lap 19. After his lone pit stop, taken a lap after Button's, he ran sixth, but the key to his result would be where he was after the others had made their second stops. The answer was second, and there he stayed, finishing 13 seconds behind Button

SPA-FRANCORCHAMPS ROUND 12   DATE: 2 SEPTEMBER 2012

Laps: **44** • Distance: **191.414 miles/308.052km** • Weather: **Sunny & warm**

Pos	Driver	Team	Result	Stops	Qualifying Time	Grid
1	Jenson Button	McLaren	1h29m08.530s	1	1m47.573s	1
2	Sebastian Vettel	Red Bull	1h29m22.154s	1	1m48.792s	10
3	Kimi Raikkonen	Lotus	1h29m33.864s	2	1m48.205s	3
4	Nico Hulkenberg	Force India	1h29m36.373s	2	1m48.855s	11
5	Felipe Massa	Ferrari	1h29m38.375s	2	1m49.147s	14
6	Mark Webber	Red Bull	1h29m39.774s	2	1m48.392s	12
7	Michael Schumacher	Mercedes	1h30m01.904s	2	1m49.081s	13
8	Jean-Eric Vergne	Toro Rosso	1h30m07.395s	2	1m49.354s	15
9	Daniel Ricciardo	Toro Rosso	1h30m11.512s	2	1m49.543s	16
10	Paul di Resta	Force India	1h30m12.313s	2	1m48.890s	9
11	Nico Rosberg	Mercedes	1h30m13.641s	2	1m50.181s	23**
12	Bruno Senna	Williams	1h30m20.059s	2	1m50.088s	17
13	Kamui Kobayashi	Sauber	1h31m04.649s	3	1m47.876ls	2
14	Vitaly Petrov	Caterham	43 laps	2	1m51.967s	19
15	Timo Glock	Marussia	43 laps	2	1m52.336s	20
16	Charles Pic	Marussia	43 laps	1	1m53.493s	22
17	Heikki Kovalainen	Caterham	43 laps	2	1m51.739s	18
18	Pedro de la Rosa	HRT	43 laps	3	1m53.030s	21
R	Narain Karthikeyan	HRT	29 laps/accident	2	1m54.989s	24
R	Pastor Maldonado	Williams	4 laps/accident	1	1m47.893s	6*
R	Sergio Perez	Sauber	0 laps/accident	0	1m48.219s	4
R	Fernando Alonso	Ferrari	0 laps/accident	0	1m48.313s	5
R	Lewis Hamilton	McLaren	0 laps/accident	0	1m48.394s	7
R	Romain Grosjean	Lotus	0 laps/accident	0	1m48.538s	8

FASTEST LAP: SENNA, 1M52.822S, 138.869MPH/223.488KPH ON LAP 43 • RACE LEADERS: BUTTON 1–44 • * 3-PLACE GRID PENALTY ** 5-PLACE GRID PENALTY

Romain Grosjean shows how not to do it as he flies his Lotus over Fernando Alonso's Ferrari.

but 12 seconds ahead of Raikkonen with Hulkenberg close behind.

Maldonado doubled his embarrassment as he completed only four laps before

hitting Marussia's Timo Glock at La Source on the first lap after the field was released by the safety car, and the damage would force him out a few laps later.

ITALIAN GP

The media all wanted a slice of Lewis Hamilton at Monza, but the main issue for them before the race was his indecision regarding his team for 2013. By Sunday afternoon, he was happy to talk, but only about his dominant victory.

McLaren's charge through the second half of the season continued apace at Monza. Ferrari had looked strong but failed to deliver, with Alonso's run hampered by a broken rear roll bar that left him 10th on the grid. So it was that Lewis Hamilton and Jenson Button filled the front row, with Felipe Massa starting third, his best grid position for ages, amid growing speculation about whether he would keep his Ferrari drive for 2013.

Massa made a storming getaway, splitting the McLarens and even making a bid to pass Hamilton at the first chicane. Hamilton, though, kept him out wide and forced the Brazilian to lift off the throttle a fraction and so tuck in to second place. Alonso was also on the move, up to sixth past Paul di Resta, Nico Rosberg, Kamui Kobayashi and Kimi Raikkonen by the start of lap 2.

With Michael Schumacher struggling for grip in fourth, the leading trio escaped. Sebastian Vettel moved into fourth on lap 4, then caught Button. Three laps later, Alonso passed him too. Yet the driver moving up the order fastest was Sergio Perez, who had started 12th, as one of just four drivers on the harder tyre, but by lap 8 was up to eighth. He then held ground, before gaining a further place when Schumacher was first to pit, and another when Raikkonen followed him in, and stayed out as everyone else came in for fresh rubber, taking the lead when Hamilton pitted on lap 23. Perez pitted six laps later and rejoined in eighth, but he and all the others moved up one place when Button retired from second on lap 33, with fuel pick-up problems snuffing out his slim title aspirations.

Another driver in trouble before then was Alonso, who was edged out on to the grass by Vettel, holing the floor of his Ferrari and bending a damper mount. Vettel would collect a drive-through penalty for this, while Alonso motored on, his handling never as good again. On lap 40, Massa let him

Massa split the McLarens into the first chicane but could do nothing about Hamilton.

MONZA ROUND 13
DATE: **9 SEPTEMBER 2012**

Laps: **53** • Distance: **190.800 miles/307.063km** • Weather: **Dry & warm**

Pos	Driver	Team	Result	Stops	Qualifying Time	Grid
1	Lewis Hamilton	McLaren	1h19m41.221s	1	1m24.010s	1
2	Sergio Perez	Sauber	1h19m45.577s	1	1m24.901s	12
3	Fernando Alonso	Ferrari	1h20m01.815s	1	1m25.678s	10
4	Felipe Massa	Ferrari	1h20m10.888s	1	1m24.247s	3
5	Kimi Raikkonen	Lotus	1h20m12.102s	1	1m24.855s	7
6	Michael Schumacher	Mercedes	1h20m12.480s	2	1m24.540s	4
7	Nico Rosberg	Mercedes	1h20m14.771s	2	1m24.833s	6
8	Paul di Resta	Force India	1h20m22.278s	1	1m24.304s	9*
9	Kamui Kobayashi	Sauber	1h20m25.119s	1	1m25.109s	8
10	Bruno Senna	Williams	1h20m29.365s	1	1m25.042s	13
11	Pastor Maldonado	Williams	1h20m29.903s	2	1m24.820s	22**
12	Daniel Ricciardo	Toro Rosso	1h20m31.537s	1	1m25.312s	14
13	Jerome d'Ambrosio	Lotus	1h20m57.082s	1	1m25.408s	15
14	Heikki Kovalainen	Caterham	52 laps	2	1m26.382s	17
15	Vitaly Petrov	Caterham	52 laps	2	1m26.887s	18
16	Charles Pic	Marussia	52 laps	2	1m27.073s	20
17	Timo Glock	Marussia	52 laps	2	1m27.039s	19
18	Pedro de la Rosa	HRT	52 laps	1	1m27.629s	23
19	Narain Karthikeyan	HRT	52 laps	1	1m27.441s	21
R	Mark Webber	Red Bull	51 laps/tyre damage	1	1m24.809s	11
R	Nico Hulkenberg	Force India	50 laps/brakes	1	No time	24
R	Sebastian Vettel	Red Bull	47 laps/alternator	2	1m24.802s	5
R	Jenson Button	McLaren	32 laps/fuel pick-up	1	1m24.133s	2
R	Jean-Eric Vergne	Toro Rosso	8 laps/accident	0	1m25.441s	16

FASTEST LAP: ROSBERG, 1M27.239S, 148.540MPH/239.053KPH ON LAP 53 • RACE LEADERS: HAMILTON 1-23, 29–53; PEREZ 24–28 • 5-PLACE GRID PENALTY ** 10-PLACE GRID PENALTY

by for second, as Hamilton cruised in the lead, but Alonso wasn't to keep this place as Perez closed in and went past into Ascari on lap 46.

Victory helped Hamilton move into second spot in the title race but third place for the Spaniard meant he was still more than a win in front.

SINGAPORE GP

This should have been a famous victory for Lewis Hamilton, but gearbox failure handed it instead to Sebastian Vettel and so changed the complexion of the title battle, as promotion to third place kept Fernando Alonso in the driving seat.

McLaren's late-season ascendancy was shown for the second race in succession by Lewis Hamilton qualifying on pole position and leading away from the starting grid. For him, however, unlike at Monza, this one didn't have the desired result as he started lap 23 in the lead, shadowed by Sebastian Vettel, yet didn't complete it, his gearbox giving up the ghost.

And so not only did Red Bull's Vettel inherit the lead and race on to win as he pleased, but the balance of power in the title race swung away from the English racer, his failure to score leaving him languishing 45 points off Fernando Alonso's championship lead. Had they finished as they were, that gap would have come down to 22.

As Marina Bay is a street circuit, and there isn't the track width that makes for easy overtaking, qualifying on pole is the first hurdle cleared. So Hamilton had reason to be pleased when he outpaced Pastor Maldonado *et al* on the Saturday evening. Then, at the start, he put his McLaren's nose ahead and kept it there. The Williams racer wasn't so successful, muscled out of the way by Vettel, and falling behind Jenson Button as well before the lap was out. Felipe Massa, starting from 13th, was forced to pit at the end of lap 1 with a puncture but fought back up to score.

Unflustered at the front, his MP4-27 clearly using its tyres less heavily than his rivals as he made his first pit stop later than they did, Hamilton was cruising.

After the leading McLaren pulled over, the outcome of the race was given another twist when the safety car was deployed from lap 31 to 37 after Narain Karthikeyan slammed his HRT into a wall. This enabled the drivers of the tyre-hungry Red Bulls and Ferraris to change from a three-stop to a two-stop strategy, and, better still for them, Maldonado retired. Then, no sooner had the race gone green again than the safety car was redeployed, this time because Michael Schumacher had slammed into the rear of Jean-Eric Vergne's Toro Rosso. Once this was cleared, Vettel was able to motor clear of Button, with Alonso off the pace but delighted to finish third to keep his momentum. Less than four seconds back, Paul di Resta scored a career-best fourth.

MARINA BAY ROUND 14

DATE: 23 SEPTEMBER 2012

Laps: **59** • Distance: **185.980 miles/299.306km** • Weather: **Hot & humid**

Pos	Driver	Team	Result	Stops	Qualifying Time	Grid
1	Sebastian Vettel	Red Bull	2h00m26.144s	2	1m46.905s	3
2	Jenson Button	McLaren	2h00m35.103s	2	1m46.939s	4
3	Fernando Alonso	Ferrari	2h00m41.371s	2	1m47.216s	5
4	Paul di Resta	Force India	2h00m45.207s	2	1m47.241s	6
5	Nico Rosberg	Mercedes	2h01m00.928s	2	No time	10
6	Kimi Raikkonen	Lotus	2h01m01.903s	2	1m48.261s	12
7	Romain Grosjean	Lotus	2h01m02.842s	2	1m47.788s	8
8	Felipe Massa	Ferrari	2h01m08.973s	3	1m48.344s	13
9	Daniel Ricciardo	Toro Rosso	2h01m11.964s	2	1m48.774s	15
10	Sergio Perez	Sauber	2h01m16.763s	2	1m48.505s	14
11	Mark Webber	Red Bull	2h01m33.319s*	3	1m47.475s	7
12	Timo Glock	Marussia	2h01m58.062s	2	1m51.370s	20
13	Kamui Kobayashi	Sauber	2h02m03.285s	3	1m49.933s	17
14	Nico Hulkenberg	Force India	2h02m05.557s	3	1m47.975s	11
15	Heikki Kovalainen	Caterham	2h02m14.111s	3	1m51.137s	19
16	Charles Pic	Marussia	2h02m39.069s*	2	1m51.762s	21
17	Pedro de la Rosa	HRT	58 laps	3	1m53.355s	24**
18	Bruno Senna	Williams	58 laps/engine	3	No time	22**
19	Vitaly Petrov	Caterham	57 laps	4	1m50.846s	18
R	Jean-Eric Vergne	Toro Rosso	38 laps/accident	2	1m48.849s	16
R	Michael Schumacher	Mercedes	38 laps/accident	2	No time	9
R	Pastor Maldonado	Williams	36 laps/hydraulics	3	1m46.804s	2
R	Narain Karthikeyan	HRT	30 laps/spun off	1	1m52.372s	23
R	Lewis Hamilton	McLaren	22 laps/gearbox	1	1m46.362s	1

FASTEST LAP: HULKENBERG, 1M51.003S, 102.203MPH/164.480KPH ON LAP 52 RACE LEADERS: HAMILTON 1–11, 15–22; BUTTON 12–14; VETTEL 23–59
• * 20S PENALTY ** 5-PLACE GRID PENALTY

Race winner Sebastian Vettel was the beneficiary of Lewis Hamilton's retirement.

JAPANESE GP

For Sebastian Vettel it was the perfect result in more ways than one, as not only did he lead every lap from pole, set fastest lap and win the race, but title rival Fernando Alonso was taken out at the first corner on lap 1.

Fernando Alonso arrived at Suzuka knowing that he didn't have the best car and that, although he had a 29-point advantage over Sebastian Vettel with six races to run, he was certainly going to need some luck if both the Red Bulls and the McLarens proved faster again.

Starting from seventh on the grid wasn't great, Alonzo being pushed back by both Sauber drivers out-qualifying him. Fortunately, this became sixth when a gearbox change forced Jenson Button back from third to eighth, with the Red Bulls locking out the front row. However, this all became immaterial as they arrived at the first corner and the Spaniard spun out of the race with a puncture after being clipped by Kimi Raikkonen's Lotus as they turned in.

What would have made it all the more galling for Alonso was that a couple of cars ahead of him were also in trouble and he would have benefited from their demise, had he been allowed to do so. Romain Grosjean had been at it again, notching up his seventh first-corner accident of the season by hitting Mark Webber and pitching him into a spin. At least the Australian was able to rejoin, unlike Alonso.

Grosjean had to pit for a 10-second stop-go penalty. Another casualty was Nico Rosberg, who got only as far as Turn 2 before he was hit by Bruno Senna's Williams.

There were no such problems for Vettel as he led the early laps, pulling clear of the driver who was sending the fans wild with excitement, Kamui Kobayashi. The Japanese driver's future with Sauber was in the balance, so this was his moment to stake his claim and he was taking his chance to shine well, followed by Button, Felipe Massa (another driver looking to cement his drive for 2013), and Raikkonen. Behind them, there was a lively battle between Lewis Hamilton and Sergio Perez, with the English driver declaring the Mexican "crazy" for one of his moves.

Massa, Vettel and Kobayashi all had reason to feel delighted with their afternoon's racing.

SUZUKA ROUND 15

DATE: 7 OCTOBER 2012

Laps: 53 • Distance: **191.224 miles/307.746km** • Weather: **Dry & bright**

Pos	Driver	Team	Result	Stops	Qualifying Time	Grid
1	Sebastian Vettel	Red Bull	1h28m56.242s	2	1m30.839s	1
2	Felipe Massa	Ferrari	1h29m16.881s	2	1h32.293s	10
3	Kamui Kobayashi	Sauber	1h29m20.780s	2	1m31.700s	3
4	Jenson Button	McLaren	1h29m21.340s	2	1m31.290s	8*
5	Lewis Hamilton	McLaren	1h29m42.732s	2	1m32.327s	9
6	Kimi Raikkonen	Lotus	1h29m46.666s	2	1m32.208s	7
7	Nico Hulkenberg	Force India	1h29m47.401s	2	No time	15*
8	Pastor Maldonado	Williams	1h29m48.606s	2	1m32.512s	12
9	Mark Webber	Red Bull	1h29m50.917s	2	1m31.090s	2
10	Daniel Ricciardo	Toro Rosso	1h30m03.161s	2	1m32.954s	14
11	Michael Schumacher	Mercedes	1h30m04.011s	2	1m32.469s	23**
12	Paul di Resta	Force India	1h30m19.702s	2	1m32.327s	11
13	Jean-Eric Vergne	Toro Rosso	1h30m24.887s	2	1m33.368s	19†
14	Bruno Senna	Williams	1h30m24.951s	3	1m33.405s	16
15	Heikki Kovalainen	Caterham	52 laps	2	1m34.657s	17
16	Timo Glock	Marussia	52 laps	2	1m35.213s	18
17	Vitaly Petrov	Caterham	52 laps	3	1m35.432s	22
18	Pedro de la Rosa	HRT	52 laps	2	1m35.385s	20
19	Romain Grosjean	Lotus	51 laps/gearbox	2	1m31.898s	4
R	Charles Pic	Marussia	37 laps/engine	2	1m35.429s	21
R	Narain Karthikeyan	HRT	32 laps/chassis	1	1m36.734s	24
R	Sergio Perez	Sauber	18 laps/spun off	1	1m332.022s	5
R	Fernando Alonso	Ferrari	0 laps/accident	0	1m32.114s	6
R	Nico Rosberg	Mercedes	0 laps/accident	0	1m32.625s	13

FASTEST LAP: VETTEL, 1M35.774S, 135.630MPH/218.276KPH ON LAP 52 • RACE LEADERS: VETTEL 1–53 • † 3-PLACE GRID PENALTY * 5-PLACE GRID PENALTY ** 10-PLACE GRID PENALTY

The first round of pit stops went well for Massa as he was able to emerge second, with Kobayashi and Button dropping to third and fourth. Hamilton then moved on to Button's tail but came under attack from Perez, who spun off at the hairpin when he tried a passing move. No one could touch Vettel, though, and the greatest excitement in the closing laps was Kobayashi managing to resist Button's best efforts to claim third.

KOREAN GP

Sebastian Vettel arrived in Korea with two wins in a row to his name, and the long journey out from the capital to Yeongam was made worthwhile when he added a third. Red Bull Racing had introduced new parts that made the RB8s faster still as they locked out a one-two finish.

The modifications in question centred on a new sidepod layout, introduced with the express aim of adding downforce and also stalling the diffuser. Technical chief Adrian Newey reckoned that these modifications were worth a couple of tenths of a second as the extra rear downforce helped to balance the car, and this could easily have been so as Mark Webber took pole for the team and Sebastian Vettel lined up outside him on the grid, having qualified less than a tenth of a second slower. The best of the rest was McLaren's Lewis Hamilton, a further tenth in arrears.

At the start of the race, Vettel made a better getaway than Webber and dived up the inside of the Australian into Turn 1. That was it, he was into the lead, and it was soon clear that his rivals would be unable to do anything about it as his RB8 maintained the advantage that it had displayed in qualifying.

Hamilton had hoped to take advantage of Webber's slow start too but, as he looked for a way past on the outside, so Fernando Alonso pushed his Ferrari up the inside to grab third. Echoing this gain for Ferrari, Felipe Massa demoted Kimi Raikkonen's Lotus to slot into fifth place at Turn 3.

Much as Romain Grosjean had assaulted Fernando Alonso at Spa, so Kamui Kobayashi thumped Nico Rosberg's Mercedes, also at Turn 3, then bounced across and collected Jenson Button, forcing the McLaren driver out of the race. Matters were far calmer at the front and Vettel was able to stretch away.

The Yeongam circuit offers passing opportunities into Turn 1 at the start but, during the race, only into Turn 3 and sometimes into Turn 4. So the order remained static from here on, with only Hamilton on the move. Sadly for him this wasn't up the order but down it, as a rear anti-roll bar had broken and his MP4-27's handling deteriorated as a result. His best efforts were rewarded only with 10th place as excessive tyre wear forced him to pit for a third set of tyres.

YEONGAM ROUND 16

DATE: **14 OCTOBER 2012**

Laps: **55** • Distance: **191.783 miles/308.645km** • Weather: **Cloudy but warm**

Pos	Driver	Team	Result	Stops	Qualifying Time	Grid
1	Sebastian Vettel	Red Bull	1h36m28.651s	2	1m37.316s	2
2	Mark Webber	Red Bull	1h36m36.882s	2	1m37.242s	1
3	Fernando Alonso	Ferrari	1h36m42.595s	2	1m37.534s	4
4	Felipe Massa	Ferrari	1h36m48.819s	2	1m37.884s	6
5	Kimi Raikkonen	Lotus	1h37m05.390s	2	1m37.625s	5
6	Nico Hulkenberg	Force India	1h37m13.952s	2	1m38.266s	8
7	Romain Grosjean	Lotus	1h37m23.463s	2	1m37.934s	7
8	Jean-Eric Vergne	Toro Rosso	1h37m38.240s	2	1m39.340s	16
9	Daniel Ricciardo	Toro Rosso	1h37m40.438s	2	1m39.084s	21*
10	Lewis Hamilton	McLaren	1h37m48.343s	3	1m37.469s	3
11	Sergio Perez	Sauber	1h37m48.713s	2	1m38.460s	12
12	Paul di Resta	Force India	1h37m53.099s	2	1m38.643s	14
13	Michael Schumacher	Mercedes	1h37m57.892s	2	1m38.513s	10
14	Pastor Maldonado	Williams	54 laps	1	1m38.725s	15
15	Bruno Senna	Williams	54 laps	2	1m39.443s	17
16	Vitaly Petrov	Caterham	54 laps	2	1m40.207s	18
17	Heikki Kovalainen	Caterham	54 laps	2	1m40.333s	19
18	Timo Glock	Marussia	54 laps	2	1m41.371s	20
19	Charles Pic	Marussia	53 laps	2	1m41.317s	24**
20	Narain Karthikeyan	HRT	53 laps	1	No time	23
R	Pedro de la Rosa	HRT	16 laps/throttle	0	1m42.881s	22
R	Kamui Kobayashi	Sauber	16 laps/crash damage	0	1m38.594s	13
R	Nico Rosberg	Mercedes	1 lap/accident	0	1m38.361s	9
R	Jenson Button	McLaren	0 laps/accident	0	1m38.441s	11

FASTEST LAP: WEBBER, 1M42.037S, 123.102MPH/198.114KPH ON LAP 54 • RACE LEADERS: VETTEL 1–55 • * 5-PLACE GRID PENALTY ** 10-PLACE GRID PENALTY

Chassis modifications helped Sebastian Vettel leave his rivals in his wake as he won.

With Webber unable to catch, let alone pass Vettel, the order at the front remained unchanged and, with Alonso finishing third, the German moved into the championship lead, by six points from the Spaniard. Ferrari's 27-point haul moved it ahead of McLaren in the constructors' championship rankings.

INDIAN GP

Sebastian Vettel made it four wins on the trot, but title challenger Fernando Alonso pulled off the drive of the race as he rose from fifth on the grid to finish second and so keep the title race on the boil.

Red Bull Racing arrived for the second Indian GP on a roll, and the speed of the RB8s in qualifying ensured that they locked out the front row for the third race in a row.

At the start, though, all eyes were trained on Fernando Alonso's pace away from standstill, as he was starting fifth and needed to pass the McLarens and Mark Webber to take a shot at Vettel. While Vettel checked on Webber's position, then claimed the line into the first corner despite the Australian having made a better getaway, Jenson Button powered past Lewis Hamilton. Further back, Jean-Eric Vergne locked up and clouted the rear of Michael Schumacher's Mercedes.

Out of Turn 3, Hamilton got a tow and passed Button for third. Not content to hang around behind the McLarens for long, Alonso also used the slipstream and these three world champions showed their skills in the most mesmerising overtaking and counter-overtaking action through the next few corners, with Button completing lap 1 in third from Alonso, then Hamilton. Helped by this scrapping, the Red Bulls were away and gone.

Three laps later, Alonso used his DRS to pass Button for third down the long straight towards Turn 4. Hamilton followed suit on lap 6 as Button struggled for grip, realising that his MP4-27 was eating its tyres. As a consequence, he was the first of the front-runners to come in for fresh rubber in this one-stop strategy race, but getting stuck behind Romain Grosjean's Lotus on his return to the fray dropped him further behind those setting the pace ahead.

Alonso was next to pit, from third, and he was still third after Webber, Hamilton and then Vettel pitted. This was how it was expected to stay, but Webber was struggling increasingly to get his RB8's KERS to work, which allowed Alonso to hunt him down and pass him to take the extra five points that second place brought and so restrict his points loss to clear winner Vettel. So, with

four wins in a row for the German, the gap between them was now down to 13 points.

The victory was a landmark one for Renault, as it was the 150th time that one of its engines had powered the winning car. Renault's first-ever victory, in 1979, by Jean-Pierre Jabouille, was doubly momentous as it was the first by a turbocharged engine.

Mark Webber holds off Fernando Alonso, but neither could stop Sebastian Vettel.

BUDDH INTERNATIONAL ROUND 17 DATE: 28 OCTOBER 2012

Laps: **60** • Distance: **190.925 miles/307.265km** • Weather: **Warm but overcast**

Pos	Driver	Team	Result	Stops	Qualifying Time	Grid
1	Sebastian Vettel	Red Bull	1h31m10.744s	1	1m25.283s	1
2	Fernando Alonso	Ferrari	1h31m20.181s	1	1m25.773s	5
3	Mark Webber	Red Bull	1h31m23.961s	1	1m25.327s	2
4	Lewis Hamilton	McLaren	1h31m24.683s	1	1m25.544s	3
5	Jenson Button	McLaren	1h31m37.010s	1	1m25.659s	4
6	Felipe Massa	Ferrari	1h31m55.418s	1	1m25.857s	6
7	Kimi Raikkonen	Lotus	1h31m55.971s	1	1m26.236s	7
8	Nico Hulkenberg	Force India	1h32m05.742s	1	1m26.241s	12
9	Romain Grosjean	Lotus	1h32m06.847s	1	1m26.136s	11
10	Bruno Senna	Williams	1h32m25.719s	1	1m26.331s	13
11	Nico Rosberg	Mercedes	1h32m32.438s	1	No time	10
12	Paul di Resta	Force India	1h32m33.559s	1	1m26.989s	16
13	Daniel Ricciardo	Toro Rosso	1h32m36.808s	1	1m26.777s	15
14	Kamui Kobayashi	Sauber	1h32m37.239s	1	1m27.219s	17
15	Jean-Eric Vergne	Toro Rosso	59 laps	2	1m27.525s	18
16	Pastor Maldonado	Williams	59 laps	2	1m26.713s	9
17	Vitaly Petrov	Caterham	59 laps	1	1m28.756s	19
18	Heikki Kovalainen	Caterham	59 laps	1	1m29.500s	20
19	Charles Pic	Marussia	59 laps	1	1m30.662s	24
20	Timo Glock	Marussia	58 laps	1	1m29.613s	21
21	Narain Karthikeyan	HRT	58 laps	1	1m30.593s	23
22	Michael Schumacher	Mercedes	55 laps/gearbox	2	1m26.574s	14
R	Pedro de la Rosa	HRT	42 laps/brakes	1	1m30.592s	22
R	Sergio Perez	Sauber	20 laps/puncture	2	1m26.360s	8

FASTEST LAP: BUTTON, 1M28.203S, 129.982MPH/209.186KPH ON LAP 60 • RACE LEADERS: VETTEL 1-60

ABU DHABI GP

This was a race that came alive due to a varied set of circumstances, leaving Lewis Hamilton frustrated, Kimi Raikkonen less than overjoyed at winning, Fernando Alonso frustrated at coming second and Sebastian Vettel elated at rising from last to third.

McLaren hit top form again as Lewis Hamilton rocketed to a dominant pole position at Yas Marina. He then looked in total control until his car coasted to a halt, as it had in Singapore, leaving him with nothing.

This put Kimi Raikkonen's Lotus into the lead, but the biggest beneficiary really was Fernando Alonso, as it also elevated the Ferrari driver to second place, offering him an even greater haul of points for his championship tally, while points leader Sebastian Vettel was way down the order. The reigning world champion had qualified third fastest, then had his time disallowed as there wasn't enough fuel left in the tank for the scrutineers to take a sample. His penalty was to start from the back of the grid. It was a gift to Alonso, offering him the chance to take the championship lead. However, at the time Hamilton pulled off, Vettel had climbed to 12th place, in spite of a damaged front wing, and was clearly far from finished.

Meanwhile, most eyes were focused on whether Raikkonen could stay in front and so score a victory in his comeback year and also the first for the Lotus name since 1987. His engineer offered some instruction and was slapped down, Kimi saying, "Leave me alone, I know what to do ..." And indeed he did, even though Alonso closed to within one second.

Vettel's charge looked to have stopped when he caught Button yet couldn't pass him, but he found a way at Turn 11 with four laps to go. To say that Alonso was less than delighted to be joined on the podium by his title rival would be an understatement. "Never lift," said Vettel to the team when on the slow-down lap, and he was true to that.

Williams was pleased to have both drivers score, but Pastor Maldonado expected more. He ran third until lap 23, but his hopes of staying there were thwarted when his FW34's KERS failed and he fell to fifth.

Late in the race, Caterham's hopes of overhauling Marussia in the constructors' championship rankings looked good, as

YAS MARINA ROUND 18 — DATE: 4 NOVEMBER 2012
Laps: 55 • Distance: 189.738 miles/305.355km • Weather: Hot & dry

Pos	Driver	Team	Result	Stops	Qualifying Time	Grid
1	Kimi Raikkonen	Lotus	1h45m58.667s	1	1m41.260s	4
2	Fernando Alonso	Ferrari	1h45m59.519s	1	1m41.582s	6
3	Sebastian Vettel	Red Bull	1h46m02.830s	2	No time	24*
4	Jenson Button	McLaren	1h46m06.454s	1	1m41.290s	5
5	Pastor Maldonado	Williams	1h46m11.674s	1	1m41.226s	3
6	Kamui Kobayashi	Sauber	1h46m18.743s	1	1m42.606s	15
7	Felipe Massa	Ferrari	1h46m21.563s	1	1m41.723s	8
8	Bruno Senna	Williams	1h46m22.209s	1	1m42.330s	14
9	Paul di Resta	Force India	1h46m22.827s	3	1m42.218s	12
10	Daniel Ricciardo	Toro Rosso	1h46m26.130s	2	1m42.765s	16
11	Michael Schumacher	Mercedes	1h46m26.742s	2	1m42.289s	13
12	Jean-Eric Vergne	Toro Rosso	1h46m33.573s	2	1m44.058s	17
13	Heikki Kovalainen	Caterham	1h46m46.431s	1	1m44.956s	18
14	Timo Glock	Marussia	1h46m55.140s	1	1m45.426s	21
15	Sergio Perez	Sauber	1h46m55.435s	3	1m42.084s	11
16	Vitaly Petrov	Caterham	1h47m03.262s	1	1m45.151s	20
17	Pedro de la Rosa	HRT	1h47m10.445s	1	1m45.766s	22**
R	Charles Pic	Marussia	41 laps/engine	1	1m45.089s	19
R	Romain Grosjean	Lotus	37 laps/accident	2	1m41.778s	9
R	Mark Webber	Red Bull	37 laps/accident	1	1m40.978s	2
R	Lewis Hamilton	McLaren	19 laps/fuel pressure	0	1m40.630s	1
R	Narain Karthikeyan	HRT	7 laps/accident	0	1m46.382s	23
R	Nico Rosberg	Mercedes	7 laps/accident	1	1m41.603s	7
R	Nico Hulkenberg	Force India	0 laps/accident	0	1m42.019s	10

FASTEST LAP: VETTEL, 1M43.964S, 119.502MPH/192.320KPH ON LAP 54 • RACE LEADERS: HAMILTON 1-19; RAIKKONEN 20-55 • * STARTED FROM PITS AS DISQUALIFIED FOR FINISHING QUALIFYING SESSION WITH INSUFFICIENT FUEL LEFT ** STARTED FROM PITS

Alonso is pensive as Raikkonen and Vettel show their delight at taking first and third.

Heikki Kovalainen reached the 12th place required. However, this was for one lap only, as he lost out to Michael Schumacher, who was fighting back from making an extra stop to have a punctured tyre replaced, and the Finn ended the race 13th, leaving the team two more races in which to pull off the feat.

UNITED STATES GP

Sebastian Vettel was anxious to win, but he was beaten by an inspired Lewis Hamilton at the Circuit of the Americas, while Fernando Alonso gave it everything to finish third for Ferrari and so keep his world title hopes alive heading off to the final round.

Hosting its first grand prix, the Circuit of the Americas outside Austin not only impressed the teams and drivers but provided a great race in front of extremely welcoming and enthusiastic fans, making it a complete success.

Sebastian Vettel qualified on pole ahead of Lewis Hamilton, with title challenger Fernando Alonso, who arrived in Texas 10 points in arrears, only eighth fastest. This was music to Vettel's ears as the young German looked to wrap up his third F1 title in three years here rather than risk keeping it open until the final round in Brazil, where anything can and often does happen.

On race morning, though, news broke that Felipe Massa's gearbox had a broken seal and so he would be hit with a five-place grid penalty, which not only advanced team-mate Alonso by one grid position but moved the Spaniard to the clean side of the track.

Alonso then did his utmost and rocketed into fourth place at the start as Vettel led into and out of Turn 1, the hairpin on the crest of a hill that many worried would be the scene of a collision or two. Mark Webber powered past Hamilton to grab second place and so Red Bull Racing had reason to smile as the Australian afforded Vettel a buffer. This lasted only until lap 4, though, when Hamilton motored past. From that point on, the race was only between Vettel and Hamilton, the rest just bit-part players. On lap 17, Webber pulled off, his alternator having failed.

Hamilton hunted down Vettel and, when HRT's Narain Karthikeyan got in the way on lap 42, pounced to take the lead with a decisive move into Turn 12, then held on all the way to the finish to make it two US GP wins in a row, albeit with the previous one having been at Indianapolis Motor Speedway in his rookie F1 season, 2007.

Alonso finished third, trailed home by Massa, but relieved to have dropped only three points to Vettel and thus keep his own hopes of a third F1 title alive. Behind this

Vettel leads the field into Turn 1 for the first time, with Webber having got past Hamilton.

AUSTIN ROUND 19

DATE: **18 NOVEMBER 2012**

Laps: **56** • Distance: **191.634 miles/308.405km** • Weather: **Sunny to start & warm**

Pos	Driver	Team	Result	Stops	Qualifying Time	Grid
1	**Lewis Hamilton**	McLaren	1h35m55.269s	1	1m35.766s	2
2	**Sebastian Vettel**	Red Bull	1h35m55.944s	1	1m35.657s	1
3	**Fernando Alonso**	Ferrari	1h36m34.498s	1	1m37.300s	7
4	**Felipe Massa**	Ferrari	1h36m41.282s	1	1m36.937s	11*
5	**Jenson Button**	McLaren	1h36m51.701s	1	1m37.616s	12
6	**Kimi Raikkonen**	Lotus	1h36m59.694s	1	1m36.708s	4
7	**Romain Grosjean**	Lotus	1h37m05.582s	1	1m36.587s	8*
8	**Nico Hulkenberg**	Force India	1h37m09.061s	1	12m37.141s	6
9	**Pastor Maldonado**	Williams	1h37m09.794s	1	1m37.842s	9
10	**Bruno Senna**	Williams	1h37m10.402s	1	1m37.604s	10
11	**Sergio Perez**	Sauber	1h37m19.610s	1	1m38.206s	15
12	**Daniel Ricciardo**	Toro Rosso	1h37m20.140s	1	1m39.114s	18
13	**Nico Rosberg**	Mercedes	1h37m20.779s	1	1m38.501s	17
14	**Kamui Kobayashi**	Sauber	55 laps	1	1m38.437s	16
15	**Paul di Resta**	Force India	55 laps	2	1m37.665s	13
16	**Michael Schumacher**	Mercedes	55 laps	1	1m36.794s	5
17	**Vitaly Petrov**	Caterham	55 laps	1	1m40.809s	21
18	**Heikki Kovalainen**	Caterham	55 laps	1	1m41.166s	22
19	**Timo Glock**	Marussia	55 laps	1	1m40.056s	19
20	**Charles Pic**	Marussia	54 laps	1	1m40.664s	20
21	**Pedro de la Rosa**	HRT	54 laps	1	1m42.011s	23
22	**Narain Karthikeyan**	HRT	54 laps	1	1m42.740s	24
R	**Mark Webber**	Red Bull	16 laps/alternator	0	1m36.174s	3
R	**Jean-Eric Vergne**	Toro Rosso	14 laps/suspension	0	1m37.879s	14

FASTEST LAP: VETTEL, 1M39.347S, 124.132MPH/199.772KPH ON LAP 56 • RACE LEADERS: VETTEL 1-41; HAMILTON 42-56 • * 5-PLACE GRID PENALTY

pair, Jenson Button worked his way forward to fifth after losing ground off the grid and so falling from 12th - the legacy of a throttle problem in qualifying - to 15th. Among

those he passed were the Lotus drivers Kimi Raikkonen and Romain Grosjean, who finished sixth and seventh, the Frenchman having spun early in the race.

BRAZILIAN GP

This was an extraordinary end to an extraordinary season. Button mastered the changing conditions to win the day, but Hulkenberg led, Hamilton was knocked out of the lead and Vettel, who'd been spun to the tail, took sixth to pip Alonso to the title.

Everything seemed to favour Sebastian Vettel as he began the race not only three places ahead of Fernando Alonso but also with a 13-point advantage. However, with drizzle falling just before the start and 25 points for a win, Alonso still had a chance. Hamilton made a perfect getaway, but the situation tilted in Alonso's favour, for he flew away from seventh on the grid while Vettel dawdled.

Felipe Massa passed Button through Turn 1, but it was what happened into Turn 4 that shaped the race. Vettel was cautious going in, Raikkonen swerved to miss him and Vettel turned in, leaving Bruno Senna nowhere to go. Hit by the Williams, he spun and, with floor damage, it looked as though his race was run and this would gift Alonso the title as long as he finished in the top three. In fact, although Vettel's straight-line speed was hampered, he was soon picking off the tailenders.

Button swiftly demoted Massa and then took the lead on lap 6, but Hamilton used DERS to go back in front at the end of the start/finish straight, only to be passed again. This time Button stayed ahead.

The drizzle turned to rain and almost everyone came in on lap 11 for intermediates. Button elected to continue on slicks, his highly tuned senses serving him well. Nico Hulkenberg, running third ahead of Alonso, was the only other driver to copy this and they ran first and second as the others started to lap faster. The rain then faded, and those on inters found their tyres overheating, meaning that they would have to change to slicks.

Hulkenberg passed Button for the lead on lap 18 and they found themselves 45 seconds clear, but this advantage was wiped out when the safety car came out as there was debris on the track. Hulkenberg controlled the restart and soon had to contend with Hamilton, who had passed Button. They swapped places on lap 48

INTERLAGOS ROUND 20

DATE: 25 NOVEMBER 2012

Laps: 71 • Distance: 190.067 miles/305.884km • Weather: **Light drizzle, then rain**

Pos	Driver	Team	Result	Stops	Qualifying Time	Grid
1	**Jenson Button**	McLaren	1h45m22.656s	2	1m12.513s	2
2	**Fernando Alonso**	Ferrari	1h45m25.410s	3	1m13.253s	7
3	**Felipe Massa**	Ferrari	1h45m26.271s	3	1m12.987s	5
4	**Mark Webber**	Red Bull	1h45m27.592s	3	1m12.581s	3
5	**Nico Hulkenberg**	Force India	1h45m28.364s	3	1m13.206	6
6	**Sebastian Vettel**	Red Bull	1h45m32.109s	4	1m12.760s	4
7	**Michael Schumacher**	Mercedes	1h45m34.563s	4	1m14.334s	13
8	**Jean-Eric Vergne**	Toro Rosso	1h45m51.309s	4	1m14.619s	17
9	**Kamui Kobayashi**	Sauber	1h45m53.906s	3	1m14.380s	14
10	**Kimi Raikkonen**	Lotus	70 laps	3	1m13.298s	8
11	**Vitaly Petrov**	Caterham	70 laps	3	1m17.073s	19
12	**Charles Pic**	Marussia	70 laps	3	1m18.104s	22
13	**Daniel Ricciardo**	Toro Rosso	70 laps	5	1m14.574s	15
14	**Heikki Kovalainen**	Caterham	70 laps	5	1m17.086s	20
15	**Nico Rosberg**	Mercedes	70 laps	4	1m13.489s	9
16	**Timo Glock**	Marussia	70 laps	4	1m17.508s	21
17	**Pedro de la Rosa**	HRT	69 laps	3	1m19.699s	24*
18	**Narain Karthikeyan**	HRT	69 laps	4	1m19.576s	23
19	**Paul di Resta**	Force India	68 laps/accident	3	1m14.121s	10
R	**Lewis Hamilton**	McLaren	54 laps/accident	3	1m12.458s	1
R	**Romain Grosjean**	Lotus	5 laps/accident	2	1m16.967s	18
R	**Pastor Maldonado**	Williams	1 lap/accident	0	1m13.174s	16**
R	**Bruno Senna**	Williams	0 laps/accident	0	1m14.219s	11
R	**Sergio Perez**	Sauber	0 laps/accident	0	1m14.234s	12

FASTEST LAP: HAMILTON, 1M18.069S, 123.467MPH/198.701KPH ON LAP 38 • **RACE LEADERS:** HAMILTON 1–5, 7, 48–54; BUTTON 6, 8–17, 55–71; HULKENBERG 18–47 • * 5-PLACE GRID PENALTY ** 10-PLACE GRID PENALTY

Button and Hulkenberg were 40 seconds clear until the safety car was deployed.

when Hulkenberg half spun, but later he slid into Hamilton at Turn 1 when trying to get back ahead. Hamilton was out, and a drive-through penalty dropped Hulkenberg down the order, allowing Button to take victory. Massa had let Alonso through to second, but this wasn't enough, as Vettel cruised home sixth to take the title.

The fingers and the T-shirts say it all as Red Bull Racing celebrates at Interlagos after the 2012 Brazilian GP. Sebastian Vettel's sixth place was enough to seal his, and the team's, third straight championship win.

FINAL RESULTS 2012

POS	DRIVER	NAT		CAR-ENGINE	R1	R2	R3	R4	R5
1	SEBASTIAN VETTEL	GER		RED BULL-RENAULT RB8	2	11	5	1PF	6
2	FERNANDO ALONSO	SPA		FERRARI F2012	5	1	9	7	2
3	KIMI RAIKKONEN	FIN		LOTUS-RENAULT E20	7	5F	14	2	3
4	LEWIS HAMILTON	GBR		McLAREN-MERCEDES MP4-27	3P	3P	3	8	8
5	JENSON BUTTON	GBR		McLAREN-MERCEDES MP4-27	1F	14	2	18	9
6	MARK WEBBER	AUS		RED BULL-RENAULT RB8	4	4	4	4	11
7	FELIPE MASSA	BRA		FERRARI F2012	R	15	13	3	9
8	ROMAIN GROSJEAN	FRA		LOTUS-RENAULT E20	R	R	6	3	4F
9	NICO ROSBERG	GER		MERCEDES F1 W03	12	13	1P	5	7
10	SERGIO PEREZ	MEX		SAUBER-FERRARI C31	8	2	11	11	R
11	NICO HULKENBERG	GER		FORCE INDIA-MERCEDES VJM05	R	9	15	12	10
12	KAMUI KOBAYASHI	JPN		SAUBER-FERRARI C31	6	R	10F	13	5
13	MICHAEL SCHUMACHER	GER		MERCEDES F1 W03	R	10	R	10	R
14	PAUL DI RESTA	GBR		FORCE INDIA-MERCEDES VJM05	10	7	12	6	14
15	PASTOR MALDONADO	VEN		WILLIAMS-RENAULT FW34	13	19	8	R	1P
16	BRUNO SENNA	BRA		WILLIAMS-RENAULT FW34	16	6	7	R	R
17	JEAN-ERIC VERGNE	FRA		TORO ROSSO-FERRARI STR7	11	8	16	14	12
18	DANIEL RICCIARDO	AUS		TORO ROSSO-FERRARI STR7	9	12	17	15	13
19	VITALY PETROV	RUS		CATERHAM-RENAULT CT01	R	16	18	16	17
20	TIMO GLOCK	GER		MARUSSIA-COSWORTH MR01	14	17	19	19	18
21	CHARLES PIC	FRA		MARUSSIA-COSWORTH MR01	15	20	20	R	R
22	HEIKKI KOVALAINEN	FIN		CATERHAM-RENAULT CT01	R	18	23	17	16
23	JEROME D'AMBROSIO	BEL		LOTUS-RENAULT E20	-	-	-	-	-
24	NARAIN KARTHIKEYAN	IND		HRT-COSWORTH F112	NQ	21	22	21	R
25	PEDRO DE LA ROSA	SPA		HRT-COSWORTH F112	NQ	22	21	20	19

SCORING

1st	25 points
2nd	18 points
3rd	15 points
4th	12 points
5th	10 points
6th	8 points
7th	6 points
8th	4 points
9th	2 points
10th	1 point

	R1	R2	R3	R4	R5
RED BULL-RENAULT	2/4	4/11	4/5	1/4	6/11
FERRARI	5/R	1/15	9/13	7/9	2/15
McLAREN-MERCEDES	1/3	3/14	2/3	8/18	8/9
LOTUS-RENAULT	7/R	5/R	6/14	2/3	3/4
MERCEDES	12/R	10/13	1/R	5/10	7/R
SAUBER-FERRARI	6/8	2/R	10/11	11/13	5/R
FORCE INDIA-MERCEDES	10/R	7/9	12/15	6/12	10/14
WILLIAMS-RENAULT	13/16	6/19	7/8	R/R	1/R
TORO ROSSO-FERRARI	9/11	8/12	16/17	14/15	12/13
CATERHAM-RENAULT	R/R	16/18	18/23	16/17	16/17
MARUSSIA-COSWORTH	14/14	17/20	19/20	19/R	18/R
HRT-COSWORTH	NQ/NQ	21/22	21/22	20/21	19/R

R6	R7	R8	R9	R10	R11	R12	R13	R14	R15	R16	R17	R18	R19	R20	TOTAL
4	4PF	RP	3	5	4F	2	R	1	1PF	1	1P	3F	2PF	6	281
3	5	1	2P	1P	5	R	3	3	R	3	2	2	3	2	278
9	8	2	5F	3	2	3	5	6	6	5	7	1	6	10	207
5	1	19	8	R	1P	R	1P	RP	5	10	4	RP	1	RPF	190
16	16	8	10	2	6	1P	R	2	4	R	5F	4	5	1	188
1P	7	4	1	8	8	6	R	11	9	2PF	3	R	R	4	179
15	6	10	16	4	12	9	5	4	8	2	4	6	7	4	122
R	2	R	6	18	3	R	-	7	R	7	9	R	7	R	96
2	6	6F	15	10	10	11	7F	5	R	R	11	R	13	15	93
11	3	9	R	6	14	R	2	10	R	11	R	15	11	R	66
8	12	5	12	9	11	4	R	14F	7	6	8	R	8	5	63
R	9	R	11	4	18	13	9	13	3	R	14	6	14	9	60
R	R	3	7	7F	R	7	6	R	11	13	R	11	16	7	49
7	11	7	R	11	12	10	8	4	12	12	12	9	15	19	46
R	13	12	16	15	13	R	11	R	8	14	16	5	9	R	45
10	17	10	9	17	7	12F	10	18	14	15	10	8	10	R	31
12	15	R	14	14	16	8	R	R	13	8	15	12	R	8	16
R	14	11	13	13	15	9	12	9	10	9	13	10	12	13	10
R	19	13	NS	16	19	14	15	19	17	16	17	16	17	11	0
14	R	NS	18	22	21	15	17	12	16	18	20	14	19	16	0
R	20	15	19	20	20	16	16	R	19	19	R	20	12		0
13	18	14	17	19	17	17	14	15	15	17	18	13	18	14	0
-	-	-	-	-	-	13	-	-	-	-	-	-	-	-	0
15	R	18	21	23	R	R	19	R	R	20	21	R	22	18	0
R	R	17	20	21	22	18	18	17	18	R	R	17	21	17	0

R6	R7	R8	R9	R10	R11	R12	R13	R14	R15	R16	R17	R18	R19	R20	TOTAL
/4	4/7	4/R	1/3	5/8	4/8	2/6	R/R	1/11	1/9	1/2	1/3	3/R	2/R	4/6	460
/6	5/10	1/16	2/4	1/12	5/9	5/R	3/4	3/8	2/R	3/4	2/6	2/7	3/4	2/3	400
/16	1/16	8/19	8/10	2/R	1/6	1/R	1/R	2/R	4/5	10/R	4/5	4/R	1/5	1/R	378
/R	2/8	2/R	5/6	3/18	2/3	3/R	5/13	6/7	6/R	5/7	7/9	1/R	6/7	10/R	303
/R	6/R	3/6	7/15	7/10	10/R	7/11	6/7	5/R	11/R	13/R	11/R	11/R	13/16	7/15	142
/R	3/9	9/R	11/R	4/6	14/18	13/R	2/9	10/13	3/R	11/R	14/R	6/15	11/14	9/R	126
/8	11/12	5/7	12/R	9/11	11/12	4/10	8/R	4/14	7/12	6/12	8/12	9/R	8/15	5/19	109
/R	13/17	10/12	9/16	15/17	7/13	12/R	10/11	18/R	8/14	14/15	10/16	5/8	9/10	R/R	76
/R	14/15	11/R	13/14	13/14	15/16	8/9	12/R	9/R	10/13	8/9	13/15	10/12	12/R	8/13	26
/R	18/19	13/14	17/NS	16/19	17/19	14/17	14/15	15/19	15/17	16/17	17/R	13/16	17/18	11/14	0
/R	20/R	15/NS	18/19	20/22	20/21	15/16	16/17	12/16	16/R	18/19	19/20	14/R	19/20	12/16	0
/R	R/R	17/18	20/21	21/23	22/R	18/R	18/19	17/R	18/R	20/R	21/R	17/R	21/22	17/18	0

FORMULA ONE RECORDS

MOST STARTS

DRIVERS

325	Rubens Barrichello	(BRA)	161	Ayrton Senna	(BRA)
308	Michael Schumacher	(GER)	159	Heinz-Harald Frentzen	(GER)
256	Riccardo Patrese	(ITA)	158	Martin Brundle	(GBR)
	Jarno Trulli	(ITA)		Olivier Panis	(FRA)
247	David Coulthard	(GBR)	152	John Watson	(GBR)
230	Giancarlo Fisichella	(ITA)	149	Rene Arnoux	(FRA)
229	Jenson Button	(GBR)	147	Eddie Irvine	(GBR)
210	Gerhard Berger	(AUT)		Derek Warwick	(GBR)
208	Andrea de Cesaris	(ITA)	146	Carlos Reutemann	(ARG)
204	Nelson Piquet	(BRA)	144	Emerson Fittipaldi	(BRA)
201	Jean Alesi	(FRA)	135	Jean-Pierre Jarier	(FRA)
199	Alain Prost	(FRA)	132	Eddie Cheever	(USA)
198	Fernando Alonso	(SPA)		Clay Regazzoni	(SWI)
197	Mark Webber	(AUS)	128	Mario Andretti	(USA)
194	Michele Alboreto	(ITA)		Nico Rosberg	(FIN)
187	Nigel Mansell	(GBR)	126	Jack Brabham	(AUS)
185	Nick Heidfeld	(GER)	123	Ronnie Peterson	(SWE)
180	Ralf Schumacher	(GER)	119	Pierluigi Martini	(ITA)
177	Kimi Raikkonen	(FIN)	116	Damon Hill	(GBR)
176	Graham Hill	(GBR)		Jacky Ickx	(BEL)
175	Jacques Laffite	(FRA)		Alan Jones	(AUS)
173	Felipe Massa	(BRA)	114	Keke Rosberg	(FIN)
171	Niki Lauda	(AUT)		Patrick Tambay	(FRA)
165	Jacques Villeneuve	(CDN)	112	Denny Hulme	(NZL)
163	Thierry Boutsen	(BEL)		Jody Scheckter	(RSA)
162	Mika Hakkinen	(FIN)	111	John Surtees	(GBR)
	Johnny Herbert	(GBR)	110	Lewis Hamilton	(GBR)

CONSTRUCTORS

851	Ferrari
724	McLaren
643	Williams
515	Lotus
469	Toro Rosso (nee Minardi)
418	Tyrrell
409	Prost (nee Ligier)
394	Brabham
383	Arrows
378	Force India (nee Jordan, then Midland, then Spyker)
345	Sauber (including BMW Sauber)
317	Benetton
301	Renault
281	Red Bull (nee Stewart, then Jaguar Racing)
230	March
208	Mercedes GP (nee BAR, then Honda Racing, then Brawn GP)
197	BRM
132	Osella

Michael Schumacher burst on to the Formula One scene late in the 1991 season when he made his debut for Jordan at Spa-Francorchamps.

Nigel Mansell had been threatening to win for a while before he took top spot for Williams in the 1985 European GP at Brands Hatch.

MOST WINS

DRIVERS

91 Michael Schumacher	(GER)	**16** Stirling Moss	(GBR)	Ronnie Peterson	(SWE)
51 Alain Prost	(FRA)	**15** Jenson Button	(GBR)	Jody Scheckter	(RSA)
41 Ayrton Senna	(BRA)	**14** Jack Brabham	(AUS)	**9** Mark Webber	(AUS)
31 Nigel Mansell	(GBR)	Emerson Fittipaldi	(BRA)	**8** Denny Hulme	(NZL)
30 Fernando Alonso	(SPA)	Graham Hill	(GBR)	Jacky Ickx	(BEL)
27 Jackie Stewart	(GBR)	**13** Alberto Ascari	(ITA)	**7** Rene Arnoux	(FRA)
26 Sebastian Vettel	(GER)	David Coulthard	(GBR)	Juan Pablo Montoya	(COL)
25 Jim Clark	(GBR)	**12** Mario Andretti	(USA)	**6** Tony Brooks	(GBR)
Niki Lauda	(AUT)	Alan Jones	(AUS)	Jacques Laffite	(FRA)
24 Juan Manuel Fangio	(ARG)	Carlos Reutemann	(ARG)	Riccardo Patrese	(ITA)
23 Nelson Piquet	(BRA)	**11** Rubens Barrichello	(BRA)	Jochen Rindt	(AUT)
22 Damon Hill	(GBR)	Felipe Massa	(BRA)	Ralf Schumacher	(GER)
21 Lewis Hamilton	(GBR)	Jacques Villeneuve	(CDN)	John Surtees	(GBR)
20 Mika Hakkinen	(FIN)	**10** Gerhard Berger	(AUT)	Gilles Villeneuve	(CDN)
19 Kimi Raikkonen	(FIN)	James Hunt	(GBR)		

CONSTRUCTORS

219 Ferrari	**12** Mercedes GP (including Honda	**2** Honda
181 McLaren	Racing + Brawn GP)	**1** BMW Sauber
114 Williams	**10** Alfa Romeo	Eagle
79 Lotus	**9** Ligier	Hesketh
35 Brabham	Maserati	Lotus*
Red Bull (including Stewart)	Matra	Penske
Renault	Mercedes	Porsche
27 Benetton	Vanwall	Shadow
23 Tyrrell	**4** Jordan	Stewart
17 BRM	**3** March	Toro Rosso
16 Cooper	Wolf	

MOST WINS IN ONE SEASON

Michael Schumacher holds the record of 13 wins in a season, but Sebastian Vettel came close in 2011, when he won 11 for Red Bull Racing.

DRIVERS

13	Michael Schumacher	2004	**7**	Fernando Alonso	2005		Jim Clark	1965
11	Michael Schumacher	2002		Fernando Alonso	2006		Juan Manuel Fangio	1954
	Sebastian Vettel	2011		Jim Clark	1963		Damon Hill	1994
9	Nigel Mansell	1992		Alain Prost	1984		James Hunt	1976
	Michael Schumacher	1995		Alain Prost	1988		Nigel Mansell	1987
	Michael Schumacher	2000		Alain Prost	1993		Kimi Raikkonen	2007
	Michael Schumacher	2001		Kimi Raikkonen	2005		Michael Schumacher	1998
8	Mika Hakkinen	1998		Ayrton Senna	1991		Michael Schumacher	2003
	Damon Hill	1996		Jacques Villeneuve	1997		Michael Schumacher	2006
	Michael Schumacher	1994	**6**	Mario Andretti	1978		Ayrton Senna	1989
	Ayrton Senna	1988		Alberto Ascari	1952		Ayrton Senna	1990

CONSTRUCTORS

15	Ferrari	2002		Ferrari	2007	**7**	Ferrari	1952
	Ferrari	2004		McLaren	1998		Ferrari	1953
	McLaren	1988		Red Bull	2010		Ferrari	2008
12	McLaren	1984		Williams	1986		Lotus	1963
	Red Bull	2011		Williams	1987		Lotus	1973
	Williams	1996	**8**	Benetton	1994		McLaren	1999
11	Benetton	1995		Brawn GP	2009		McLaren	2000
10	Ferrari	2000		Ferrari	2003		McLaren	2012
	McLaren	2005		Lotus	1978		Red Bull	2012
	McLaren	1989		McLaren	1991		Tyrrell	1971
	Williams	1992		McLaren	2007		Williams	1991
	Williams	1993		Renault	2005		Williams	1994
9	Ferrari	2001		Renault	2006			
	Ferrari	2006		Williams	1997			

MOST POLE POSITIONS

DRIVERS

68	Michael Schumacher	(GER)
65	Ayrton Senna	(BRA)
36	Sebastian Vettel	(GER)
33	Jim Clark	(GBR)
	Alain Prost	(FRA)
32	Nigel Mansell	(GBR)
29	Juan Manuel Fangio	(ARG)
26	Mika Hakkinen	(FIN)
	Lewis Hamilton	(GBR)
24	Niki Lauda	(AUT)
	Nelson Piquet	(BRA)
22	Fernando Alonso	(SPA)
20	Damon Hill	(GBR)
18	Mario Andretti	(USA)
	Rene Arnoux	(FRA)
17	Jackie Stewart	(GBR)

16	Stirling Moss	(GBR)
	Kimi Raikkonen	(FIN)
15	Felipe Massa	(BRA)
14	Alberto Ascari	(ITA)
	Rubens Barrichello	(BRA)
	James Hunt	(GBR)
	Ronnie Peterson	(SWE)
13	Jack Brabham	(AUS)
	Graham Hill	(GBR)
	Jacky Ickx	(BEL)
	Juan Pablo Montoya	(COL)
	Jacques Villeneuve	(CDN)
12	Gerhard Berger	(AUT)
	David Coulthard	(GBR)
11	Mark Webber	(AUS)
10	Jochen Rindt	(AUT)

CONSTRUCTORS

207	Ferrari
154	McLaren
127	Williams
107	Lotus
51	Renault
47	Red Bull
39	Brabham
16	Benetton
14	Tyrrell
12	Alfa Romeo
11	BRM
	Cooper
10	Maserati
9	Ligier
	Mercedes GP (including Brawn GP + Honda Racing + BAR)
8	Mercedes
7	Vanwall
5	March
4	Matra
3	Force India (+ Jordan)
	Shadow
	Toyota
2	Lancia
1	BMW Sauber
	Toro Rosso

Ayrton Senna was the king of pole position, but here, Alain Prost gets the better of him into the first corner at Adelaide in 1988.

FASTEST LAPS

DRIVERS

76	Michael Schumacher	(GER)
41	Alain Prost	(FRA)
37	Kimi Raikkonen	(FIN)
30	Nigel Mansell	(GBR)
28	Jim Clark	(GBR)
25	Mika Hakkinen	(FIN)
24	Niki Lauda	(AUT)
23	Juan Manuel Fangio	(ARG)
	Nelson Piquet	(BRA)
21	Gerhard Berger	(AUT)
19	Fernando Alonso	(SPA)
	Damon Hil	(GBR)
	Stirling Moss	(GBR)
	Ayrton Senna	(BRA)
18	David Coulthard	(GBR)
17	Rubens Barrichello	(BRA)
15	Felipe Massa	(BRA)
	Clay Regazzoni	(SWI)
	Jackie Stewart	(GBR)
	Sebastian Vettel	(GER)
14	Jacky Ickx	(BEL)
	Mark Webber	(AUS)
13	Alberto Ascari	(ITA)
	Alan Jones	(AUS)
	Riccardo Patrese	(ITA)
12	Rene Arnoux	(FRA)
	Jack Brabham	(AUS)
	Lewis Hamilton	(GBR)
	Juan Pablo Montoya	(COL)
11	John Surtees	(GBR)

CONSTRUCTORS

226	Ferrari
151	McLaren
131	Williams
71	Lotus
40	Brabham
35	Benetton
31	Renault
29	Red Bull
22	Tyrrell
15	BRM
	Maserati
14	Alfa Romeo
13	Cooper
12	Matra
11	Mercedes GP (including Brawn GP + BAR + Honda Racing)
	Prost (including Ligier)
9	Mercedes
7	March
6	Vanwall

MOST POINTS (THIS FIGURE IS GROSS TALLY, I.E. INCLUDING SCORES THAT WERE LATER DROPPED)

DRIVERS

1566	Michael Schumacher	(GER)
1364	Fernando Alonso	(SPA)
1054	Sebastian Vettel	(GER)
999	Jenson Button	(GBR)
913	Lewis Hamilton	(GBR)
848.5	Mark Webber	(AUS)
798.5	Alain Prost	(FRA)
786	Kimi Raikkonen	(FIN)
704	Felipe Massa	(BRA)
658	Rubens Barrichello	(BRA)
614	Ayrton Senna	(BRA)
535	David Coulthard	(GBR)
485.5	Nelson Piquet	(BRA)
482	Nigel Mansell	(GBR)
420.5	Niki Lauda	(AUT)
420	Mika Hakkinen	(FIN)
399.5	Nico Rosberg	(GER)
385	Gerhard Berger	(AUT)
360	Damon Hill	(GBR)
	Jackie Stewart	(GBR)
329	Ralf Schumacher	(GER)
310	Carlos Reutemann	(ARG)
307	Juan Pablo Montoya	(COL)
289	Graham Hill	(GBR)
281	Emerson Fittipaldi	(BRA)
	Riccardo Patrese	(ITA)
277.5	Juan Manuel Fangio	(ARG)
275	Giancarlo Fisichella	(ITA)
274	Jim Clark	(GBR)
273	Robert Kubica	(POL)
261	Jack Brabham	(AUS)
259	Nick Heidfeld	(GER)
255	Jody Scheckter	(RSA)
248	Denny Hulme	(NZL)
246.5	Jarno Trulli	(ITA)
242	Jean Alesi	(FRA)

CONSTRUCTORS

5248.5	Ferrari
4691.5	McLaren
2756	Williams
1952.5	Red Bull (including Stewart + Jaguar Racing)
1382	Renault
1352	Lotus
1026	Mercedes GP (including BAR + Honda Racing + Brawn GP)
877.5	Benetton
854	Brabham
711	Sauber (including BMW Sauber)
617	Tyrrell
551	Force India (including Jordan + Midland + Spyker)
439	BRM
424	Prost (including Ligier)
333	Cooper
303	Lotus*
278.5	Toyota
174	Toro Rosso
171.5	March
167	Arrows
155	Matra

Alain Prost set the first of his 41 fastest laps for Renault in the 1981 French GP.

Juan Manuel Fangio claimed the last of his five drivers' titles in 1957, a year when his greatest drive for Maserati came at the German GP.

MOST DRIVERS' TITLES

7	Michael Schumacher	(GER)		Jim Clark	(GBR)		Denis Hulme	(NZL)
5	Juan Manuel Fangio	(ARG)		Emerson Fittipaldi	(BRA)		James Hunt	(GBR)
4	Alain Prost	(FRA)		Mika Hakkinen	(FIN)		Alan Jones	(AUS)
3	Jack Brabham	(AUS)		Graham Hill	(GBR)		Nigel Mansell	(GBR)
	Niki Lauda	(AUT)	1	Mario Andretti	(USA)		Kimi Raikkonen	(FIN)
	Nelson Piquet	(BRA)		Jenson Button	(GBR)		Jochen Rindt	(AUT)
	Ayrton Senna	(BRA)		Giuseppe Farina	(ITA)		Keke Rosberg	(FIN)
	Jackie Stewart	(GBR)		Lewis Hamilton	(GBR)		Jody Scheckter	(RSA)
	Sebastian Vettel	(GER)		Mike Hawthorn	(GBR)		John Surtees	(GBR)
2	Fernando Alonso	(SPA)		Damon Hill	(GBR)		Jacques Villeneuve	(CDN)
	Alberto Ascari	(ITA)		Phil Hill	(USA)			

MOST CONSTRUCTORS' TITLES

16	Ferrari	2	Brabham		BRM
9	Williams		Cooper		Matra
8	McLaren		Renault		Tyrrell
7	Lotus	1	Benetton		Vanwall
3	Red Bull		Brawn		

NB To avoid confusion, the Renault stats listed are based on the team that evolved from Benetton in 2002 and include those stats that have happened since, plus those from Renault's first spell in F1 between 1977 and 1985. The figures for Benetton and Toleman, from which it metamorphosed in 1986, are listed as Benetton. The Lotus stats are solely for the team that ran from 1958 to 1994, with the 2012 Lotus team listed as Lotus*. Conversely, the stats for Red Bull Racing include those of the Stewart and Jaguar Racing teams from which it evolved. Likewise, Force India's stats include those of Jordan, Midland and Spyker, and Scuderia Toro Rosso's include those of its forerunner Minardi.

2013 FILL-IN CHART

DRIVER	TEAM	Round 1 – 17 March AUSTRALIAN GP	Round 2 – 24 March MALAYSIAN GP	Round 3 – 14 April CHINESE GP	Round 4 – 21 April BAHRAIN GP	Round 5 – 12 May SPANISH GP	Round 6 – 26 May MONACO GP	Round 7 – 9 June CANADIAN GP	Round 8 – 30 June BRITISH GP
1 SEBASTIAN VETTEL	Red Bull								
2 MARK WEBBER	Red Bull								
3 FERNANDO ALONSO	Ferrari								
4 FELIPE MASSA	Ferrari								
5 JENSON BUTTON	McLaren								
6 SERGIO PEREZ	McLaren								
7 KIMI RAIKKONEN	Lotus								
8 ROMAIN GROSJEAN	Lotus								
9 NICO ROSBERG	Mercedes								
10 LEWIS HAMILTON	Mercedes								
11 NICO HULKENBERG	Sauber								
12 ESTEBAN GUTIERREZ	Sauber								
14 PAUL DI RESTA	Force India								
15 BRUNO SENNA*	Force India								
16 PASTOR MALDONADO	Williams								
17 VALTTERI BOTTAS	Williams								
18 JEAN-ERIC VERGNE	Toro Rosso								
19 DANIEL RICCIARDO	Toro Rosso								
20 VITALY PETROV*	Caterham								
21 CHARLES PIC	Caterham								
22 TIMO GLOCK	Marussia								
23 MAX CHILTON	Marussia								

124

SCORING SYSTEM: 25, 20, 15, 10, 8, 6, 4, 3, 2, 1 POINTS
FOR THE FIRST 10 FINISHERS IN EACH GRAND PRIX

* UNCONFIRMED AT TIME OF GOING TO PRESS

Round 9 – 7 July GERMAN GP	Round 10 – 21 July TBC*	Round 11 – 28 July HUNGARIAN GP	Round 12 – 25 Aug BELGIAN GP	Round 13 – 8 Sep ITALIAN GP	Round 14 – 22 Sep SINGAPORE GP	Round 15 – 6 Oct KOREAN GP	Round 16 – 13 Oct JAPANESE GP	Round 17 – 27 Oct INDIAN GP	Round 18 – 3 Nov ABU DHABI GP	Round 19 – 17 Nov UNITED STATES GP	Round 20 – 24 Nov BRAZILIAN GP	POINTS TOTAL

Kimi Raikkonen won his first grand prix for more than three years when he won in Abu Dhabi in 2012 ahead of Alonso and Vettel.

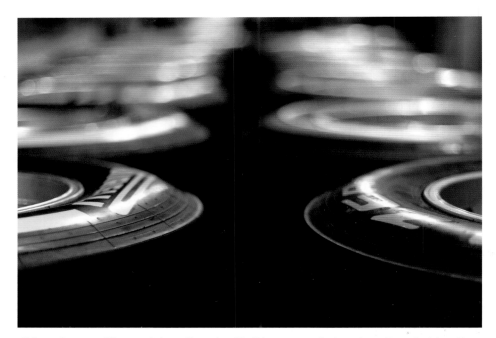

Major performance differences between the various Pirelli tyre compounds always keeps the racing interesting.

The publishers would like to thank the following sources for their kind
permission to reproduce the pictures in this book.

Getty Images: /Julian Finney: 77

LAT Photographic: 61TL, 61R, 61B, 63TL, 63R, 63B, 118, 119, 121, 122, 123; /Charles Coates: 12, 13, 15, 16, 24,
29, 33, 37, 39, 42, 47, 49, 51, 96, 102, 110, 113, 114-115; /Glenn Dunbar: 3, 18, 28, 41, 43, 44-45, 52, 53, 56, 90-91,
100-101, 104, 120; /Steve Etherington: 10, 22-23, 30, 31, 95, 97, 103, 105, 106, 126-127; /Andrew Ferraro: 6-7,
21, 25, 26, 36, 40, 46, 50, 58-59, 98, 112; /Andy Hone: 11, 14, 17, 27, 54, 92, 94, 107, 108, 109, 111, 128; /Daniel
Kalisz: 38, 48, 55; /Alastair Staley: 35, 57; /Steven Tee: 5, 8-9, 19, 20, 32, 34, 64-65, 66-67, 88-89, 93, 99